MASSIVELY BETTER HEALTHCARE

MASSIVELY BETTER HEALTHCARE

THE INNOVATOR'S GUIDE TO TACKLING
HEALTHCARE'S BIGGEST CHALLENGES

HALLE TECCO, MBA, MPH

COLUMBIA UNIVERSITY PRESS
NEW YORK

Columbia University Press
Publishers Since 1893
New York   Chichester, West Sussex
cup.columbia.edu

Library of Congress Cataloging-in-Publication Data
Names: Tecco, Halle author
Title: Massively better healthcare :
the innovator's guide to tackling healthcare's biggest challenges /
Halle Tecco.
Description: New York : Columbia University Press, [2026] |
Includes bibliographical references and index.
Identifiers: LCCN 2025025438 | ISBN 9780231222365 hardback |
ISBN 9780231564182 epub
ISBN 9780231565097 (PDF)
Subjects: LCSH: Medical care—United States |
Public health—United States | Health services administration—
United States
Classification: LCC RA395.A3 T43 2026
LC record available at https://lccn.loc.gov/2025025438

Cover design: Drue Wagner
Cover art: Ángeles Aldariz / Adobe Stock

GPSR Authorized Representative: Easy Access System Europe,
Mustamäe tee 50, 10621 Tallinn, Estonia, gpsr.requests@easproject.com

TO BEAR AND JEFF, MY SUN AND MOON.

THIS WORK WAS ONLY POSSIBLE BECAUSE OF YOUR

ENDLESS LOVE AND SUPPORT.

NEVER DOUBT THAT A SMALL GROUP OF THOUGHTFUL,

COMMITTED CITIZENS CAN CHANGE THE WORLD;

INDEED, IT'S THE ONLY THING THAT EVER HAS.

—MARGARET MEAD

CONTENTS

PREFACE

Who Are You to Do This?

I always wondered why somebody doesn't do something about that.
Then I realized I was somebody.
—LILY TOMLIN

The fluorescent lights hummed quietly overhead, casting a sterile glow across the sea of cubicles. I sat in mine, a fresh-faced graduate student intern at Apple's Cupertino, California, headquarters in 2010, tasked with overseeing the healthcare category of the nascent App Store. (That Apple entrusted a novice like me with this role said less about my qualifications and more about how little the company prioritized the sector at the time.)

My fingers tapped the keyboard of my iPhone (3GS!) as I opened yet another uninspired medical app. To my left, separated by a four-foot partition, sat Linda Kim. The energy and enthusiasm radiating from her cubicle completely contrasted with the silence in mine. Linda covered the gaming segment, and the excitement in her voice as she discussed the latest apps in her category was palpable.

I leaned back in my chair, my gaze drifting between my screen and the sign in our department that read "Love Is in the Detail." Not only were there nine gaming apps for every medical app on the App Store at the time, but the quality of the gaming apps was light-years ahead. The app developers Linda worked with used every native feature of the iPhone in creative new ways. The healthcare apps on my screen, in contrast, felt like afterthoughts—outsourced projects lacking the same passion and ingenuity. It was clear where the love (and the detail) was being lavished, and it wasn't on healthcare.

As I looked at another mediocre medical app, frustration gnawed at me. I knew the market size of every other category in the App Store *combined* paled in comparison to the ginormous healthcare industry. If the US healthcare system were a country, it would be the fourth-largest economy in the world. The disconnect between this massive opportunity and the dearth of innovation before me was maddening.

At that moment, in my tiny cubicle, I had an idea. If only we could channel the creativity and innovation surrounding me *into healthcare.*

So, I did what any self-respecting, healthcare-obsessed business student would do. I hatched a plan.

That fall, I went back to business school to develop a concept to fuel innovation in this sector by bringing together tech entrepreneurs and healthcare experts. I assumed that those entrepreneurs building cool things in gaming, social media, and other tech segments would come and build cool things in healthcare if they knew the sheer size of the opportunity and had the support of healthcare experts to do it. I came up with the name *Rock Health*, after the Rock Center for Entrepreneurship at Harvard Business School, where I spent many days and nights working on the business plan.

I dreamed of supporting impactful, mission-driven health startups that would change healthcare.

Instead, I faced closed door after closed door.

I was up against the old guard of healthcare: healthcare veterans who scoffed at any newcomers, staunchly defending their entrenched hold on the system. (I affectionately refer to them as the "Cranky Old Guard"—a.k.a. the C.O.G.)

Breaking into the sector meant fitting into a predetermined mold—one that, as a young woman and someone without a medical background, I didn't fit into.

But I didn't give up. I brought on a cofounder, Nate Gross, who was completing a joint MD/MBA and shared my audacious vision (figure 0.1). Together, we pitched group after group and . . . still weathered a storm of rejections. (Nate went on to help start

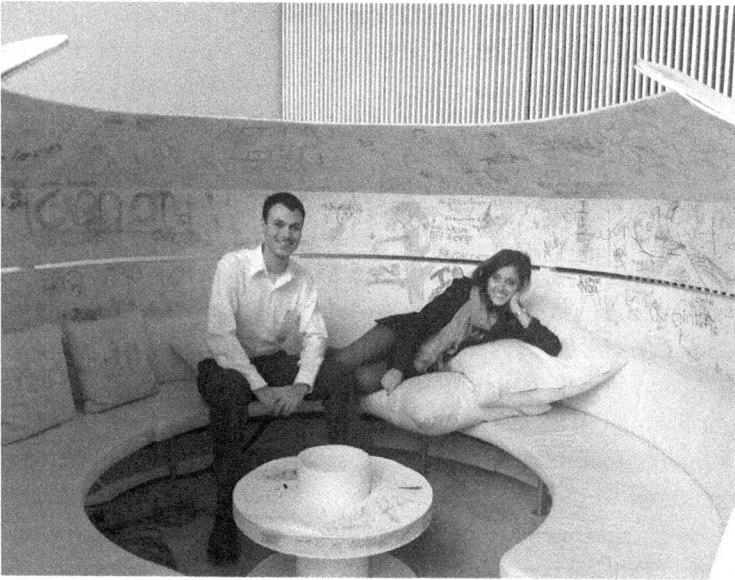

Figure 0.1 Nate and me promoting Rock Health on the MIT campus.

Doximity, a now publicly traded digital health company, and is still on the board of Rock Health.)

One time after a pitch, the venture capitalist (VC) sat there, arms crossed, letting the silence stretch until it felt suffocating. Then, with a dismissive sneer, he said something I can still hear clearly today: "But who are *you* to do this?" At that moment, imposter syndrome hit me in full force. My confidence evaporated, leaving me hollow and defeated. Who *was* I to do this? To think I could actually change healthcare?

I left in tears. Outside the VC's Back Bay office, Nate reminded me that we had to focus on the believers. He said, "If they don't want to work with us, then it's clear they weren't the right partner anyway."

We honed our pitch and focused on finding those who shared our enthusiasm for change.

Then, we finally caught our break. We got introduced to Aneesh Chopra and Todd Park at the White House. Aneesh was the first chief technology officer (CTO) of the United States and Todd was CTO of the US Department of Health and Human Services (HHS). They were working on something called the Blue Button initiative to enable veterans and Medicare beneficiaries to instantly download their health records. They invited us to speak at a conference and introduce our concept to attendees. Our pitch was a hit. It resonated so strongly that we rushed to register the Rock Health domain name on the spot.

Soon after, Dr. Michael Matly and the team at the Mayo Clinic got behind our vision and offered to fund us. With their generous support, Rock Health, the first startup incubator and seed fund dedicated to digital health, was born. We were scrappy, passionate, and determined to help fix healthcare. Having a brand like the Mayo Clinic on board helped us attract other like-minded backers, including Kaiser Permanente, the California HealthCare Foundation, Nike, and more.

The early days at Rock Health were so much fun. We built an incredible community that was welcoming to "outsiders." We worked with extraordinary founders—some who have since built massive organizations that have reshaped their corners of healthcare. Many of their stories you will hear in this book.

Together, we became part of the "new guard" of healthcare: a group determined to dismantle broken systems and rebuild something better. As I looked back at my journey from that cubicle at Apple to the emerging community we were building at Rock Health, I made a promise to myself. If I ever became part of the old guard, I would do it differently. I would remember the frustration of that young intern, staring at mediocre healthcare apps, and use my position to keep pushing for the changes we so desperately need. I would open doors instead of shutting them, welcome fresh perspectives instead of defending the status quo, and never forget that love is in the details.

BECOMING AN INSIDER

Looking back at my early days in this sector, I can't help but cringe at some of the things I said and did. I made assumptions that were way off base, made investments that failed miserably, and occasionally stepped on toes I didn't even know existed.

I was often underestimated and dismissed as an outsider who couldn't possibly understand the complexities of healthcare. One time, a healthcare reporter even shamed me—in an article—for dressing too casually at a healthcare conference. I never felt like I belonged, and I rarely felt welcomed.

So I doubled down. When I realized my MBA was only giving me part of the picture, I went back to school (at age thirty-four!) to get my master of public health (MPH). I wanted to understand the science of protecting and improving the health of populations, to see the forest and not just the trees. I didn't just aim to be a good healthcare investor anymore; I wanted to change healthcare.

As I kept learning, I kept sharing. At Rock Health, we hosted conferences to bring people together and began publishing industry reports to help disseminate information. We were the first to start tracking every single digital health deal to have longitudinal data on industry trends. I also started a podcast and a blog, and I talked to anyone who wanted to learn with me. I found that I loved working with students, so I created and started teaching a class at Columbia Business School in 2015 and at Harvard Medical School in 2024.

As my experiences in the sector accumulated, I realized that being an insider isn't about knowing all the answers. It's about asking better questions and earnestly attempting to understand how healthcare works. It's about using your position to open doors for others and challenging the status quo when it needs to be challenged.

In writing this book, I oscillated between feeling like I had so much knowledge to share and feeling like I didn't know enough.

That about sums up working in healthcare—no matter how much experience you accumulate, becoming an expert in every corner of it is a Sisyphean task. It's a never-ending loop of learning and relearning, which is exactly what makes navigating it both thrilling and daunting.

So I guess I'm an insider now. And I'm committed to using whatever influence I've gained to push for the changes we so desperately need.

THE PHASES OF WORKING IN HEALTHCARE INNOVATION

Since I started working in healthcare, I've seen a revolving door of fellow bright-eyed optimists eager to make their mark. And some of them, with brilliant ideas and a zealous drive for change, do just that. But as the years go by, I've also watched many of these enthusiastic innovators gradually become disillusioned and jaded and eventually bow out, leaving their visions unfulfilled.

I've recognized a pattern of phases that many of us, perhaps you too, experience. These aren't sequential steps but rather emotional stages we find ourselves cycling through as we attempt to make a meaningful impact.

Blind Optimism

We burst onto the scene brimming with enthusiasm, convinced that our fresh perspectives and bold ideas are precisely what healthcare needs. The status quo seems ripe for disruption, and we're chomping at the bit to shake things up. This is the time when audacious goals get set and the potential for impact feels limitless. I love this feeling—the exhilaration of believing we can move mountains and transform healthcare as we know it.

Despair and Disillusionment

Then reality sets in. As we start to grasp how truly messed up and rigged the healthcare system is, it's easy to become overwhelmed and discouraged. We slam into walls of resistance, get tangled in bureaucratic red tape, and find ourselves drowning in regulations that make even the simplest tasks feel impossible. This is the point at which I've seen folks throw in the towel and go work elsewhere, their once-fervent drive extinguished by the realities of healthcare.

Battle-Scarred Skepticism

Those of us who manage to claw our way through despair and disillusionment emerge on the other side a bit worse for wear but undeniably wiser. We've seen enough to know that there are no easy answers in healthcare, and we approach new ideas with a healthy dose of skepticism. We may be more reluctant to try new things, or perhaps we're just exhausted. This phase is about learning to pick our battles and focusing our energy on areas where it can drive the most significant impact.

Enlightened Determination

If we're fortunate and persistent, we eventually reach a state I call "enlightened determination." This mindset allows us to make meaningful, sustainable progress despite healthcare's challenges. We've learned to discern which levers can be pulled from within the system and which ones require bending the frame itself. We stop trying to fix everything at once and instead focus on what's both possible and catalytic. Most important, we've found a way to maintain our drive and commitment, even when faced with inevitable setbacks and roadblocks.

I've cycled through these phases more times than I can count, even swaying between optimism and skepticism within a single project. And I've watched as colleagues and friends do the same. Some have found their way to enlightened determination, whereas others have chosen to leave healthcare, their passion doused by just how hard it is.

My goal with this book is to equip you with the tools, strategies, and mindset that will help you reach the state of enlightened determination as efficiently as possible. Although I wrote this primarily for entrepreneurs and innovators looking to make an impact in healthcare, this book is for anyone who wants to understand and improve our system—whether you're a provider, patient, investor, or simply someone who cares about the state of healthcare in America.

Here's how we'll approach this:

Part I, "US Healthcare: Make It Make Sense," is an overview of healthcare. We'll discuss what's ailing our healthcare system, do a deep dive into critical stakeholders and their modus operandi, and talk about healthcare's sleeping giant. This foundation is necessary because we need to thoroughly understand the problems before we can effectively solve them.

In Part II, "The Anatomy of Healthcare Innovation," we'll take a closer look at healthcare innovation. In doing so, I'll share the four pathways to innovation and a simple checklist for evaluating new opportunities. We'll look at the reasons why innovating in healthcare is hard, and hopefully I'll convince you to use this difficulty to your advantage. Finally, we'll discuss failure and why things sometimes go sideways.

In Part III, "The New Rules of Building Massively Better Healthcare," we'll dive into the four big lessons I've gleaned from the remarkable founders and healthcare leaders with whom I've had the privilege of learning. These four rules are as follows:

- Work from the inside out, not the outside in
- Align the margin and the mission
- Be a good steward of health data
- Invest in evidence

By the end of this book, you'll have gained new insight and inspiration for making a real, lasting impact. I'm honored to be your guide on this journey, but the ideas and strategies presented in this book are a culmination of everything I've learned from my peers over the years. My role has been to synthesize and share these learnings, building on the foundation laid by those who have dedicated their lives to making healthcare massively better.

ALL HANDS ON DECK

I believed this when I was sitting in a cubicle at Apple, and I still believe it today: Healthcare needs all the talent we can get to solve some pretty big problems.

The challenges are plentiful, and the wins often feel scarce. But a different view emerges if we step back and see the bigger picture. It's the gestalt, the sum greater than its parts, where our individual impact intertwines and contributes to collective progress.

This book is an invitation to join that progress and lend your distinct perspective and talents to the ongoing story of healthcare transformation. Whether you're a seasoned clinician, a technical entrepreneur, or simply someone who cares about a healthier future, there's a place for you in this effort.

And if someone ever asks, "But who are *you* to do this?"—let your work be the answer.

PART I

US HEALTHCARE: MAKE IT MAKE SENSE

1

THE DIRE NEED FOR HEALTHCARE INNOVATION

Every system is perfectly designed to get the results it gets.
—W. EDWARDS DEMING

Healthcare in the United States delivers essential services that not only sustain lives and communities but also employs one in nine Americans.[1] Yet the US healthcare system creaks under the strain of enormous challenges. Escalating costs, limited access, and the rising burden of chronic disease expose cracks in the foundation of healthcare.

Most of us have had frustrating, confusing, expensive, or even devastating experiences as patients and caregivers. We've seen firsthand how the current system fails to meet our needs, and many of us have faced the burden of medical debt, navigated confusing insurance policies, or struggled to access the care we need.

The reality is that our healthcare system is broken. Consider the following:

- **Unchecked expenditures:** Unchecked healthcare expenditures continue to devour nearly one-fifth of our nation's gross domestic product (GDP), growing faster than our economy. If this trend continues, access to care will become increasingly restricted and funding for other priorities like education, infrastructure, and social programs will be threatened. Warren Buffet appropriately called ballooning healthcare costs a "hungry tapeworm on the American economy."

- **Sick care:** Our healthcare system operates with outdated models and practices ill-suited to our needs. A reactive "sick care" mindset dominates, focusing on costly crises over prevention. This creates a vicious cycle of illness and ever-higher spending.
- **Inequities:** Healthcare remains full of inequities. Structural barriers related to factors like geography, race, and economic status prevent many individuals from realizing their full health potential.

This chapter has three goals. First, to expose the deep flaws within our current healthcare system—its staggering costs, inadequate outcomes, and the paradox of simultaneously overusing, underusing, and misusing care. Second, to examine the systemic issues perpetuating these problems, including our reactive sick care approach. Finally, to highlight the pervasive health inequities that plague our nation, making a case for why change is overdue.

My hope is that by the time you finish this chapter, you will be (as I am) all-in for a wholesale transformation of healthcare.

AMERICANS SPEND MORE ON HEALTHCARE BUT GET LESS HEALTH OUT OF IT

Despite living in one of the wealthiest, most advanced societies on the planet, Americans end up with comparatively dismal health outcomes:

- **Life expectancy:** Americans live shorter lives than people in almost all other high-income countries.[2]
- **Chronic disease:** The United States has the highest rate of people with multiple chronic conditions and an obesity rate nearly twice the Organization for Economic Cooperation and Development (OECD) average.[3]
- **Maternal and infant mortality:** The United States has the highest infant and maternal mortality rates of any high-income country. In fact,

our maternal mortality rate is more than three times the rate in most other high-income countries, with nearly twenty-four maternal deaths for every one hundred thousand live births.[4]

- **Mental health:** About one-quarter of US adults have a mental health diagnosis such as anxiety or depression.[5] Meanwhile, untreated mental illnesses cost about $300 billion a year in lost productivity.[6] This is one of the highest rates among high-income countries.

Even more upsetting, indeed shocking, is that behind this depressing data isn't an underfunded healthcare system. The opposite is true. We're *overpaying* for these outcomes.

The United States has a uniquely expensive healthcare system, with per capita spending far surpassing any other OECD member country (figure 1.1).

Understanding why the US system is so expensive requires looking beyond simple individual choices and examining deeper, interconnected aspects of US life.

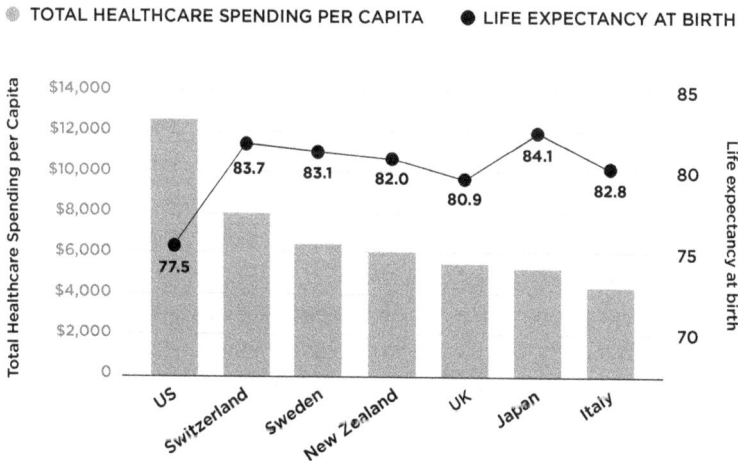

TOTAL HEALTHCARE SPENDING PER CAPITA ● LIFE EXPECTANCY AT BIRTH

Figure 1.1 Americans spend more and get less.

WHY IS HEALTHCARE SO EXPENSIVE
IN THE UNITED STATES?

Poor health and high healthcare costs create a vicious cycle. As medical bills go up and up and up, Americans become less and less able to access the very care that might keep them healthy to begin with. Every neglected health issue that goes unattended when it first presents can become a future health crisis, driving up costs for the system as a whole. Our flawed healthcare model fuels this destructive feedback loop, in which affordability and health are perpetually at odds.

When we talk about why healthcare is so expensive, each stakeholder is quick to blame the others. But the reality is that high medical bills reflect a perfect storm of demographic, economic, and systemic factors:

- **A reactive versus proactive approach:** Much of our healthcare system focuses on treating diseases and conditions after they occur (a "*sick* care system") rather than focusing on prevention (an actual "*health* care system"). More on this shortly.
- **Administrative complexity:** The administrative costs associated with managing US healthcare are significantly higher than in countries with simpler, more unified healthcare systems.[7] Administrative costs drive 30 percent of excess spending.[8] Not only does administrative waste deplete funds desperately needed for patient care, but it also drains providers of precious time and energy.
- **An aging population:** Although life-saving treatments now allow patients to survive events like heart attacks, longer lifespans come with new health challenges, creating ongoing demand for healthcare services. Older individuals typically require more frequent and extensive medical care, resulting in higher per capita healthcare expenditures. In fact, people age fifty-five and older account for 30 percent of the population but 56 percent of total health spending.[9]

- **Chronic disease:** The rise in chronic health conditions also contributes to increased healthcare costs, as managing these conditions requires ongoing, usually lifelong, medical care.
- **Obesity:** Adults with obesity have annual medical costs twice as high as those who are not obese.[10] The Centers for Disease Control and Prevention (CDC) estimates that obesity alone costs the US healthcare system nearly $173 billion annually.[11]
- **Defensive medicine:** Fear of malpractice lawsuits may lead doctors to order extra tests and procedures to protect themselves from potential legal action.[12] Some studies estimate that defensive medicine costs our country $45.6 billion annually.[13]
- **Lack of price transparency:** In many cases, patients (and even clinicians) only know the cost of treatments *after* the service has been provided. This lack of transparency makes it difficult for patients to make informed decisions about their care and for providers to consider cost-effectiveness when recommending treatments.
- **Limited competition:** Patients typically have limited options when choosing providers or services, particularly in emergencies or when restricted by insurance networks. This reduced competition can lead to higher prices, as providers have less need to compete on cost.
- **Misaligned incentives:** Our healthcare system often rewards increasing costs rather than controlling them. For example, health insurance companies are required by law to spend a fixed percentage (usually 80%) of the premiums they collect on medical care. This means their profits are tied to the total amount spent: the higher the healthcare costs, the more money they're allowed to keep. So, insurers may have little financial incentive to push prices down. At the same time, healthcare providers operating under a fee-for-service model are incentivized to increase the volume of services (more on this in chapters 2 and 6).

These factors create a system in which costs spiral out of control for both individuals and society as a whole. For many Americans, this translates to a single major illness pushing them into debilitating medical debt. Let's take a closer look at how medical debt wreaks havoc on American families.

MEDICAL DEBT: THE NUMBER ONE REASON FOR BANKRUPTCY IN THE UNITED STATES

Americans are contacted by debt collectors about medical bills more than any other type of debt.[14] Medical bills are the most common reason for bankruptcy, disproportionately affecting those already struggling financially.[15] Medical debt deepens inequity and the healthcare affordability crisis in our country. It doesn't just impact low-income families, however. Many otherwise financially secure middle-class families go bankrupt too, if they are unlucky enough to suffer a medical crisis.

The sheer desperation that medical debt inflicts on Americans is captured clearly in the rise of crowdfunding platforms like GoFundMe, where more than one-third of campaigns are created to raise money for medical bills. Although these campaigns sometimes provide financial relief (about 12 percent raise their target amounts), their existence is a clear and damning indication of how our healthcare system has utterly failed us.[16]

Tragically, the threat of crushing medical debts can further complicate patient health. Debt becomes a barrier for many to recover from an illness and thereafter maintain good health. Those burdened with debt struggle to afford future medical care or delay treatment for new or persisting problems. Medical debt can damage credit scores, affecting economic opportunities like securing housing or leasing a car.[17]

A stigma also surrounds debt and bankruptcy, which are treated as moral failings and often are attributed to the irresponsibility of the individual rather than to the flaws in the US healthcare system. The truth is most people are forced to decide between debt and their health. They take on debt to pay for their medications. Or, bankruptcy becomes a means of securing a life-saving surgery. Healthcare in this country often traps people in an impossible choice, robbing them of dignity and well-being.

Some innovators are starting to address this problem.

BOX 1.1.

In the Trenches: Undue Medical Debt

Jerry Ashton and Craig Antico spent decades as debt collection executives, chasing payments from individuals often struggling with financial hardship. They encountered countless Americans trapped under mountains of a particular type of debt: unpayable medical bills.

With their insider knowledge of the debt-buying industry, they realized they were distinctly qualified to help those in need and made a complete career 180.

They devised a clever solution to this healthcare crisis. They would buy vast bundles of medical debt, belonging to those least able to pay, on the secondary market for a steep discount (it costs roughly $1 to retire $100 in debt) and then simply to erase it. Beneficiaries receive a letter informing them that some or all of their debt has been erased, with no tax consequences or penalties. And just like that, they're free of medical debt.

Founded in 2014, Undue Medical Debt (formerly RIP Medical Debt) is a New York–based 501(c)(3).[18] Although its approach is ultimately a creative Band-Aid on a flawed system, its impact is undeniable. More than $20 billion in medical debt has been wiped out for more than thirteen million Americans, helping restore hope and dignity to individuals battered by a system that is simply too expensive and demonstrating how innovative thinking can create a significant impact even within the constraints of our current system.

WAIT, ARE WE OVERUSING OR UNDERUSING HEALTHCARE SERVICES?

A symptom of how confusing the state of US healthcare has become is that most of us cannot answer the question: Are we providing too much care, too little, or the wrong kind? The answer is yes—to all three. That's right; we're simultaneously overusing, underusing, and misusing healthcare services. This paradox creates inefficiencies and, unfortunately, missed opportunities for better health outcomes.

Underuse

We *underuse* healthcare whenever patients do not receive the care they need. This could be due to high costs, lack of access, or engagement barriers like health literacy. For example, 44 percent of Americans say they didn't go to a doctor when they were sick or injured because of cost.[19] About one-quarter of adults say they or a family member have cut pills in half, skipped doses of medicine, or have not filled a prescription because of cost.[20] Down the line, this underutilization can translate to delayed diagnoses, worsening conditions, or expensive emergency care—a cycle we desperately need to break.

Overuse

We *overuse* healthcare when people get medical services from which they are unlikely to benefit or, worse, they receive services that could potentially cause harm. Researchers estimate that one-third of all US healthcare spending produces no patient benefit at all.[21] This can include unnecessary or duplicative tests and treatments that drive up costs without a corresponding improvement in health outcomes.

Evidence suggests that higher spending is not necessarily correlated with better outcomes. In fact, there is often no correlation between spending and quality.[22] The implication is that unnecessary services drive costs without improving patient care.

Misuse

Finally, the *misuse* of healthcare harms patients. The Institute of Medicine defines misuse as "the failure to properly execute clinical care plans and procedures," also known as *malpractice*. Despite advancements in medical technologies and knowledge, a study from the Johns Hopkins University School of Medicine suggests that medical errors are the third-leading cause of death in the United States after heart disease and cancer.[23] Surgical errors, inappropriate treatments, and avoidable complications endanger lives and are a waste of healthcare dollars.

OUR SICK CARE SYSTEM

As Clayton M. Christensen said in his seminal book *The Innovator's Prescription*, "Nearly all Americans are cared for by business models that profit from patients' sickness, rather than wellness."[24]

What does that mean? We have a system that operates in crisis mode and takes care of us when we're sick, but not one that promotes health in the first place. Emphasis on treatment over prevention misses opportunities to catch problems early.

This reactive healthcare model is a relic of how we managed the primary health threats of yesteryear. A century ago, the most common cause of death was *infectious diseases* (also known as *communicable diseases*), such as influenza, tuberculosis, and diphtheria. Our healthcare system was initially designed to address these acute illnesses—conditions that develop suddenly and last a short time.[25]

But today, we face a new threat: *chronic diseases* (also known as *noncommunicable diseases*, NCDs), which account for eight of the ten leading causes of death.[26] Chronic diseases develop more slowly, often worsen over time, and result from genetic, physiological, environmental, and behavioral factors.[27]

Despite this change in what's killing us, our healthcare system still largely operates on the legacy model, focusing on treating illness rather than promoting health and preventing disease in the first place. This misalignment results in missed early intervention and prevention opportunities, ultimately leading to poorer health outcomes and higher costs. At the same time, these high costs mean medically disenfranchised folks may skip routine visits or ignore early signs of illness, ultimately driving poorer outcomes and reliance on more expensive acute care down the line.

To make things worse, our systems are fragmented. This is especially troubling for individuals managing multiple chronic conditions or utilizing emergency or ambulatory care across various providers. Consequently, *coordinated care*, the organized delivery of healthcare services among multiple providers, becomes important but difficult. A lack of care coordination can lead to:

- Worse health outcomes for patients
- Increased use of emergency care
- Medication errors
- Medical errors
- Poor transitions of care from hospital to home[28]

Meanwhile, our everyday environment exacerbates—and often creates—health challenges. These *social determinants of health* majorly influence health outcomes. For example, highly processed, calorie-dense foods saturate the market, from supermarket aisles to fast food restaurants, contributing to rising obesity, diabetes, and other chronic illnesses. This national trend is worse in food deserts, where fresh, healthy options are scarce and unaffordable. Additionally, most communities are built for cars, not pedestrians or cyclists, encouraging sedentary lifestyles that negatively affect our physical and mental health.

Finally, our fragile public health system is unable to fully address these challenges. Public health works to protect and improve the health of communities through disease prevention, health education, and population-wide interventions. However, years of underfunding have left public health departments understaffed and ill-equipped to handle major outbreaks, let alone provide sustained and effective programs that promote health. When public health succeeds, its victories often go unnoticed, making it hard to maintain support and funding, leaving us vulnerable to immediate threats like disease outbreaks and long-term health crises.

HEALTH EQUITY AND THE DISPARITY DIVIDE

Although healthcare disparities are often viewed through the lens of race and ethnicity, they also occur across socioeconomic status, age, language, gender, disability, sexual identity and orientation—and even geography. In fact, we have a system in which your zip code has a bigger influence on your life expectancy than your genetic code.[29]

As a result, we're paying a premium for a healthcare system that struggles to deliver consistent, high-quality care to *all* citizens.

Think of rural communities struggling with doctor deserts, where the nearest hospital is two hours away. Consider communities of color disproportionately burdened by air pollution, facing higher rates of respiratory conditions like asthma and chronic obstructive pulmonary disease.[30] Or low-income families battling medical bills, forced to choose between life-preserving medications and groceries, their health held hostage by financial hardship.

These are the lived experiences of millions of Americans and reminders of the deep-seated inequities embedded in our healthcare system. The human cost—in shorter lifespans, more days, months, or years spent sick, and loved ones in need of care and unable to access it—is immeasurable.

And the price tag for society as a whole is immense. Deloitte estimates that the direct medical costs associated with health inequities is $320 billion.[31] Plus, it's tough to work when you're sick. Chronic conditions, which disproportionately burden people from marginalized backgrounds, can lead to 10 to 70 percent productivity loss; this number is even higher for people suffering from pain or depression.[32] That's a lot of talent, creativity, and potential sidelined by health incquities.

But the good news is that closing the health equity gap doesn't just give everyone a fair chance at a healthy, productive life. It could also add $2.8 trillion to the US GDP and five million more people to the workforce.[33]

Addressing these health disparities requires much more than innovation, but at a minimum, innovation must not make existing disparities worse. Without prioritizing inclusivity in our innovations' very designs, any tool risks widening those gaps further. It's hard enough to solve enormous problems of injustice without our healthcare unintentionally adding fuel to the fire.

A CALL FOR INNOVATION

Our current healthcare system, built on foundations laid long ago, is ill-equipped to meet the challenges of today, let alone those of the future. We cling to outdated models that prioritize treating illnesses over proactive health promotion. A mindset focused on costly sick care leaves us perpetually playing catch-up, throwing resources at crises rather than at innovations to nurture lasting well-being.

This reactive approach creates a vicious cycle. Unaddressed health issues become full-blown medical emergencies, driving up costs and overwhelming the system. Prevention fades into the background, and the potential for early intervention—which could save lives and money—remains untapped.

These systemic failures undermine our health and hurt our wallets. Stagnant systems fail to address the social conditions that shape, even determine, our well-being. They fail to prioritize the needs of underserved communities, exacerbating health disparities. And unfortunately, they miss countless opportunities to keep people healthy in the first place.

This leaves us unprepared for the challenges ahead, from an aging population to the growing burden of chronic disease. We risk drowning under ever-rising costs while health outcomes fail to improve. The divide widens, and with it the urgency for change becomes ever more acute.

As a country and as a society, we confront both an economic imperative—reining in costs—and a moral imperative—recognizing that a healthy population is the foundation of a just and prosperous society. This moment demands courage and ambition. History will look back on our era with admiration or disappointment, depending on whether or not we rise to this challenge and start to solve these problems.

The need for bold new ideas could not be more apparent. The choice to innovate has become less a question of "Should we?" and more a matter of "How do we?"

To solve healthcare's problems, we first need to understand how the system works. The next chapter breaks down the major players in US healthcare. We'll look at their roles, challenges, and how they fit together—setting us up to spot opportunities for real change.

TL;DR

- **The US healthcare system is failing across multiple dimensions:** Americans spend more on healthcare than any other OECD member country, yet our health outcomes lag behind.
- **Medical debt devastates US families:** Medical expenses are the leading cause of bankruptcy in the United States, highlighting the costly financial impact of our healthcare system on individuals and families.
- **Healthcare delivery suffers from fundamental inefficiencies:** Our healthcare system simultaneously provides too much, too little, and the wrong kind of care, creating inefficiencies and missed opportunities for better health outcomes.
- **Our reactive approach creates a vicious cycle:** Our sick care system, focusing on treatment rather than prevention, creates a vicious cycle of illness and ever-higher spending. Fragmented care, social determinants of health, and an underfunded public health system further compound these problems.
- **Healthcare disparities persist as a systemic failure:** Health disparities rooted in socioeconomic factors, race, and geography are a stain on our healthcare system and economy. Closing the health equity gap could add $2.8 trillion to the US GDP.

2

HEALTHCARE'S NOT-SO-SIMPLE FOOD CHAIN

America's healthcare system is neither healthy, caring, nor a system.

—WALTER CRONKITE

'll never forget when the price of a medication at the pharmacy made me think I needed my hearing checked.

While working on this book, I had an annual skin check with my dermatologist. I asked her about a persistently dry, irritated patch on the back of my arm. She knew what this was: eczema, an extremely common skin condition. I left the office with a prescription for a topical cream, thinking I would pick up the medication and get back to work.

If only it were that simple.

I arrived at the pharmacy, stood in line, and showed the pharmacist my ID. They had it in stock already—great! I was pulling out my credit card to pay and preparing to wish the pharmacist a good day when what he said stopped me in my tracks. Surely, I'd heard him wrong.

"That's going to be $275," he said. "Your insurance covered $40." A two-week supply for $275. Never mind that eczema is often a chronic condition. I had major sticker shock.

Okay, do I really need this Rx? I wondered, already beginning to make my peace with the itch. Noticing my hesitation, a different pharmacist swept in to save my day (and my wallet) with the words, "Wait one second!"

She typed something into her computer and, moments later, declared, "Good news! I got it down to $25.50."

Once again, my hearing must be failing me, I thought. *How on earth could a price go from a $275 co-pay with insurance to $25.50 out of pocket? The same product. The same pharmacy. An 11 times difference. Make it make sense!*

On my walk home, with my medication in hand, I pulled out my phone and shared the story on social media. I was curious whether others had similar experiences with seemingly random prescription prices. Thousands (and I'm not exaggerating when I say *thousands*!) of people replied, sharing similar stories and frustrations about absolutely wild price differences in their prescription medication.

This experience isn't unique. Every day, Americans face countless quirks, complexities, and challenges just trying to get and stay well. How we receive care, where we get it, and how much it costs can vary depending on factors opaque to most of us.

We're all part of the healthcare system, but many of us don't understand it enough to be able to navigate it, much less change it. Even those of us who have worked in this sector can't possibly grasp all of it. Given all the disparate systems, fiefdoms, and regulations in American healthcare, we can only dream of becoming experts in our own little corners.

Just think about the sheer number of stakeholders involved in filling a prescription—a common task for most Americans. First, your doctor (stakeholder one) prescribes a medication developed by a pharmaceutical company (stakeholder two) and approved by the US Food and Drug Administration (FDA; stakeholder three). The drug is then distributed by wholesalers (stakeholder four) to pharmacies. Your health insurance company (stakeholder five) then determines your coverage and out-of-pocket costs based on the formulary and pricing negotiated by the pharmacy benefit managers (PBMs; stakeholder six). All this before you (stakeholder seven) even set foot in the pharmacy (stakeholder eight).

Each of these stakeholders has distinct needs and incentives. Knowing more about them helps explain why the US healthcare system is so complicated. As you will see, these complexities are often the result of historical quirks and piecemeal policies that have shaped our system over time.

In this chapter, I'll provide a condensed overview of US healthcare by looking at three major categories of stakeholders: providers, payers, and pharma. In the next chapter, we'll talk about the fourth P—patients.

Although I will do my best to help you make sense of US healthcare, I must admit that I can't truly do that. US healthcare simply *doesn't make sense*. However, after reading this chapter, I do hope you'll be able to move on to the rest of this book with a better understanding of the root causes of healthcare's complexity—and more confidence to help address them.

PROVIDERS

Let's go back to my dermatology visit for a moment. When she saw the rash on my arms, my doctor knew, from her expertise, that it was eczema. She made a diagnosis and logged the process accordingly in the practice's electronic health record (EHR). Based on current treatment standards and my symptoms, she wrote me a prescription.

With this process, my doctor participated in an evolving approach to providing care. In the past, providers relied on intuition and trial-and-error to diagnose and treat conditions (called "intuitive medicine"). Today patients are instead treated based on what works for some or most people ("empirical medicine") or sometimes with "precision medicine," in which case diseases are diagnosed more precisely—based on the individual—and interventions are delivered more effectively for each patient.

That's not the only place where my dermatologist's work is influenced by broader trends. From how she is paid to even why she may have chosen to be a dermatologist (as opposed to another specialty), her medical career is shaped by history and imbalances of power across the provider spectrum.

Providers: How We Receive Care

Today's doctors, nurses, and other healthcare professionals work in various care settings, from hospitals to urgent care centers. These entities and businesses influence how they provide care. We can broadly divide the type of care into three buckets: primary care, acute care, and specialty care (table 2.1). Let's dive in.

PRIMARY CARE Primary care is the core of healthcare delivery, serving as the central point of contact for patients throughout their lives. Its main goals are prevention, early detection, and management of chronic diseases.

TABLE 2.1
Types of Providers

Type of Providers	Goal	Examples
Primary care	Prevention, early detection, chronic disease management	Routine checkups, vaccinations, screenings, diabetes management, hypertension
Acute care	Immediate, short-term treatment for urgent or severe conditions	Emergency room visits, hospitalizations for infections, labor and delivery, surgery
Specialty care	Focused expertise on specific body systems or conditions	Cardiology, oncology, dermatology, neurology

Even though primary care is the only medical specialty for which a greater supply produces improvements in population health, longer lives, and greater health equity, the United States faces a shortage of primary care providers (PCPs), particularly in rural and underserved areas.[1] An estimated 100 million Americans don't have a regular PCP, a number that nearly doubled from 2014 to 2023.[2]

Why? We can find the answer on both the supply and demand side:

- Demand is growing for primary care services as the population grows and ages and the prevalence of chronic diseases increases.
- PCPs have lower salaries than specialty care providers and face high rates of burnout.[3]
- Fewer doctors are choosing to work in primary care, and lately, PCPs have been more likely to quit than other types of doctors.[4]

Today, primary care is predominantly delivered by larger, multiprovider practices. Much patient care is administered by nurse practitioners (NPs) and physician assistants (PAs), along with staff physicians. These practices are typically affiliated with larger health systems, in which intrasystem care coordination takes precedence over the relationship-based primary care model of years past.

ACUTE CARE If primary care is generally concerned with preventative health, acute care comes into play when things go wrong. Although you might go to a primary care provider for a lingering cough, acute care providers take over if your cough suddenly makes it difficult to breathe.

Acute care can include the following:

- **Hospitals:** Whether you're going to the ER with severe abdominal pain or getting X-rays done of a possible broken bone, a lot of acute care happens in the hospital. According to the American Hospital Association

(AHA), nearly one million beds are available in US hospitals.[5] Like most other US care settings, hospitals are mainly private. Almost half of all US hospitals are nonprofit—but this doesn't mean they don't profit. More on this distinction later in the chapter.

- **Hospital-at-home:** For some acute care patients, a hospital stay has been the main option available to them—but not anymore. Since 2020, the Centers for Medicare and Medicaid Services has promoted at-home hospital care through the Acute Hospital Care At Home program. Per the AHA, this innovative care model has reduced costs, improved outcomes, and, understandably, improved patient experiences.[6]
- **Urgent care:** More and more, you can't turn around in a US city without running face-first into an urgent care clinic. The number of urgent care centers now exceeds eleven thousand not including clinics inside retail stores or freestanding emergency rooms.[7] As primary care shortages keep more Americans from an established doctor-patient relationship, more patients receive acute care from the NPs and PAs largely staffing these on-demand clinics to fill in the gaps. However, there are questions about the quality of care some of these centers provide. For instance, a 2018 Pew Charitable Trusts and CDC study found that urgent care centers overprescribed antibiotics.[8]

SPECIALTY CARE Last, there's specialty care. Like my dermatologist, nearly nine out of every ten US physicians are specialists today.[9] They provide services ranging from consultations to outpatient procedures. They're often focused on solving specific problems in specific organ systems—from psychiatric disorders to musculoskeletal health. The United States is home to many of the world's leading specialists, which is why wealthy patients from around the world travel here for complex treatments at institutions like Mayo Clinic, MD Anderson, Memorial Sloan Kettering, and the Cleveland Clinic.

Our nation has an abundance of specialist care. Much of it, however, is concentrated in cities and major medical centers. Rural patients have fewer specialists per capita and longer travel distances for care.[10] One of the biggest improvements to specialist access has been internet connectivity. With the rise of telehealth, patients are no longer limited to the providers in their immediate area. Similarly, local providers have better access to the best possible specialty consults for their patient cases.

Increasingly, telehealth-based startups have been reshaping specialty care. In 2020, my dermatologist started seeing patients via telemedicine. Specialists like her went from offering teledermatology at a rate of 15 percent in 2016 to 80 percent at the height of pandemic restrictions.[11] The expanded specialist access doesn't stop there. With this innovation, the virtual women's health clinic Maven has expanded access to and research on the pregnancy benefits of virtual doula care.[12] Condition-specific providers—such as virtual-first cardiology platform Heartbeat Health, in which I'm an investor—have found easier ways to make high-quality care accessible to more people.

Even with improved digital access, however, patients still face barriers like insurance coverage limitations, high out-of-pocket costs, and confusing referral requirements that can make it difficult for patients to utilize these specialists, whether in-person or virtually.

Providers: Credentialing

Annually, around twenty-nine thousand newly minted physicians graduate from US medical schools.[13] They join a diverse clinical workforce, including an estimated 4.7 million registered nurses.[14] Other professionals on the provider side include the following:

- **NPs and PAs:** As I mentioned earlier, these provider professionals have increasingly stepped in to fill physician-shaped gaps in many care settings. NPs are among the fastest-growing medical professions.[15] Today, they work in medical specialties beyond primary care, especially psychiatry, women's health, and emergency medicine.

- **Allied health professions:** Broadly speaking, the allied health professions encompass clinicians beyond nursing and medicine. This category includes radiology technicians, dietitians, speech-language pathologists, audiologists, paramedics, physical therapists, counselors, and occupational therapists.
- **Community health workers:** These public health workers serve as ambassadors for the healthcare system in their local community. They advocate for individuals' care, identify and deliver culturally relevant health resources to low-income areas and communities of color, and connect individuals to necessary social services.
- **Health coaches:** This category comes with a stigma—and a large reason is accreditation, which I'll touch on more in a moment. Increasingly, startups and even primary care practices have begun offering health coaching services.[16] Other health coaches work independently as service providers, often finding clients on social media and through referrals. Although professional standards exist for this role, such as the National Board–certified Health and Wellness Coach credential, most health coaches in the United States don't have this kind of formal training.[17] Of course, the potential exists for health coaches to help people through healthy habit-building and evidence-based practices. But patients risk falling for flashy marketing and promises an untrained service provider may be unqualified to deliver.

When thinking about medical credentialing, the first organization that probably comes to mind is the American Medical Association (AMA).

Admittedly, the AMA evokes complicated feelings for many of us in healthcare. Yes, it was founded in the nineteenth century to raise the standards in healthcare by standardizing medical education and licensing.[18] Since then, however, the AMA has lobbied to artificially restrict the number of medical graduates, contributing to our critical clinician shortage.[19] The organization also worked against the push to allow PAs and NPs to step in and fill those gaps.[20]

The AMA also has a complex and troubling history of racial discrimination, including excluding Black physicians for nearly a century and being responsible for the closure of many Black medical schools, which has had significant long-term impacts on diversity in the medical profession.[21]

Providers: Biggest Challenges

Providers take on a lot to stay afloat and keep us all healthy. How they juggle (or fail to juggle) these challenges determine what healthcare looks like.

- **Clinician shortages:** This is the big one. The Association of American Medical Colleges suggests that by 2034 we'll be left with a shortfall of between 37,800 and 124,000 physicians.[22] We're also facing a nursing shortage, which is expected to intensify as our population ages and needs more and more care. The following challenges—especially burnout and medical school costs—feed into these shortages, while a strained workforce further exacerbates challenges like care delays and burnout. It's a vicious cycle, and we can't intervene fast enough.
- **Burnout:** With any job, mental health is tied to endurance and performance. This is especially true for the people tasked with caring for us. Yet studies conducted since the pandemic suggest that nearly three out of four healthcare workers in the United States have symptoms of depression.[23] The reasons are manifold. Providers are spending more time fighting with their EHRs than ever, cutting into both patient and personal time. Plus, many providers feel disenchanted with US healthcare's inefficiencies and inequities (you likely are feeling this way, too). Making healthcare providers' day-to-day jobs more sustainable is vital to stemming shortages—and ensuring that the providers sticking around can do their critical jobs well. Companies like Marvin Behavioral Health, in which I'm an investor, are addressing this issue by offering mental health services tailored to the clinician workforce.
- **Care coordination:** Providers often need to organize patient care activities and share information with a patient's other providers to achieve

safer and more effective care. The challenge stems from the fragmented nature of our healthcare system. Providers must manage disjointed systems with varying processes between primary care and specialty sites. Patients often struggle to understand referral reasons, appointment procedures, and follow-up steps. Information exchange is inconsistent: Specialists may receive unclear referral reasons or incomplete test results, while primary care physicians often lack feedback on specialist visits. The complexity extends to navigating health system affiliations and insurance networks, which directly affects a provider's ability to give and receive referrals. This fragmentation leads to inefficient care delivery, increased provider frustration, and, ultimately, compromised patient care.

- **Costs and competition of medical training:** The average total cost of medical school is more than $200,000.[24] Given the limited number of spots, many hopeful doctors take what they can get, regardless of the debt. The heavy burden of medical training is part of the reason why many clinicians are drawn toward more lucrative specialties—and away from the stereotypically more thankless field of primary care.

- **Malpractice considerations:** America is a litigious country. The risk of lawsuits is especially high in medicine. Physicians spend an average of 3.2 percent of their income on malpractice insurance, which has almost become mandatory.[25] The stress from anticipating or dealing with such litigation has led to a specific form of burnout: medical malpractice stress syndrome.[26]

- **Rising cybersecurity threats:** Ransomware attacks and other cybersecurity breaches against healthcare systems have increased for years. At best, these kinds of events can compromise sensitive health information. At worst, they can cripple hospital infrastructure and put lives at risk. Healthcare systems must be vigilant and invest significant resources into cybersecurity assets and policies to avoid these disasters. With every potential employee computer being a liability, bigger health systems have more ground to cover, risk-wise.

- **Consolidation:** Speaking of big health systems, many have been growing because of increased mergers and acquisitions across healthcare. Larger regional healthcare systems have been swallowing up smaller practices as the costs of maintaining a brick-and-mortar private practice have become untenable for many independent providers. At the same time, many US healthcare delivery organizations have sold to private equity (PE), with $1 trillion invested in the past decade.[27] Why would this be a concern? More research is needed, but one Harvard Medical School study found that PE-owned hospitals perform worse on several quality measures—including fall and infection risk—and may lead to higher prices.[28]

- **Low margins:** Despite the high cost of care, healthcare providers generally operate with low margins. For example, nonprofit hospitals have an operating margin of 1–2 percent, barely breaking even.[29] Low margins make it challenging for providers to invest in new technologies, improve facilities, or offer competitive salaries, which in turn can exacerbate other issues like clinician shortages and burnout.[30] This financial pressure also contributes to the trend of consolidation as smaller providers struggle to remain independent in this challenging economic environment.

Providers: How Did We Get Here?

Our healthcare system didn't always look like this. To better understand how we got here, let's take a glance at where we came from.

Today, individual providers don't have an enormous amount of power, but many of the large provider institutions do. That tug-of-war has been going on for the past three centuries.

In the eighteenth century, physicians had what sociologist Paul Starr calls "professional sovereignty"—the freedom to practice how they liked.[31] But that also meant many of these professionals went unchecked, sometimes performing abusive procedures and offering ineffective patent medicines (what we know today as snake oil— and its salesmen).[32]

Over the course of the next two centuries, with the rise of licensing standards and the AMA, doctors and other providers began to professionalize, trading some of their power for trust and institutional authority. For more on how this shift occurred, I'd recommend reading Starr's *The Social Transformation of American Medicine*—it's considered to be the definitive history of the US healthcare system.

The twentieth century brought massive changes. The Hill-Burton Act of 1946 funded the construction of hospitals, nursing homes, and other health facilities across the country, creating more than seventy thousand new hospital beds.[33] The establishment of Medicare and Medicaid (1965) then significantly expanded access to healthcare for elderly and low-income Americans.

What followed was a tidal wave of consolidation. Hospital systems got bigger and bigger. PE firms started buying up medical practices. As with many other areas of American life, healthcare became overwhelmingly corporate. Today, an estimated 80 percent of physicians now work for hospitals or corporations—a complete 180 from the independent practice model of the past.[34]

This history helps explain why my dermatologist visit looked the way it did, and why changing healthcare is so hard. We're dealing with centuries of accumulated structures, incentives, and power dynamics that aren't easy to untangle.

PAYERS

Let's revisit how I ended up at my dermatologist's office. Yes, I was looking to have a skin checkup, but I didn't have an established dermatologist at the time. To find a specialist, I had to do some research.

As is the case for most patients searching for a provider, the key deciding factor was insurance coverage. I needed to find someone *in-network*, meaning a provider who has a contract with my insurance plan to provide services at prenegotiated rates. Luckily, my health plan had a directory of approved local providers.

BOX 2.1.

For-Profit Versus Nonprofit Hospitals: Is There a Difference?

Corporations evoke a lot of specific ideas in the American imagination. There's bloated bureaucracy and top-down hierarchies. But the strongest association, I'm willing to bet, is between corporations and profit, or even greed.

That's where it can be easy to get confused. Some see this as a binary, associating for-profit healthcare companies with greed and waste and nonprofit hospitals with good. Of course, it's not so black and white. You can find efficiency, innovation, and high-quality care at both for-profit *and* nonprofit healthcare organizations. You also can find waste, inefficiency, and greed at both.

Nonprofit hospitals or health plans certainly can be profitable; they just can't distribute said profit to shareholders. Many nonprofit hospitals are indeed "rolling in money," to quote physician-journalist Elisabeth Rosenthal.[35] A study published in Health Affairs found that mean operating profits were $58.6 million for nonprofit hospitals and $43.4 million for for-profit hospitals.[36] But nonprofit hospitals use those profits to provide charity care, right? Actually, some nonprofit hospitals have been found to have worse ratios of charity care to total expenses than for-profit hospitals. In addition, 86 percent of nonprofit hospitals do not provide more charity care than the value of their tax exemption.[37] Although 49 percent of hospitals are nonprofit, they may not necessarily be fulfilling the charitable mission that their tax-exempt status implies.

So are for-profit hospitals the answer? They offer the potential for a focus on operational efficiency and increased access in underserved areas (for-profit hospitals have actually been shown to serve more Medicaid patients, especially in rural markets).[38] This model, however, presents an unavoidable trade-off as profitability and shareholder satisfaction become core driving factors, alongside—and sometimes instead of—the quality of care provided. Not to mention, for-profit hospitals are legally allowed to refuse care to patients who cannot afford treatment (once they are out of immediate danger).

In truth, the tax status of an organization is not the leading indicator of the quality of care it delivers. Both nonprofit and for-profit hospitals exist on lists of the best hospitals in the country as well as lists of the worst.

Lately, we've seen the rise of the public benefit corporation (PBC) model in healthcare. Compared with C corps, which are structured to maximize shareholder value, PBCs work for the public good by serving the interests of those involved in and affected by the corporations (including employees, customers, and the planet).[39] Notable healthcare PBCs include the following:

- Life science cloud software company **Veeva** (which was the first public company to convert to a PBC)
- Independent primary care network **Aledade**
- Publicly traded biotechnology company **United Therapeutics**
- Community-based care company **Waymark**
- Prescription glasses company **Warby Parker**

If my plan's directory hadn't been accurate or if its network of providers had been more limited, however, I might not have been so lucky. I was grateful for my insurance at that moment, even though I hadn't chosen it. Like many married people in the United States, I'm on my spouse's insurance plan.

Of course, my plan didn't just help me find my care; it also covered a large portion of the medical bill (also known as a claim). And payment still only grazes the surface of what payers do in healthcare. They also:

- Enroll patients in health insurance coverage
- Determine patient eligibility (check if the member's plan covers the requested service)
- Collect premiums (monthly or annual fees paid by enrolled members for their insurance coverage)

- Negotiate and set rates for healthcare services
- Process claims (medical bills) for coverage and reimbursement for care
- Pay providers using collected premiums
- Manage financial risk, particularly for catastrophic or high-cost care, by spreading the risk across a large pool of members
- Handle prior authorization requests, which is when providers must get advance approval from the insurance company before performing certain procedures, prescribing specific medications, or ordering expensive tests.

Payers: How We Pay for Care

Today, just over half (53.7 percent) of Americans receive health insurance through their employer, followed by 37.8 percent on Medicaid and Medicare (split evenly between the two). Roughly 10 percent of Americans purchase their coverage directly from an insurance company or through a federal or state marketplace like Healthcare.gov. The remaining folks have a mix of Tricare, Veterans Affairs (VA) benefits, or no coverage at all. Some people are covered by more than one type of health insurance during the year, resulting in a total that exceeds 100 percent (see figure 2.1).[40]

This is where it gets even more confusing, so stick with me. We'll start by dissecting the channels by which someone receives insurance—from their employer, the government, or directly. This doesn't necessarily dictate, however, who is administering or underwriting said insurance behind the scenes. Commercial health plans, for instance, provide insurance through all three channels. Let's dive in.

EMPLOYMENT-BASED INSURANCE Although most US employees switch jobs every four years, most of us rely on our jobs, or our partners' jobs, for health coverage.[41]

Employer-based insurance	53.7%
Medicaid	18.9%
Medicare	18.9%
Marketplace coverage	9.9%
Uninsured	8.3%
TRICARE	2.4%
VA	1.0%

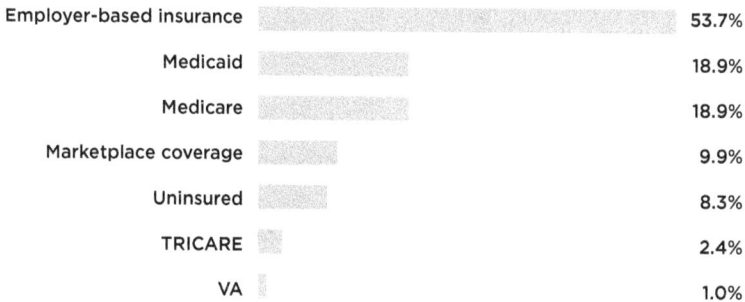

Figure 2.1 Health insurance by coverage type.

Why do we tie health insurance to employment? The answer is a historical quirk that seemingly won't go away. During World War II, the government set price and wage controls to prevent inflation. The Stabilization Act of 1942 excluded "insurance and pension benefits in a reasonable amount," which in turn inspired employers to offer health insurance and pension benefits as a perk to attract employees.[42] This trend laid the foundation for our employer-based insurance system.

Fast forward to today, and employer-based insurance has become a massive expense, and possible distraction, for businesses. In fact, it's the second-highest expense for most companies, right behind wages. Warren Buffett famously said that General Motors was "a health and benefits company with an auto company attached," and the Starbucks CEO once shared that the company spends more on healthcare than on coffee beans.

With healthcare being such a significant expense, employers must choose carefully how they structure their health benefits. And they have a few options. They can set up a *fully-insured* plan, in which an employer contracts with a commercial payer who administers the plan and underwrites the financial risk for the healthcare costs of employees.

Alternatively, most companies with more than one thousand employees choose to self-insure. With *self-insured* plans, an employer effectively acts like an insurer and underwrites the financial risk for employee healthcare costs. To protect against catastrophic losses, self-insured employers typically purchase *stop-loss insurance*. Self-insured employers will also work with a *third-party administrator* (TPA) to handle the day-to-day operations of the health plan the employer underwrites. Federal law (the Employee Retirement Income Security Act of 1974, or ERISA) exempts private, self-insured employers from most state insurance laws, including *reserve requirements* (minimum funds insurers must maintain to ensure that they can pay claims), mandated benefits (specific benefits plans must cover, like birth control), premium taxes (state taxes charged on insurance premiums), and other consumer protection regulations.[43]

Small employers (generally less than fifty employees) aren't completely out of options regarding health benefits. Qualified Small Employer Health Reimbursement Arrangement (QSEHRA) programs allow these businesses to offer nontaxed reimbursement of certain health expenditures to employees who maintain minimum essential coverage. There's also the growing Individual Coverage HRA (ICHRA) option, which is available to employers of any size.

To learn more about employment-based insurance, check out KFF's comprehensive Employer-Sponsored Health Insurance 101.[44]

GOVERNMENT-SPONSORED INSURANCE Government-sponsored health insurance covers more than one-third of the US population.[45] Notice I refer to these as government-*sponsored* and not government-*run* plans. That's because many of these plans, although paid for by the government, are run by private commercial health plans.

- **Medicaid (18.9 percent):** A joint federal and state program that provides health coverage to low-income individuals and families, including children, pregnant women, elderly individuals, and people with disabilities. Most states rely on managed care organizations (MCOs) run by private companies to manage their state Medicaid program.[46] Eligibility and specific coverage varies by state.

- **Medicare (18.9 percent):** A federal health insurance program primarily for people ages sixty-five or older, as well as some younger people with disabilities. It consists of four parts: Part A (hospital insurance), Part B (medical insurance), Part C (Medicare Advantage plans offered by private companies), and Part D (prescription drug coverage).[47] (If you've ever struggled to remember the difference between Medicare and Medicaid, here's a tip: we *care* for the elderly and *aid* the poor.)

- **TRICARE (2.6 percent):** A health insurance program for active duty service members, their families, and military retirees. It functions similarly to private insurance, offering various plans with different levels of coverage and costs, allowing beneficiaries to receive care from both military and civilian providers.

- **VA (1 percent):** The Veterans Health Administration is a government-run healthcare system that provides services to eligible veterans and their families. It offers a wide range of services, including primary care, mental health care, specialty care, and long-term care, with a focus on meeting the specific needs of veterans.

- **Indian Health Service (IHS):** IHS provides direct medical and public health services to members of federally recognized Native American Tribes and Alaska Native people. People are technically considered uninsured if they only have coverage through the IHS, as IHS coverage is not considered comprehensive.

MARKETPLACE COVERAGE Thanks to the Affordable Care Act (ACA), getting health insurance outside of an employer's offerings is easier than it once was. Plan shoppers can compare insurance companies, metal tiers, and network options through a federal or state marketplace (e.g., healthcare.gov).

Yet if you've ever been self-employed, unemployed, or looked for insurance outside of your work's benefits, you know the struggle. Without employer contributions to bear some of the premium burden, enrollees in marketplace plans can spend hundreds or even thousands of dollars a month for insurance that sometimes doesn't even cover all the care they need.

Plus, unlike employer-sponsored health insurance, which uses pretax dollars, if you purchase insurance directly, you pay for it with post-tax dollars. This tax difference is one of the reasons direct purchase insurance is significantly more expensive than a similar plan through an employer.

THE UNINSURED Uninsured rates vary from state to state, along with public coverage options. As of 2023, Massachusetts had the lowest uninsured rate at 3.1 percent, while Texas had the highest at 18.6 percent.[48]

Most people who are uninsured have at least one worker in the family, but they do not have access to coverage through their job. Predictably, most uninsured nonelderly adults cite the high costs of commercial insurance as their reason for being uninsured.[49]

Especially vulnerable populations include poor adults in states without expanded Medicaid coverage and people who are ineligible for federally funded coverage, including Medicaid and private premium subsidies.

Laws like the Emergency Medical Treatment and Labor Act of 1986 mandate that even uninsured people have the right to treatment in emergency situations—but that's the bare minimum. Plus, despite their vulnerability, uninsured patients often pay the highest price for care compared with public and private payers.[50]

Still, we've made incredible progress in lowering the uninsured rate in the United States, largely thanks to policies like the ACA. In 2013, the year before Medicaid expansions and federal premium subsidies went into effect, the number of uninsured people was a whopping 45.2 million. In the next decade, that number fell to 26.4 million.[51] May we keep building on this progress in years to come.

BOX 2.2.

Commercial Health Plans and the Medical Loss Ratio

If you've ever received health insurance from your employer, you've likely held a card with one of the brand names (like UnitedHealth or Aetna) on the front. These are two examples of commercial health insurance companies—a category that has grown dramatically in both size and influence in our lifetime. In fact, the revenues of the six largest for-profit health insurance companies accounted for a staggering 30 percent of total US health spending in 2023, up from less than 10 percent in 2011.[52]

Four of the top 20 companies on the 2024 Fortune 500 list are health insurance giants: UnitedHealth Group, CVS Health (Aetna), Cigna, and Elevance Health (formerly Anthem).

This concentration of power gives insurers enormous leverage in negotiating prices with providers and setting premiums for consumers. Although economies of scale can increase efficiency, the resulting oligopolistic structure raises concerns about reduced competition and inflated prices.

To understand how these insurers grew so large, we need to look at the rules that govern them. One of the most important is the medical loss ratio (MLR), introduced by the ACA in 2010.[53]

This requirement mandates that insurers spend at least 80–85 percent of premium revenues (the amount you pay each month for health insurance) on "clinical services" and "quality improvement," capping insurers' profits and overhead. If insurers don't meet the MLR threshold, they must rebate the difference to customers. The MLR formula is shown in figure 2.2.[54]

$$\text{MLR} = \frac{\text{Total Medical Spend} + \text{Quality Improvements}}{\text{Premium Revenue} - \text{Allowable Deductions}}$$

Figure 2.2 The medical loss ratio formula.

(continued on next page)

(*continued from previous page*)

The numerator includes anything paid out for medical service claims plus any expenses for activities that improve healthcare (a.k.a. quality improvement activity).

The denominator includes premium revenue minus allowable deductions (federal and state taxes and licensing and regulatory fees, with adjustments for risk, risk corridors, and reinsurance).

Although it was intended to ensure that a substantial portion of premiums goes toward actual healthcare, the MLR has also created incentives (and disincentives) that don't always align with improving healthcare outcomes or reducing costs.

For instance, because insurers keep only 15–20 percent of premiums for administrative costs and profits, they have an incentive to increase overall healthcare spending. Why? Because when total spending goes up, 15–20 percent becomes a bigger number. Bigger pie, bigger slice.

On the flipside, it disincentivizes nonclinical programs like nutrition or social support, which are generally considered administrative expenses and not medical spending, meaning they don't typically count toward the numerator of the MLR equation.[55] This creates a financial disincentive for insurers to invest in these important areas, despite their potential to improve health outcomes and reduce long-term costs.

Some people also point to MLR as a driver of vertical consolidation, in which health plans acquire provider organizations. As Ann Somers Hogg of the Christensen Institute points out, "By integrating provider organizations into their parent companies, insurers can retain a portion of their medical 'costs' as revenue for another line of business."[56]

Payers: Biggest Challenges

Payers have major responsibilities to patients, providers, and the US government. The following are just some of the major challenges they contend with:

- **Rising cybersecurity threats:** Health data is extremely appealing to cybercriminals, which creates a huge cybersecurity threat given the large amounts of sensitive data health plans harbor and the many potential points of vulnerability they need to manage. This is especially true for payer organizations, many of which are among the biggest operations in the nation.

- **Claims system:** In most industries, purchasing a service is straightforward: you receive an invoice and make a payment. Healthcare operates on a fundamentally different model. There are thousands of health insurance plans in the United States, each with distinct pricing agreements negotiated with providers. As a result, healthcare services aren't simply invoiced but instead are submitted as claims for reimbursement. This creates a poor experience for patients. Billing errors are abundant—not to mention the huge costs involved in administrating the entire thing.[57]

- **Regulatory pressure:** Although it's a big one, the ACA is not the only regulation that governs how payers function. Other significant laws payers need to nimbly account for include Medicare reforms involving prior authorization and interoperability. For instance, a 2020 reform required payers to give patients direct access to their claims and encounter data through a Patient Access API.[58]

- **Quality ratings:** Those of us on employer plans don't get to choose our insurance. We just hope that the human resources team picks a good one. But how do potential plan enrollees evaluate the insurer they're considering? That's why health plan star ratings exist. These quality ratings, which range from one to five stars, are based on how members rate their experiences, how well a plan's network provides care, and how efficiently the plan is administered. Payers need to keep an eye on care gaps and their internal functions to maintain attractive public-facing ratings year after year. That includes maintaining customer satisfaction, which health insurers don't do too well.

- **Reputation:** Surveys indicate that less than half of Americans are fully satisfied with their health insurance.[59] Payers are often viewed as faceless bureaucracies more focused on denying care than supporting it.

Negative headlines about coverage denials, billing issues, or automation missteps can erode trust and damage a plan's brand.

- **Automation:** Payers are increasingly turning to automation to speed up their claims processing. The goal is eventually for payers to be more efficient in serving members and providers and to save on administrative costs. However, during this transition period, as payers test the limits of artificial intelligence (AI) integrations in their workflows, they risk getting into hot water. We've seen this in how Medicare Advantage plans have come under fire for their use of automated prior authorization, which has resulted in frequent and harmful denials of lifesaving care.[60]

This multipayer system, unlike the streamlined single-payer or socialized models seen in peer nations, is a uniquely American beast with its own set of quirks and challenges.

Although public and private payers strive to provide coverage and manage costs, the system's inherent complexities and misaligned incentives can create barriers to care, leaving patients and providers grappling with confusion, delays, and financial burdens.

Payers: How Did We Get Here?

Reforms and failed proposals from the past century or so have turned America's public and private payers into the powerful entities they are today.

Private health insurance, as we know it today, largely began during the Great Depression. Blue Cross introduced one of the first offerings in 1929 when Baylor University hospital administrators were seeking a way to make their services more accessible. The plan provided up to 21 days of coverage for hospitalization annually if patients prepaid 50 cents a month. It was an immediate success, quickly enrolling people across the city and inspiring similar programs nationwide.

Then, during World War II, price and wage controls led employers to offer health insurance as a perk to attract employees outside of these limitations. This trend laid the foundation for our employer-based insurance system.

Also during World War II, Congress revisited the idea of more broadly operating health insurance as part of Social Security, but the proposed bill did not pass. Just after the end of the war, President Harry S. Truman championed this cause, but to no avail. Instead, a policy mandating hospitals provide a "reasonable volume" of charitable care was passed.[61]

In 1961, the AMA launched a major campaign against Medicare, known as Operation Coffee Cup. The effort featured Ronald Reagan recording speeches warning against "socialized medicine."[62] Despite this opposition, Medicare was signed into law in 1965 by President Johnson, quickly enrolling nearly 20 million elderly Americans in the first three years.[63]

The 1970s saw a series of health reform proposals, the most contentious of which was Senator Ted Kennedy's bipartisan national health insurance bill, which he returned to sponsoring again and again over the course of the decade. By the end of 1977, President Jimmy Carter pushed Kennedy to preserve a larger role for private payers and minimize federal spending in his plan, but Kennedy resisted.

Most recently, in 2010, President Barack Obama signed the ACA into law, mandating that all individuals have health insurance by 2014 (the Trump administration reversed this in 2017).

The ACA also introduced Health Insurance Marketplaces (also known as Exchanges) to facilitate health insurance purchases for individuals and small businesses.

This history helps explain why my health insurance comes through my husband's job and why we have this tangled mix of public and private coverage. We're dealing with decades of regulations and piecemeal solutions that have become permanent features of US healthcare.

Some health systems have taken an innovative approach to healthcare delivery by offering their own insurance plans. These *payviders*—a portmanteau of payer and provider—combine both roles under one roof.

This model has existed for a while in the United States, with around three hundred US health systems currently offering health plans of their own.[64]

One of the oldest and most recognizable payviders is Kaiser Permanente. As of October 2024, Kaiser Permanente's health plan had 12.5 million members. It consistently earns high marks from the National Committee for Quality Assurance (NCQA) and has a strong reputation for keeping costs low and quality high, which it credits to this integrated model.

Here are a few reasons health systems might decide to pursue the payvider model:

- **Coordinated care:** Integrating primary, secondary, and hospital care can lead to better-coordinated care and potentially better health outcomes.
- **Aligned incentives:** With prepayment from each member, payviders are motivated to focus on prevention, health promotion, and effective management of both acute and chronic conditions.
- **Improved efficiency:** By integrating care and coverage, payviders may require fewer resources for billing and administrative overhead.
- **Improved patient experience:** Streamlined healthcare delivery and simplified billing can lead to happier patients. In fact, Kaiser Permanente was ranked the best health plan in a 2024 Insure.com survey.[65]

Over the past decade, pioneering payviders like Kaiser Permanente, Geisinger Health, Providence, UPMC, and Intermountain Health have seen significant growth, demonstrating the potential success of this integrated model. Their ability to align incentives, control costs, and maintain high-quality care has made them stand out. More recently, tech-forward insurance companies like Oscar Health have entered from the opposite direction—starting as insurers and then building their own care delivery capabilities through telehealth.

Yet we haven't seen widespread adoption of the payvider model, which raises a good question: Why not?

PHARMA

With 60 percent of American adults taking at least one prescription drug and 25 percent taking four or more, the pharmaceutical industry—from pharm to table—is an enormous player in our healthcare system.[66] And an expensive one too: Americans spent a whopping $722.5 billion in 2023 on prescription drugs, or roughly $2,163 per person.[67]

At the pharmacy, picking up my topical ointment, I had a complicated interaction with this world. The most straightforward aspect of this interaction was with the pharmacist, who received the prescription from my doctor and filled it when I came in.

But behind that should-be-simple transaction were several stakeholders. There was my insurance—although technically, it wasn't my health insurance spitting out that shocking $275 price tag. Instead, this was the intermediary between pharmacies and insurance—the PBM, which manages my prescription benefits. Then there was the wholesaler, who moved the drug from the manufacturer to my pharmacy. And, finally, there was the company that created this medication and helped decide the list price in the first place.

Pharma: How We Develop and Distribute Medications

The US pharmaceutical industry leads the world in developing cutting-edge medicines, particularly in areas of unmet medical need. Fueled by extensive research and development (R&D) activities, pharmaceutical companies invest billions of dollars annually to pursue new and improved treatments. But most of us don't interact with those lucrative, scientific areas of pharma. Nor do we know much about the intermediary sitting between our health plan and procuring the medications we need. We generally interact only with the last-mile distributor of drugs: retail pharmacies.

Let's look at the flow of money, products, and services in the pharmaceutical supply chain (figure 2.3).

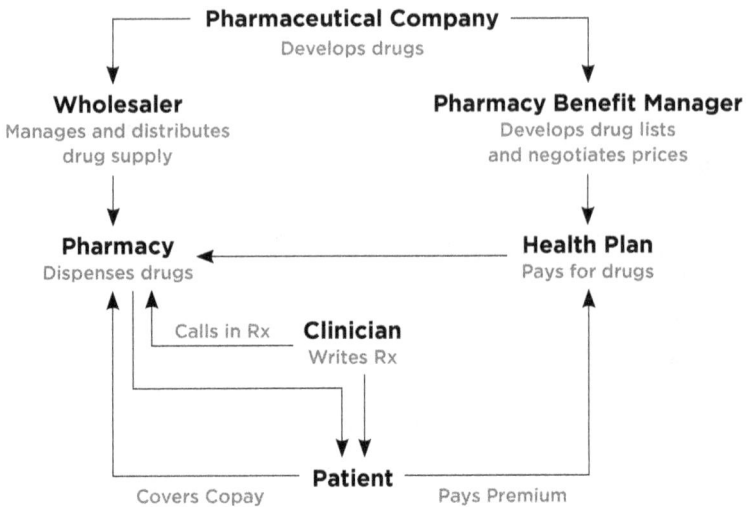

Figure 2.3 This simplified view (yes, this is simplified) illustrates how prescription drugs move through the stakeholders.

PHARMACIES AND PHARMACISTS What do you think is closer to you: your local coffee shop or a pharmacy? For the average American, it's the latter. Just under nine out of ten Americans live no farther than five miles from the nearest pharmacy.[68] As a comparison, for eight out of ten of us, the closest Starbucks is about 20 miles away.[69]

Pharmacists are some of the most frontline healthcare workers we have. They don't just dispense our medications. These professionals also administer vaccines, conduct health screenings, counsel us on how to take our medications, and help manage chronic diseases in concert with our medical providers. Pharmacists can prescribe birth control in thirty states and the District of Columbia, and they were authorized to prescribe COVID-19 treatments during the pandemic.[70]

Pharmacists are highly trained healthcare professionals, completing their doctor of pharmacy (Pharm.D.) degrees in four years and passing state licensing exams. Many also complete residencies for specialized roles in areas like oncology or critical care.

However, pharmacists face growing challenges. More than half of them experience burnout, driven by factors like understaffing, metrics-driven corporate practices, and increasing administrative burdens.[71]

Historically, many pharmacists have worked in independent, family-owned pharmacy businesses. But the 2010s saw massive consolidation as these independent pharmacies disappeared or were gobbled up or replaced by the likes of CVS, Walmart, and Walgreens.

Then, these major pharmacy chains began closing locations and restructuring their businesses. This turbulent period starting in 2021 saw the CEOs of Rite Aid, CVS, and Walgreens all replaced as their companies struggled with changing market dynamics and PBM pressures. Rite Aid filed for bankruptcy in 2023 and emerged again in 2024 with a quarter fewer stores.[72] Meanwhile, Walgreens announced it was closing twelve hundred stores and CVS shuttered nine hundred.[73]

Although pharmacy access remains strong in most communities, research shows that 15.8 million Americans live in pharmacy deserts across both urban and rural areas.[74] These pharmacy deserts disproportionately affect communities with higher proportions of racial and ethnic minorities, people with limited English proficiency, those without health insurance, and individuals with ambulatory disabilities—the same populations that have historically faced barriers to healthcare access. As consolidation and closures continue, these gaps in pharmacy access could worsen, particularly in already underserved areas.

PBMS Take a moment to pull out your health insurance card. Now, look at the back. What does it say next to prescriptions (Rx)? Is it a different name from your overall health insurer's?

That right there is your PBM, the entity your insurance contracts with to manage your pharmacy benefits. They're the ones deciding which drugs your plan covers, how much you pay for them, and where you can buy them. PBMs act as intermediaries between various segments of the pharmaceutical supply chain, including drug manufacturers, pharmacies, and payers. PBM core functions include the following:

- **Formulary design:** Develop drug lists, set coverage tiers (pricing levels), and evaluate medications for inclusion.
- **Utilization management:** Handle prior authorizations (doctor approval required before coverage), step therapy (trying preferred drugs first), and supply limits.
- **Price negotiation:** Work with manufacturers, pharmacies, and wholesalers on pricing and rebates (money paid back to reduce costs).
- **Network management:** Maintain pharmacy networks and mail-order services.[75]

The market for PBM services is highly concentrated, with three firms controlling nearly 80 percent of the market.[76] A 2024 Federal Trade Commission (FTC) report pointed out that these three largest PBMs are owned by health insurance companies.[77] Some of them even share a parent company with retail or mail-order pharmacies. Knowing this makes it a little less surprising that the cost of my prescription was higher *with* insurance than without.

The FTC report claims that this rise in vertical integration may have "created financial conflicts of interest and given large PBM-insurer-pharmacy entities the ability and incentive to preference their affiliated entities over rival entities, potentially resulting in a lessening of competition at various levels of the pharmaceutical supply chain" (figure 2.4).[78]

These relationships—and PBMs' strategic reimbursement rates—are also an important factor in the disappearance of independent pharmacies from around the United States.[79]

This is why, at a White House roundtable in 2024, billionaire entrepreneur Mark Cuban used colorful language to refer to PBMs as "s****ing on independent pharmacies." I'd recommend giving Cuban's testimony a listen to learn more about why he sees PBMs as "putting stock price over health."[80]

Parent/ Owner	CVS Health Corporation	The CIGNA Group	UnitedHealth Group Inc.	Humana
Health Insurer	Aetna	Cigna Healthcare	UnitedHealthcare	Humana
Health Care Provider	MinuteClinic, Signify Health	Evernorth Care Group	Optum Health	CenterWell
PHARMACY BENEFIT MANAGER	♥CVS caremark 34%	EXPRESS SCRIPTS 23%	Optum Rx 22%	Humana Pharmacy 7%
Drug Label Provider	Cordavis Limited	Quallent Pharmaceuticals	NUVAILA	
"PBM GPO"/ Rebate Aggregator	Zinc Health Services	Ascent Health Services	Emisar Pharma Services	Ascent (via contract)
Pharmacy-Retail	CVS Pharmacy			
Pharmacy-Mail Order	CVS Caremark Mail Service Pharmacy	Express Scripts	Optum Rx Mail Service Pharmacy	CenterWell Pharmacy
Pharmacy-Specialty	CVS Specialty Pharmacy	Accredo	Optum Specialty Pharmacy	CenterWell Specialty Pharmacy

Figure 2.4 Vertical integration of health plans and PBMs.

Stat News also has an excellent video series called Behind the Counter that explores the factors involved in pricing prescription drugs, including the complex relationship between drugmakers, insurers, and PBMs.[81]

WHOLESALERS Between your local pharmacy and drugmakers (which we'll cover in a moment) sits another intermediary: pharmaceutical wholesalers. About 92 percent of all prescription drugs in the United States flow through wholesalers, with just three companies—Cardinal Health, Cencora (formerly AmerisourceBergen), and McKesson Corporation—handling more than 90 percent of this distribution.[82]

You may not be familiar with these names, but they are far from small players. McKesson ranks as the ninth largest company in the US by 2024 revenue, Cencora is tenth, and Cardinal is fourteenth, with a combined $829 billion in revenue in 2024 alone.

These companies manage the drug supply chain, purchasing medications from manufacturers, storing them, and then distributing them to pharmacies, hospitals, and clinics across the country.

Wholesalers operate differently in the branded versus generic drug markets. For brand-name drugs, they're price-takers, typically making slim margins. But with generic drugs, wholesalers have more power to influence prices through their negotiations with manufacturers. If a generic manufacturer can't secure a contract with one of the big three wholesalers, they are effectively locked out of the market. Because generics make up 90 percent of retail prescriptions, wholesalers make more money from generics than brand-name drugs.[83]

So how do wholesalers make money with such thin margins? One way is through *forward buying*—that is, purchasing extra inventory when they anticipate a price increase, then selling at the higher price later. They also earn revenue through services they provide to pharmacies and manufacturers, from data analytics to repackaging drugs. Although wholesalers capture only about $2 of every $100 spent on prescriptions, their position in the middle of the supply chain gives them influence over which drugs make it to pharmacy shelves and at what price.

PHARMACEUTICAL COMPANIES Finally, we have the drug makers. Pharmaceutical companies have made remarkable contributions to human health and longevity:

- **Vaccines:** Through innovative vaccine development, the industry has helped eradicate smallpox and nearly eliminated several other devastating diseases. Between 1994 and 2023, childhood vaccinations alone prevented 508 million illnesses, 32 million hospitalizations, and 1.1 million deaths, saving $540 billion in direct costs and $2.7 trillion in societal costs.[84]

- **Treatments:** Breakthroughs in medications for cancer, heart disease, diabetes, HIV/AIDS, and mental health disorders have transformed once-deadly conditions into manageable ones.
- **Chronic disease management:** Daily life has improved dramatically for those with chronic conditions through medications managing allergies, asthma, arthritis, and now even obesity. These treatments allow people to live fuller, more active lives while managing their health conditions.

Pharmaceutical innovation was responsible for two-thirds of the increase in Americans' life expectancy between 2006 and 2018.[85] These gains reflect breakthrough treatments that have helped people live longer, healthier lives.

But discovering these breakthrough treatments is a risky business. Only about one in ten preclinical drugs makes it all the way to FDA approval.[86] The so-called bench-to-bedside delay often amounts to years of work on products that often never see the light of day or help a single patient.

Nevertheless, drug development remains incredibly lucrative. The biggest pharmaceutical companies boast median net income margins of 13.8 percent—nearly double the 7.7 percent average for other large S&P 500 companies.[87]

Clearly, pharmaceutical companies' early gambles are paying off, right? Well, as it turns out, much of the basic and applied research, which forms the foundation for drug development, is publicly funded by institutions like the National Institute of Health (NIH). In other words, we, the taxpayers, are seed-funding a lot of the pharma industry.

At the same time, drug prices in the United States are 2.5 times higher than elsewhere in the world.[88] Pharma is the only major healthcare stakeholder that exercises relatively unrestrained pricing

BOX 2.4.
Where Does $100 Spent on a Prescription Drug Go?

Researchers at the Leonard D. Schaeffer Center for Health Policy and Economics at the University of Southern California looked at where our prescription dollars go (figure 2.5).[92]

For every $100 spent at the pharmacy, $41 goes to the drug manufacturer (of which $15 is net profit), while another $41 is split among intermediaries (wholesalers, pharmacies, PBMs, and insurers) who move, store, and manage the product. The remaining $17 covers the actual cost to manufacture the drug.

What's striking about this split is that the organizations doing the actual scientific discovery, conducting the incredibly costly clinical trials, and taking on the enormous risks of drug development receive the same share as the combined middlemen who move, store, and manage the product. Although distribution and management are necessary functions, they don't drive medical innovation or create new treatments. Yet for every dollar that goes to the companies investing billions in R&D, another dollar goes to these intermediaries who neither discover nor manufacture these lifesaving medications.

But don't feel *too* bad for the pharmaceutical companies—they still maintain significantly higher gross margins than other players in the supply chain: 71 percent, compared with 22 percent for insurers, 20 percent for pharmacies, 6 percent for PBMs, and just 4 percent for wholesalers.

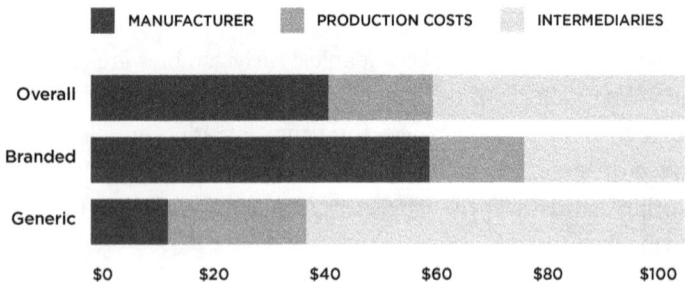

Figure 2.5 Distribution of every $100 spent at the pharmacy.

power. The industry can set the prices paid by Medicare and Medicaid for new drugs. It also has the upper hand with private insurers, who are obligated to cover many new drugs. In the European Union, in contrast, member states have stricter price controls and have more negotiating power when a new drug enters the market.[89] In Canada, the Patented Medicine Prices Review Board (PMPRB) caps the prices of patented medications by comparing them to prices in other countries to ensure Canadian prices are fair.[90]

But there's another way to look at this. In *The Great American Drug Deal*, biotech investor Peter Kolchinsky argues that expensive branded drugs should be viewed as a societal investment rather than an expense. Why? High-cost brand-name drugs are necessary to grow our pool of inexpensive generic drugs. Because brand-name drugs eventually "go generic," they become dramatically cheaper while maintaining the same benefits. In contrast, he points out, the cost of healthcare services—like colonoscopies or knee replacements—only moves in one direction: up.[91]

Pharma: Biggest Challenges

The pharmaceutical industry faces some major hurdles despite (or sometimes because of) being built on innovation:

- **Blockbuster model:** Like Hollywood, the pharmaceutical industry has long relied on the "blockbuster" drug model, in which companies invest heavily in developing and marketing drugs with the potential for annual sales exceeding $1 billion. More than half (55 percent) of approved drugs don't make enough money to recoup their development costs, meaning profits from a few drugs subsidize the rest of the business.[93] To make things more challenging, they have to recover their investment *before* the patent expires and generic competitors enter the market and bring down prices.
- **Drug discovery and development:** Drug discovery has gotten slower, riskier, and more expensive in the last few decades.[94] Some folks claim that the low-hanging fruit in drug discovery has largely been picked, making it more difficult and expensive to develop new blockbuster drugs.

This pressures companies to constantly innovate and find new revenue sources, often leading to high drug prices to recoup R&D costs. The industry is now grappling with how to adapt its business model to remain profitable while also addressing concerns about drug affordability and access.

- **Reputation:** The pharmaceutical industry faces a persistent challenge in public perception. According to an annual Gallup poll, pharma has consistently ranked as the lowest-rated or tied for the lowest-rated industry since 2016 (lower than oil and gas, the federal government, and electric/gas utilities).[95]

- **FDA approval:** With the FDA as the main gatekeeper drug companies must contend with, delays in approval processes quickly become a major headache. Take the 2024 approval of Neffy, a needle-free alternative to the EpiPen. Before finally getting greenlit, Neffy was recommended for approval but then initially was not approved, with the federal agency requesting an additional study.[96] In the meantime, patients hoping for the product amid EpiPen shortages had to simply wait.

- **Compounding pharmacies:** Compounding pharmacies are facilities that can legally produce drugs under certain circumstances, like during drug shortages. Some, however, now produce alternatives to expensive branded drugs at lower costs, filling market gaps. Pharmaceutical manufacturers increasingly assert unfair competition, arguing that compounding pharmacies act beyond their authorized purpose when mimicking commercially available drugs. The industry pushes for stricter regulation, citing safety concerns, while compounding continues to grow as a disruptive force in the pharmaceutical market, potentially eating into the profit margins of established drug companies that invest billions into getting a drug to market.

- **Counterfeit medications:** You can imagine why fake medications might be dangerous. That's why the FDA vigilantly monitors the closed US drug distribution system for counterfeits in the supply.[97] Still, the World Health Organization estimates that more than 10 percent of global pharmaceutical commerce is made up of counterfeit drugs.[98] The most common ones are the most popular and expensive, from erectile dysfunction pills to chemotherapy. Besides being dangerous, these fakes also undermine trust in the pharmaceutical industry and threaten the market power of pharma's legitimate offerings.

Pharma: How Did We Get Here?

The pharmaceutical industry has changed dramatically over the past century. The early US drug market was a mess of unregulated patent medicines and snake oil salesmen—sound familiar from our earlier discussion of providers? This led to the Pure Food and Drug Act of 1906, marking the beginning of federal drug safety oversight.[99]

The discovery of penicillin in 1928 and its subsequent mass production during World War II kicked off the modern pharmaceutical era, during which companies moved from simply manufacturing known compounds to investing heavily in R&D for new drugs.[100]

As the pharmaceutical industry grew more complex and powerful in the postwar decades, so did concerns about drug safety and effectiveness. The 1962 Kefauver-Harris Amendments helped shift us to more evidence-based drug development by requiring pharmaceutical companies to prove both safety and efficacy before FDA approval.[101] Although this dramatically improved drug safety, it also sent development costs and timelines soaring. Today, bringing a new drug to market can cost between $314 million to $4.46 billion and can take ten to fifteen years.[102]

The dawn of 1980 brought a major inflection point with the passing of the bipartisan Bayh-Dole Act.[103] This law allowed universities, businesses, and nonprofits to patent and profit from discoveries from federally funded research rather than forfeit the rights to the federal government. This created today's model, in which taxpayers fund much of the basic research while innovators handle development and commercialization. This legislation is generally considered successful as it has bolstered US economic output by $1.3 trillion, supported 4.2 million jobs, and led to more than eleven thousand new companies.[104]

Another landmark piece of legislation soon followed. The 1984 Hatch-Waxman Act streamlined generic drug approvals while preserving patent protections for new drugs.[105] Companies began to race to recoup development costs during their patent exclusivity period before facing generic competition. Today, generic drugs make up 90 percent of prescriptions but only 20 percent of prescription revenue.[106] Brand-name drugs (which cost twenty times more than generics) make up 10 percent of prescriptions and 80 percent of revenue.

The late 1980s and early 1990s saw the quiet rise of a now-powerful intermediary: the PBM. Although PBMs started in the 1950s as simple claims processors, the industry transformed as prescription drug costs climbed.[107] Insurers and employers started turning to PBMs to help manage drug benefits and negotiate better prices.

The 1990s also saw the rise of blockbuster drugs like Prozac (an antidepressant) and Lipitor (for high cholesterol), establishing the current business model, in which companies bank on developing high-revenue drugs to offset massive R&D costs. By the early 2000s, blockbusters accounted for 40–45 percent of all drug revenues.[108]

Then, in 1997, the FDA loosened restrictions on direct-to-consumer advertising (DTCA) of prescription drugs on television.[109] Before this, pharmaceutical companies had to include a drug's complete risk information in their ads—essentially impossible in a thirty-second TV spot. The 1997 guidance opened the floodgates and the impact was immediate: Pharmaceutical industry spending on TV advertising more than doubled from $310 million in 1997 to $664 million just a year later. By 2022, DTCA reached $8.1 billion.[110] (Note that the United States is one of only two countries, the other being New Zealand, that allow drug manufacturers to market prescription drugs directly to the public.)

My sticker shock at the pharmacy counter makes more sense when you consider how the market works. Pharmaceutical companies need to recoup their R&D dollars before patents expire. The rise of intermediaries explains why my pharmacist could magically cut my price by typing a few keystrokes. And although we've certainly come a long way from snake oil salesmen, we're still grappling with balancing scientific progress with affordability and access. Our current system excels at making cutting-edge drugs but often struggles to make them available to the patients who need them most.

WHERE DO WE GO FROM HERE?

After looking at how providers, payers, and pharma shape US healthcare, it's easy to feel overwhelmed. These stakeholders are massive, powerful, and entrenched in their ways. Each operates within its own tangle of incentives, regulations, and historical quirks that seem to make meaningful change impossible.

But the thing about systems built by humans is that they can be changed by humans.

Impermanence is a challenge *and* an opportunity. In our country, policymakers have limited terms. Companies rise and fall. The powers that be are not forever. On one hand, this explains why our laws and systems are set up the way they are—haphazardly. On the other, it's also why we can change the status quo instead of treating it like an inevitability.

The most important thing we can do, both as patients and innovators, is to resist our feelings of helplessness. This is an understandable reaction to the messy lattice of power and incentives you've just read about. But with this information, you can step up. You can take what you know about healthcare, pair it with your own expertise, and build new solutions.

Because we've all been patients, we intuitively understand that US healthcare doesn't quite add up. Now, with a grounding in the many challenges and competing incentives throughout the rest of the healthcare jungle, you can see even more problems to solve—and new avenues through which to solve them.

In recognizing just how messy US healthcare is, we can stop waiting for the adults to show up. We're the adults. And it's our prerogative to make things better. For ourselves and each other.

TL;DR

- **You're not too much of an outsider to "get it":** US healthcare isn't built intentionally. It's not made to make sense.
- **Each stakeholder has its own source and gradient of power:** The way power flows within and between stakeholders is shaped by a complicated history of policy, corporate growth, and institution-building.
- **Incentives are not the same as individual motivations:** These stakeholders operate in response to an intersecting network of incentives and challenges, which are often at odds with the intrinsic motivations of the individuals working in these systems.
- **Recognizing problems begets solutions:** As an innovator, by recognizing the problems underpinning our healthcare system—and not accepting them as a given—you're poised to help solve them.

3

HEALTHCARE'S SLEEPING GIANT

It is a competitive advantage to partner with patients, survivors, and caregivers
at every stage of innovation. Otherwise, you leave half the team on the bench.
—SUSANNAH FOX

My grandma was a force of nature. Although petite in stature—
she stood tall at just 4'11"—she had an enormous spirit that
craved adventure. After my grandfather died, she pursued her wan-
derlust on a shoestring budget, chaperoning student trips to far-
flung places and sending us grandkids postcards filled with tales of
vibrant markets and ancient ruins. After seventy-five years of living
in Ohio, she decided to pursue her dream of trading Midwest win-
ters for the Florida sunshine. She bought a trailer in the small town
of Inverness. And she wouldn't be alone.

Her son, my uncle, volunteered to migrate to Florida to look
after her (figure 3.1). A wanderer himself, he had held a string of
odd jobs that ranged from working on an Alaskan fishing boat to
being a gas station attendant to buying and selling merchandise on
eBay. Wherever his travels took him, however, he always seemed
to circle back to my grandma's sofa. A nomad, he was uninsured
and never established habits of care supervised by a doctor. He was
a loner, a smoker, and perhaps Grandma's favorite child. As they
planned their new life down south, they thought they could make it
work by living off her Social Security and a helping hand from Meals
on Wheels. The rest of the family talked to my grandma all the time
on the phone, and we even met her for a weekend in Tampa, but a
few years passed without any of us seeing their living conditions.

Figure 3.1 My grandma and uncle arriving in Florida.

Then came the call. Meals on Wheels was worried. They reported that the steps to the trailer were slick with moss, and they were concerned for my grandma's well-being. Alerted, the family acted, and we traveled down to check in with my grandmother and uncle in person.

What awaited us was a scene worse than we could have ever imagined. The trailer was riddled with mold, the electricity intermittent. Inside the cramped space, my uncle, now more than five hundred pounds and immobile, chain-smoked. He hadn't seen a doctor in more than a decade, his chronic illnesses left untreated. Far from taking care of his aging mother, it was my grandma, with early signs of dementia (she would often call him by my late grandpa's name), who struggled to tend to his needs.

We brought them back to Cleveland, where they lived in a makeshift bedroom in my mother's dining room. A whirlwind of doctors' appointments and navigating the social safety net followed, along with attempts to find my uncle home healthcare aides. Each effort brought a new frustration—weeks-long waits for specialists, unaffordable medications, and the ever-present worry that even with care, the damage done was irreversible.

The cracks in our healthcare system were wide enough for my uncle to slip through. By the time help was feasible, the deterioration was deep-rooted. Diagnosed with emphysema, cancer, and "failure to thrive" (a controversial label often used to describe physical, cognitive, and functional decline), he later passed away.[1] But not before costing our healthcare system hundreds of thousands of dollars in end-of-life medical and hospice care.

My uncle's story is a sobering example of how medical disenfranchisement and years of neglect can lead to devastating consequences—not just for individuals but for the entire healthcare system. It's easy to point fingers at personal choices, but when millions of Americans remain unengaged with their health, we must ask: Is the system part of the problem?

In this chapter, we'll explore this question, diving into the patient engagement challenge and how we desperately need innovation to help engage and intervene before a crisis spirals out of control. I will uncover the systemic barriers that keep people from accessing and participating in their care, along with the high cost of this disengagement for both individuals and society. But I'll also shine a light on a growing movement—a "healthcare consumer awakening"—that offers hope for a more proactive, equitable, and patient-centered future.

THE ENGAGEMENT CHALLENGE (AND OPPORTUNITY)

More than a decade ago, Rock Health became one of the first groups to study consumer adoption of digital health tools through our annual consumer survey and report. We wanted to understand consumer adoption trends, including telehealth, wearables, genetic testing, health apps, and more. As part of our 2015 Digital Health Consumer Adoption report, our team devised a framework to evaluate patient archetypes on two gradients: unhealthy to healthy and unengaged to engaged.[2]

This simple matrix helped us think through different patient populations, their needs, and the opportunities for innovation in each quadrant. It became a framework I use and share often (figure 3.2).

Let's explore each quadrant and the specific characteristics of the patients they represent.

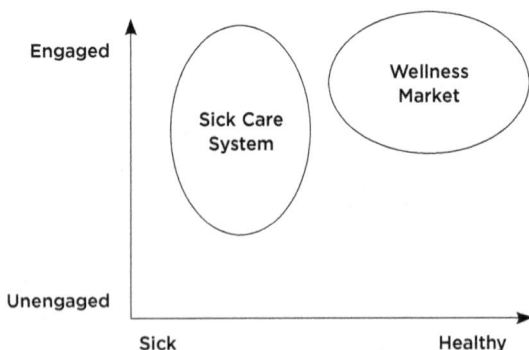

Figure 3.2 Patient engagement-health matrix.

Healthy and Engaged

- Proactive about health maintenance
- Regular participants in preventive care
- Early adopters of digital health, wellness, and longevity trends

For healthy and engaged individuals, health is a top priority. They're getting ten thousand steps a day, eating the recommended Mediterranean diet, taking various supplements, and never missing a health screening (they may even be getting additional screenings). A $1.5 trillion global wellness market caters to this group, which often has the disposable income to invest heavily in preventive health.[3]

This group, however, also includes the "worried well"—people who are healthy but excessively concerned about their health, leading to anxiety and overutilization of healthcare resources.

Sick and Engaged

- Actively managing chronic conditions or acute health issues
- Regular users of healthcare services
- Well-informed about their conditions

Sick and engaged patients are facing health problems and are actively engaged in getting better. They do their own research, ask lots of questions during appointments, and aren't afraid to get a second opinion. Many find support and share experiences through online patient communities and disease-specific forums. But unfortunately, a rising number of "influencers" peddle the illusion of quick fixes, preying on this group's desire for easy solutions to complicated health challenges.

Our current healthcare system is largely geared toward "fixing" this group rather than preventing illness in the first place.

Healthy and Unengaged

- Healthy today but not proactive about health maintenance
- Infrequent users of healthcare services
- May lack health literacy or interest in preventive care

Serving the healthy and unengaged folks in this quadrant, people like my uncle in the decades before his health declined, represents a huge missed opportunity. They're not actively engaged with the healthcare system, for reasons I'll share soon, and without regular checkups and preventive care, we miss opportunities for early intervention that could avert more serious health issues down the line.

Sick and Unengaged

- Living with untreated or poorly managed health conditions
- Infrequent or inconsistent users of healthcare services
- May face significant barriers to accessing care

The sick and unengaged people in this quadrant represent the most vulnerable group. Like my uncle in his later years, these individuals are dealing with health issues but aren't actively engaged in managing them, often because of systemic barriers. Their health issues, left untreated or poorly managed, can escalate into serious complications, leading to more frequent use of expensive emergency services for what should be preventable issues.

The upper half of the matrix shown in figure 3.2—the engaged patients—are the two groups that our healthcare system and the wellness industry have traditionally focused on. But what about the unengaged? Whether healthy or unhealthy, this group often falls through the cracks.

There's a huge opportunity in finding ways to move people to a motivated, engaged state sooner, before chronic conditions set in and while prevention is still possible. Yes, personal responsibility is important. But when American individualism means people who could be helped fall through the cracks, it's also a failure of the system—an expensive failure that would be cheaper to fix in the first place.

There are many reasons someone would be chronically unengaged with our healthcare system.[4]

- **High cost of care:** The biggest barrier to engagement is the prohibitively high cost of care in the United States. Even for those with insurance, high deductibles, copays, and out-of-pocket expenses can lead many to postpone or avoid healthcare services altogether.[5]
- **Disenfranchisement:** Over 100 million Americans—nearly one-third of our nation—are medically disenfranchised.[6] This means they do not have access to a consistent source of primary care because of a shortage of providers in their local community.
- **Socioeconomic factors:** Poverty, lack of transportation, inability to take time off work, or lack of childcare can all create significant barriers to engaging with healthcare services. These factors can make even routine checkups impossible.
- **Health literacy:** Low health literacy can make it difficult for individuals to understand medical information, navigate the healthcare system, or recognize the importance of preventive care. This can lead to disengagement from healthcare services and poorer health outcomes.[7]
- **Mistrust:** Given America's fraught history of discrimination in healthcare, it's understandable that many people find it hard to trust the medical establishment. This mistrust stems from medical racism, sexism, homophobia, classism, ableism, and other pervasive biases. Cultural insensitivity and negative personal experiences further erode trust in the healthcare system, particularly among already marginalized communities. When people don't trust their healthcare providers to see them, hear them, or treat them fairly, they're far less likely to seek care in the first place.[8]
- **Judgment and shame:** Some patients experience judgmental attitudes from healthcare providers. This judgment—whether about a stigmatized diagnosis, lifestyle choices, or adherence to treatment plans—can be

humiliating and push people away from seeking care. (For example, one study found that 15.8 percent of patients felt "shamed" by health professionals for their weight.)[9] Patients who feel judged rather than supported are less likely to engage with the healthcare system, even when they need it most.

- **Bad past experiences:** One negative encounter with the healthcare system can lower institutional trust and deter someone from seeking care for years.[10] Whether it's a misdiagnosis, a dismissive doctor, a medical error, or simply feeling unheard or disrespected, these experiences leave lasting scars.

There are both health and economic benefits to higher patient engagement. Engaged patients show better health outcomes and report higher satisfaction with their care.[11] Higher engagement leads to the following:

- **Fewer preventable deaths:** The Centers for Disease Control and Prevention estimates that up to 40 percent of the deaths from the five leading causes of death (heart disease, cancer, chronic lower respiratory diseases, stroke, and unintentional injuries) are preventable.[12] This means hundreds of thousands of early deaths could be avoided by helping people become more active in their health.
- **Higher quality of life:** Research shows that patient engagement and higher *self-efficacy* (one's belief in their ability to manage their health) may improve the quality of life for people living with chronic diseases.[13]
- **Increased productivity:** One study calculated the total cost of absenteeism to employers as $3.6 billion for smoking, $9.1 billion for physical inactivity, and $17.9 billion for obesity—and this is just among the workforce.[14]
- **Cost savings:** As the saying goes, "An ounce of prevention is worth a pound of cure." Adherence to prescribed treatment alone could save us an estimated $100 billion annually.[15]
- **Reduced disparities:** Given that vulnerable populations are most at risk for being disenfranchised, it's possible to narrow health equity gaps and improve outcomes for those who face systemic barriers to care.

Our challenge—and opportunity—lies in creating a healthcare system that effectively serves all four quadrants, with a particular focus on engaging the unengaged. Understanding *why* they are unengaged and removing those barriers is just as important (if not more!) than building new tools for engagement. But how do we create the conditions to make that possible?

BOX 3.1.

In the Trenches: Aledade

After years as a public servant, Dr. Farzad Mostashari knew one thing for sure: primary care could change lives. As the National Coordinator for Health Information Technology at the US Department of Health and Human Services and founder of the NYC Primary Care Information Project, he'd seen how a strong relationship with a primary care doctor could keep people engaged with their health.

He also saw a problem. Too many people were falling into our matrix's "unengaged" quadrants and not actively involved in their care. Dr. Mostashari believed that empowering primary care doctors could fix this.

In 2014, he founded Aledade to put this belief into action. The company (a public benefit corporation) helps independent primary care practices engage patients and succeed financially by keeping people healthy.

Aledade gives primary care doctors tools to identify and reach out to patients who might otherwise slip through the cracks. One of its primary care partners is Dr. Darrin Menard's practice in rural Scott, Louisiana.

When Dr. Menard started working with Aledade, he thought his practice was doing well managing patients' blood pressure. But Aledade's app showed their hypertension control rate was only 63 percent.

Using Aledade's workflow suggestions and guidance, Dr. Menard's team identified patients with high blood pressure who hadn't returned for follow-ups. They reached out to these patients, bringing them in for checkups and starting treatment when needed.

"Our office was able to utilize the Aledade app to identify our patients that had moderate to severely elevated blood pressure readings on their

---

(*continued on next page*)

(*continued from previous page*)

last visit with the care team," Dr. Menard explains. "Those patients were tagged, and we generated a list through the app to call those patients and have them come back in for a recheck of blood pressure and initiate therapy if needed."[16]

In just one year, the practice's hypertension control rate jumped to 90 percent. In four years, it exceeded 95 percent. The practice saw similar improvements in other areas. Pneumonia vaccination rates rose from 18 percent to 92 percent and annual wellness visits increased from 18 percent to 87 percent.

Aledade's story shows how the right software can help primary care practices better engage patients. The company's efforts helped move people from the "unengaged" to the "engaged" quadrants of our matrix by giving primary care physicians the tools Dr. Mostashari knew they needed.

PATIENTS AS STAKEHOLDERS

Patients, in theory, are the protagonists of healthcare, but they've historically had the least power. Unlike the other stakeholders, patients lack organized representation and struggle to influence policy and practice. Yet they (we) are the ones with the most at stake.

Just follow the money to Washington. The healthcare sector spends more on lobbying than any other industry.[17] In 2023, these organizations were top spenders across *all* industries:

- **$30.2 million:** The American Hospital Association represents hospitals and healthcare networks.
- **$28.6 million:** Blue Cross/Blue Shield represents 33 independent and locally operated health insurance companies.
- **$27.6 million:** Pharmaceutical Research and Manufacturers of America represents biopharmaceutical companies.
- **$21.2 million:** The American Medical Association is the largest national association of physicians.

- **$15.4 million:** Pharmaceutical Care Management Association is the national association representing pharmacy benefit managers (PBMs).

Individual companies also have a lobbying presence including Pfizer ($14.4 million), Amgen ($14.3 million), UnitedHealth Group ($10.7 million), and Cigna ($10.4 million). If these lobbying efforts weren't helping sway policies in their favor, they wouldn't continue year after year. This has been dubbed the "return on investment for lobbying"—and researchers have found that for every dollar a company spends on lobbying, its value increases by $200.[18]

So who's looking out for healthcare consumers? Patient advocacy groups like Patients for Affordable Drugs Now and Patients Rising have a presence in D.C., but they are dwarfed by industry lobbyists. In 2023, these two groups combined spent about $350,000 on lobbying—a drop in the bucket compared with corporate spending.[19]

THE GREAT HEALTHCARE CONSUMER AWAKENING

For decades, healthcare consumers have been a sleeping giant within our system—a dormant force with the potential to drive massive change. Now that giant is beginning to stir.

As medical costs continue to climb relentlessly, we, the people, are breaking out of our forced role as passive recipients—and payers—of care. Citizens are emerging as more active, vocal stakeholders, demanding affordability, transparency, and a say in healthcare spending. This shift, which we might call a "healthcare consumer awakening," could fundamentally change our sick care system.

The term *consumer* in healthcare is contentious. Some people say that it diminishes the vulnerability and humanity of patients. I would argue, however, that the term *patient* has inadvertently reinforced our passive role in our health. Yes, we are periodically patients when we are sick and need care. But we are also the ultimate consumers and payers of healthcare—every day, sick or well.

Americans pay for healthcare in many ways, often invisibly. We pay premiums, accept lower wages in exchange for employer-sponsored healthcare, and watch as 30 percent of our state tax dollars and 24 percent of our federal tax dollars flow into the healthcare system.[20] Our financial relationship with healthcare makes us consumers in the truest sense. The difference is that, unlike in other markets, we've been consumers without choice—bearing the costs without the corresponding power to make truly informed decisions or drive change.

But the healthcare consumer is finally awakening and demanding more control over healthcare. Here's why.

First and foremost, we come back to the issue of cost. For decades, healthcare expenses in the United States have outpaced inflation at an alarming rate. In 2023, national health spending grew by 7.5 percent, reaching a record $4.8 trillion—or $13,493 per person.[21] This trend has significantly outpaced wage growth, placing an ever-increasing burden on families. As healthcare consumes a larger portion of household budgets, consumers increasingly question the value they receive for their dollars.

Second, healthcare coverage is also changing. New models are putting more responsibility—and potentially more control—in the hands of consumers. Following are two examples of this change:

- **High-Deductible Health Plans (HDHPs):** HDHPs have lower premiums but expose consumers to higher out-of-pocket expenses before insurance coverage kicks in.[22] As of 2024, 27 percent of all covered workers were enrolled in an HDHP with a savings option (where people can use pretax dollars for out-of-pocket expenses), a huge increase from just 4 percent in 2006.[23]
- **Individual Coverage Health Reimbursement Arrangement (ICHRA):** Introduced in 2020, ICHRA plans allow employers to provide tax-free reimbursements for health insurance premiums and qualified medical expenses. The HRA Council reported a 171 percent increase in the number of workers with access to ICHRA from 2022 to 2023.[24] An estimated five thousand employers offered ICHRAs in 2024.[25]

HDHPs and ICHRAs have made consumers more acutely aware of their healthcare expenses. However, the National Bureau of Economic Research found that while HDHPs lead to lower healthcare costs, that's because of lower utilization and not price shopping.[26]

Third, the asymmetry of information between patients and every other stakeholder is gradually shifting toward greater patient empowerment and transparency in healthcare. The No Surprises Act, which went into effect in 2022 to protect patients against surprise medical billing, and other hospital price transparency rules have made healthcare pricing more available and predictable. We also have greater access to healthcare information than ever before. Within just two years of being launched, more than one-third of Americans were already using artificial intelligence apps, like ChatGPT, to research conditions and treatments and understand medical results.[27] We've never seen that speed of adoption before in healthcare.

Last, the relationship between insurers and the public has grown particularly strained, with 60 percent of insured adults reporting problems with their coverage.[28] These problems range from network adequacy issues (not having enough in-network doctors available) to preauthorization delays (where patients must wait for insurance company approval before getting medical care) to denied claims (where insurance companies refuse to pay for medical services after they've been provided).

In November 2024, Anthem Blue Cross Blue Shield announced it would limit reimbursements for anesthesia during surgeries and medical procedures—essentially telling Americans they might need to pay out of pocket if their surgery took longer than a given time limit, something obviously out of a patient's control. In a statement from the American Society of Anesthesiologists, Dr. Donald E. Arnold called this "just the latest in a long line of appalling behavior by commercial health insurers looking to drive their profits up at the expense of patients and physicians providing essential care."[29] The timing was particularly galling: Anthem's parent company had recently reported a 24 percent increase in its year-over-year net income to $2.3 billion.

Social media exploded with outrage at what many saw as a new low for the insurance industry. The announcement crystallized everything people dislike about health insurance companies: their focus on profits over patient care, their arbitrary rules designed to deny coverage, and their seeming indifference to human suffering. The backlash was intense and immediate. The next month, Anthem reversed course.

Still, the incident revealed deep fissures, exposing just how far removed the system has become from the foundational purpose of protecting people's health. The growing frustration erupted tragically on December 4, 2024, when UnitedHealthcare CEO Brian Thompson was targeted and killed in New York City. The bullet casings had the words "deny," "defend," and "depose" written on them—terms commonly used to describe insurer tactics to avoid paying claims. Although such violence can never be justified, the incident (along with the subsequent lionization of the suspect by many) laid bare the desperation many Americans feel with our healthcare system.

HOLDING EMPLOYERS ACCOUNTABLE
FOR HEALTHCARE SPENDING

As I discussed in the last chapter, most Americans receive health benefits through their employers. Now, people are starting to hold their employers accountable. While I was writing this book, current and former employees at Johnson & Johnson and Wells Fargo took the extraordinary step of suing these companies over alleged mismanagement of health benefits, the first lawsuits of their kind.[30]

The lawsuits allege that these companies, as fiduciaries of their employees' health plans, failed in their responsibility to be prudent stewards of these benefits. Specifically, the employees claim that their employers overpaid for prescription drugs, effectively wasting plan assets and driving up costs for employees.

This signals a new level of sophistication among employees in understanding and questioning healthcare financing and plan administration. Whether or not these lawsuits are successful, they will likely force employers nationwide to reevaluate their approach to healthcare benefits, potentially leading to more aggressive negotiation with insurers and PBMs, increased transparency, and a greater focus on cost-effectiveness in healthcare spending.

BOX 3.2.

Who Really Pays for Healthcare?

When it comes to paying for healthcare in the United States, the answer is not as simple as pointing to a single entity. The cost is spread across a network of insurers, employers, patients, and taxpayers, often in ways that are far from transparent.

Let's start with the obvious: health insurance companies. We often think of them as the "payers" in the healthcare system, the ones footing the bill. But that's not entirely accurate. Insurance companies are more like intermediaries. They use *your* monthly payment (a premium) to pay your medical claims. To stay in business, they need to profit off more customers than they pay out in claims—at least in the few years you are on their plan.

At the end of the day, they are risk-bearing financial entities and not the ones *really* paying for healthcare. In fact, they don't even "pay" the bills in the traditional sense. They get invoiced by providers and, then, maybe pay the claim.

What about employers? After all, more Americans get their health insurance through their jobs than any other way. But it's a mistake to think our employers are gifting us healthcare. Workers pay the cost of employer-sponsored health plans through lower wages and higher

---

(*continued on next page*)

(*continued from previous page*)

prices for goods and services. In other words, we're still paying for it, just not directly.

Then there are the costs we see more directly. Insurance premiums alone are staggering, averaging $8,951 annually for single coverage and $25,572 for family coverage in 2024.[31] On top of that come the copays, the deductibles, the bills that show up weeks after a doctor's visit. Americans shelled out an additional $1,514 per person in these out-of-pocket health expenses in 2023—and that's after already paying their insurance premiums.[32]

And even though we don't have socialized medicine, healthcare still accounts for a huge chunk of our taxes. Roughly a quarter of our federal tax dollars go to healthcare in some form, whether it's Medicare, Medicaid, the Children's Health Insurance Program, or subsidies for Affordable Care Act plans, along with 30 percent of our state taxes.[33]

So who actually pays for healthcare? When you think about it, the answer is obvious. We do. Every American pays for healthcare through lower wages, higher prices, out-of-pocket costs, and taxes. The burden isn't spread out evenly. A Rand Corporation study found that lower-income families spend a much bigger chunk of their income on healthcare—33.9 percent for the bottom fifth of earners, compared with only 16 percent for the top fifth.[34]

This convoluted system obscures the true cost of healthcare and makes it hard to fix the problems. When we can't clearly see who's paying and how much, it's tough to have an honest conversation about how to make the system work better.

But because we are the ones ultimately footing the bill, we also have the power to demand change. We can advocate for a healthcare system that is more transparent, more equitable, and more focused on delivering value for every dollar spent.

We need to push for policies that reduce perverse incentives and put the focus on keeping people healthy rather than just managing risk and shifting blame.

We must demand more from our insurers, employers, and policymakers. We need to insist on a system that works for us, the people paying the bills, rather than for the ones that obscure costs and perpetuate inequities.

The road to a massively better healthcare system starts with understanding who pays for it. But it ends with all of us, as patients, taxpayers, and citizens, demanding something better. We have the power to shape the future of US healthcare. It's time we used it.

THE RISE OF HEALTHCARE SHOPPING

Consumers are increasingly researching their options before making healthcare decisions, a trend that has accelerated in recent years. By doing so, consumers are taking a more active role in their care, considering factors such as quality, convenience, and value alongside price. Studies have shown that tools for price-shopping healthcare services reduce costs without leading to a decrease in quality.[35]

According to a 2024 McKinsey report, economic uncertainty has spurred consumers to become more discerning in their purchases across various industries, including healthcare:

- 45 percent of consumers report researching providers and in-network costs before choosing a health insurance plan.
- 44 percent of consumers research providers before making an appointment.
- Those who research providers look at an average of two to three options before making a decision.

This is a significant change from just a few years ago. The 2017 survey showed that only 20–30 percent of healthcare consumers conducted similar research. The near doubling of this behavior in such a short time illustrates the rapid increase in consumer engagement in healthcare decision-making.[36]

BOX 3.3.
In the Trenches: Collective Health

Ali Diab learned about healthcare's opacity the hard way. After emergency surgery, he found himself battling his health insurer over massive surprise hospital bills. While managing a difficult recovery, he was forced to become his own advocate in a system in which getting straight answers seemed impossible.

This experience led Ali and his cofounder, Dr. Rajaie Batniji, to start Collective Health to make health benefits simple, transparent, and pleasant to use. As an early investor through Rock Health and a current board member, I've watched Collective Health grow from a promising startup to a company now serving more than six hundred thousand Americans.

Collective Health empowers healthcare consumers by making their employer-sponsored insurance benefits more transparent and straightforward. The platform guides members toward smarter health decisions by providing relevant care suggestions; finding high-quality, lower-cost options for routine procedures like MRIs; and helping those with chronic conditions stay on track with their care plans.

One study showed that members using Collective Health had higher engagement with care advocacy, fewer emergency room visits, and increased use of preventive care.[37] These improvements led to meaningful savings throughout the healthcare system. When members can better understand, navigate, and use their benefits, everyone wins.

The rise of healthcare shopping is both a symptom of and catalyst for the broader consumer awakening in healthcare. It reflects growing consumer empowerment and drives further changes in how healthcare is delivered, priced, and experienced.

MORE DIRECT-TO-CONSUMER OPTIONS THAN EVER

As consumers become more active healthcare shoppers, companies are responding with an explosion of direct-to-consumer (D2C) healthcare options. These new solutions are no longer just geared toward the worried well—they're becoming mainstream.

I see this firsthand when I run my "Ohio test," asking friends and family in my home state about healthcare brands they know and use. Increasingly, they mention venture-backed healthcare startups they've discovered through provider referrals or D2C marketing—a level of brand recognition that was unimaginable a decade ago.

This isn't just anecdotal. Today, 21 percent of Americans have taken a mail-in DNA test, 53 percent own at least one wearable health tracking device, and more than half of Americans have used virtual care in the past year.[38] Mobile health apps like Noom, Flo, and MyFitnessPal saw consumer spending surge from $550 million in 2016 to $3.4 billion in 2023—a staggering 524 percent increase.[39] Even established players are shifting to D2C: Diabetes management giant Dexcom now offers a continuous glucose monitoring system called Stelo directly to consumers without a prescription.

Perhaps most excitingly, D2C healthcare is tackling areas that have long been stigmatized or difficult to access. Virtual care options now provide discreet, accessible care for needs ranging from menopause and infertility to sexual dysfunction, mental health, substance use disorder, gender-affirming care, hair loss, acne, and abortion. We're seeing a complete shift in how Americans access these sensitive but essential healthcare services—and it's about time.

WHAT'S NEXT FOR HEALTHCARE CONSUMERS

The awakening of healthcare's sleeping giant—healthcare consumers—is here, not a moment too soon. If we play our cards right, this could be what it takes to help more people realize their full health potential.

You can choose one of two sides as this unfolds. You can stand by the status quo, treating healthcare consumers as passive participants. Objects, not subjects. Or you can help activate patient engagement to reach those long marginalized by our system.

To me, the choice is clear. We need new tools and business models to make preventive health accessible and engaging. We need to hold the intermediaries accountable for how they spend our money. We need to unravel healthcare paternalism.

But we've got a long way to go. The same system failing millions of Americans isn't going to transform overnight just because we've started asking questions.

Our greatest challenge—and opportunity—is leveraging this awakening to serve our most unengaged populations. Success will lie in our ability to extend patient empowerment universally.

We have an unprecedented chance to remake a system that would have intervened before my uncle's health spiraled, that would have bolstered my grandmother in her caregiving role, and that treats every patient with the dignity and care they inherently deserve.

This is the future of healthcare we must strive toward—a vision in which the cracks in the system are sealed, prevention trumps crisis management, and patient engagement is the norm, not the exception. It's an ambitious goal, but one that the consumer awakening has brought within our reach.

TL;DR

- **Patient engagement is a challenge:** Patients range from healthy to sick and engaged to unengaged. Our healthcare system often fails those who are unengaged, leading to preventable crises and higher costs.
- **Multiple obstacles prevent engagement:** Factors like disenfranchisement, socioeconomic barriers, high costs, health literacy issues, mistrust, and negative past experiences keep people from engaging with healthcare.
- **Patients remain historically disempowered:** Despite being central to healthcare, patients have historically been the least empowered stakeholders, lacking organized representation and struggling to influence policy and practice.

- **The sleeping giant is emerging:** Healthcare consumers are becoming more informed and empowered, demanding transparency, affordability, and a say in healthcare spending.
- **This creates new opportunities:** The consumer awakening presents a new opportunity to transform healthcare. Our success will depend on extending this empowerment to all, especially the most vulnerable and unengaged populations.

PART II

THE ANATOMY OF HEALTHCARE INNOVATION

4

WHAT DOES INNOVATION LOOK LIKE?

Innovation is the ability to see change as an opportunity–not a threat.
—STEVE JOBS

In the first part of the book, we examined the urgent need for innovation in healthcare. But what exactly do we mean by "innovation"? What form does it take, and how can we recognize it when we see it?

Many of us assume the most important healthcare innovations must look cutting-edge: laser scalpels, neural implants, 3D-printed organs. This futuristic imagery of innovation can cause us to overlook, and even undervalue, less visible healthcare solutions that can yield massive returns.

We need the "skyscrapers" of innovation, obviously, but we must also work on the "power grid"—the infrastructure essential for its functioning. Many fundamental, albeit unsexy, solutions in healthcare are desperately needed. Neglecting these foundational elements can lead to problems that undermine the impact of even the most exciting new advancements.

In this chapter, we'll explore healthcare innovation and the various pathways it can follow. We'll look at examples of groundbreaking technologies, creative business models, and competitive solutions that are changing the way healthcare is delivered and experienced. I'll also introduce a framework for evaluating healthcare innovations based on three criteria: sustainability, scalability, and impact.

WHAT DO WE MEAN BY INNOVATION?

Healthcare innovation is the development and implementation of new ideas, processes, technologies, or even business models that, when done right, can measurably improve health outcomes, reduce costs, improve experiences, or increase access to healthcare.

Healthcare innovation takes many forms. Some innovations introduce something entirely new to the world, like real-time heart rate monitoring on your hand (e.g., the Oura Ring or the Apple Watch).

But innovation doesn't always mean invention. Some of the most impactful solutions come not from brand-new technologies, but from rethinking how we use what already exists. Take telemedicine: live-stream video wasn't new at the time, but applying it to doctor visits changed how and where care could be delivered. And when layered with new business models, like D2C memberships, it created entirely new ways to access care.

To help my students make sense of these different types of innovation, I created the Healthcare Innovation Pathway Matrix. It is a simple but helpful way to assess how a solution fits into the healthcare status quo.

THE FOUR PATHWAYS OF HEALTHCARE INNOVATION

This matrix looks at two key dimensions (figure 4.1). The y-axis looks at the product (or service) being introduced: "new" means groundbreaking advancements, whereas "established" means that it is already proven in healthcare or other industries. The x-axis assesses the business model or strategy: a "new" model rethinks how care is financed, delivered, or accessed, while an "established" model works within traditional structures.

No one pathway is better than the others. As you review all four quadrants, you'll see that impactful companies have come from all of them.

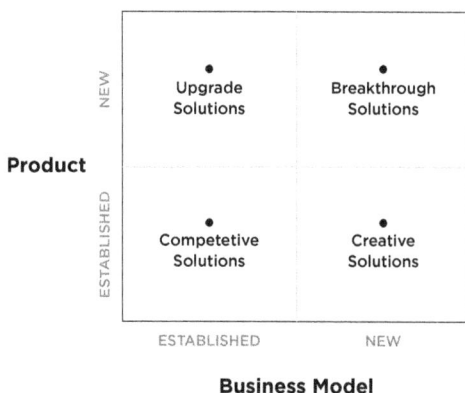

Figure 4.1 Four Pathways of Healthcare Innovation.

Of course, companies can and do bounce around among these pathways. Innovation can never truly rest in a single quadrant. What's new becomes old, and even the most game-changing ideas eventually become part of accepted practice (or not).

Although the words fit nicely in these boxes, reality is not as neat. A single solution might contain aspects that fall into different quadrants, and those placements can shift over time.

An idea might initially feel radical, but as regulations soften and adoption rates rise, does that shift its placement? Ultimately, we care more about results than tidy classifications. That is why this matrix—of breakthrough solutions, upgrade solutions, creative solutions, and competitive solutions—is best for *starting* the conversation, not providing definitive answers. Let's go through them.

Breakthrough Solutions

This quadrant showcases radical innovations in which the product and its underlying business model are entirely new to the market. Breakthrough solutions challenge the status quo and attempt to completely transform healthcare. Because of this, they are also the absolute most difficult to execute.

For example, take Dexcom, a company that made more than $4 billion in 2024 selling its continuous glucose monitoring (CGM) system for diabetes management (figure 4.2).

- **Product innovation:** Early Dexcom devices were groundbreaking. CGM technology wasn't brand new at the time, but it was bulky, invasive, and primarily meant for short-term hospital use. Dexcom upended CGM by offering discreet, wearable sensors that transmit glucose data every five minutes from the comfort of a user's home.
- **Business model disruption:** Instead of targeting just hospitals, Dexcom went direct-to-consumer. This was audacious—diabetic patients were used to finger-prick glucose checks, and many doctors were slow to recommend new products. Dexcom invested heavily in patient education and advocacy, changing the power dynamic between patients and providers.
- **The shifting position:** Initially, Dexcom fit squarely in the upper right quadrant of the matrix. Both the underlying tech and its business model were radically new. Dexcom's success, however, has shifted its position. Although its CGM technology has continued to evolve, it is less

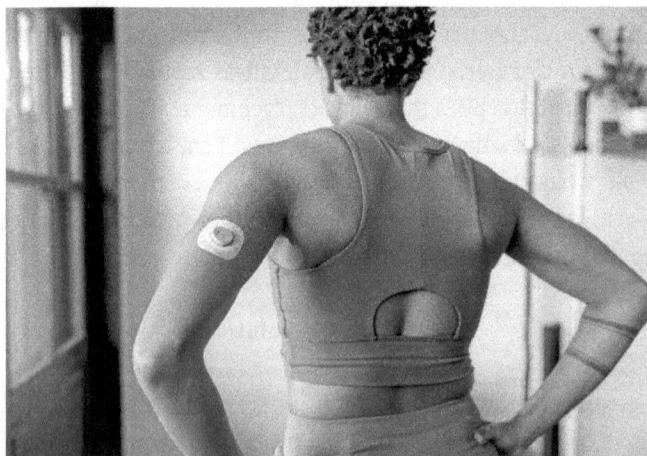

Figure 4.2 A woman stays active while wearing the Dexcom Stelo continuous glucose monitor on her arm.

cutting-edge today as rivals have emerged. Simultaneously, as health plans began to recognize the benefits of CGM and pay for it, Dexcom's subscription model started to feel less like a maverick move and more like the start of a broader trend.

That Dexcom has moved across the matrix doesn't diminish the legacy of its disruption. It demonstrates the matrix's fluidity. Dexcom is now one of the largest publicly traded healthcare technology companies. Yesterday's breakthrough often becomes tomorrow's accepted standard, underscoring why innovations don't rest in any single quadrant for long.

The potential rewards of building a breakthrough solution are enormous, but the hurdles are equally daunting. When the technology and business model are novel, you're not just selling a product but a whole new way of doing things. This means educating and convincing patients, providers, and payers about the benefits, which can be costly and time-consuming.

Innovators in this quadrant usually face the most skepticism, needing to convince wary clinicians that their technology works, prove to payers that it's worth the investment, and change patients' long-held behaviors. If the innovation involves a new medical device, as in Dexcom's case, the US Food and Drug Administration approval process can be lengthy and unpredictable. Breakthroughs require years of research and development (R&D), clinical trials, and market education before generating significant revenue, making it challenging if innovators can't secure investors who believe in their long-term vision; however, if and when successful, breakthrough solutions can completely change healthcare.

Upgrade Solutions

Upgrade solutions occur when innovative new products are introduced into proven business models, driving efficiency or enhancing the user experience. Successful upgrade solutions offer something that feels like a significant level up.

A great example is PillPack, which was founded by a pharmacist and engineer and sold to Amazon for roughly $1 billion (figure 4.3):

- **Product innovation:** PillPack found a friction point at which the current system creates unnecessary difficulties. In this case, patients, specifically those juggling multiple medications, were struggling to get and take their medications as prescribed. From managing refills and navigating insurance to physically taking the right medications at the right time, it's difficult for patients to stay adherent. And the more medications someone has, the more challenging it becomes. PillPack developed a proprietary end-to-end system to make medication adherence easier. The company synchronized prescription refills and insurance to deliver

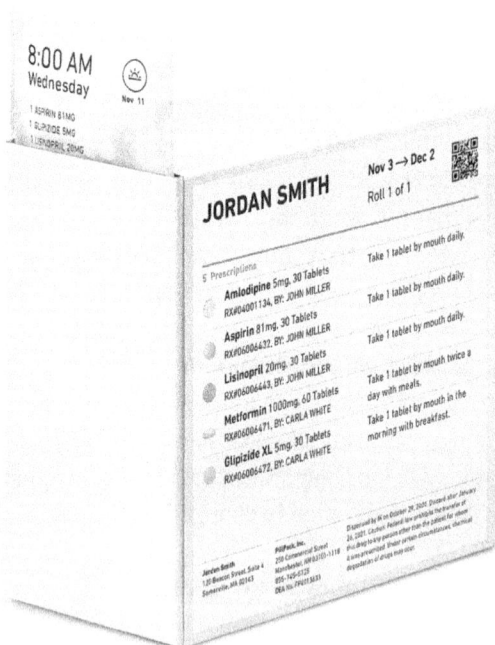

Figure 4.3 PillPack's signature dispenser shows both a daily packet of medications (marked with time and date) and a comprehensive medication list with dosing instructions.

presorted, individually dosed medication packets in a convenient dispenser to each customer every month.

- **Business model fit:** Although the service was the first of its kind, PillPack's business model looked familiar. The company accepted prescriptions from any physician, worked with existing insurance providers, and mirrored the basic setup of centralized mail-order pharmacies. This lowered barriers to adoption from all players involved—providers, payers, *and* patients—and helped PillPack scale quickly.

- **Upgrade potential:** PillPack illustrates how product upgrades can improve healthcare (after all, the bar is quite low). By scaling the pharmacist and redesigning medication management, the company improved medication adherence and health outcomes, all while making the patient experience markedly better.

Even though the business model fits existing structures, upgrade solutions involve building an entirely new product. This requires investment in R&D, infrastructure, and potential regulatory hurdles depending on the solution's nature. In the case of PillPack, it required building a new full-service pharmacy. Because upgrade solutions have an existing market they aim to fit into, the key is to make a product so vastly better than current options that it compels customers to switch.

Innovation doesn't always require shattering the entire system. PillPack's acquisition by Amazon proves the value inherent in identifying a friction point and improving upon the status quo.

Creative Solutions

Products in this quadrant innovate by introducing creative new business models or strategies to meet unaddressed needs or capture new markets. They create new workflows, bring together partners that haven't worked together before, or change how healthcare operates. The emphasis can be on reaching underserved populations or reimagining ways to deliver care or improve access. In creative solutions, the product is simply the enabler—the real innovation comes from reimagining how existing tools can solve healthcare problems in new ways.

For example, let's look at GoodRx, a publicly traded digital health company:

- **Established product:** Prescription price comparison tools aren't unique to GoodRx, nor is the software powering the platform. What distinguishes GoodRx is that the company partners with pharmacy benefit managers (PBMs) and other parties to make the contracted price at each pharmacy entirely transparent for patients.[1] These prices are displayed with list prices from savings programs, retailers, and manufacturer copay discounts so patients can see and compare the out-of-pocket medication prices at nearby pharmacies on the GoodRx website. This addresses the enormous pain point of navigating wildly disparate drug costs amid an opaque industry, allowing patients to price shop. This is not just helpful for the uninsured and underinsured: the out-of-pocket prices they reveal for patients are often better than insurance prices.
- **Business model disruption:** While providing a valuable service to patients, GoodRx generates income from pharmacies by leveraging PBMs' existing networks and collecting fees for driving customers to pharmacies. This allows GoodRx to operate outside traditional prescription insurance and offer discounts to nearly everyone. Another part of the model is the company's obsession with the consumer experience, which is evident in GoodRx's language. Instead of confusing industry language (e.g., wholesale acquisition cost, deductible, customary price), the website uses consumer-friendly language like coupon, retail price, and discount price.
- **Enabled by software:** While the company was founded by two tech veterans (one of whom previously worked at Facebook), the user experience is straightforward, making drug cost navigation easy for even the least tech-savvy patients. But it's the partnership network that enables GoodRx to create tremendous value.

Success in this quadrant hinges on overcoming inertia. GoodRx had to change consumer behavior and get patients to visit its website *before* going to their usual pharmacy. One tactic the company employed was using channel partners and placing marketing materials directly in clinics to educate patients about its price shopping tool at the point of care.

Creative solutions also require a strategy (and usually connections) to secure partnerships necessary for the new business model. Getting stakeholders to do things differently can take time and lots of convincing. When a company is new without a track record, building trust comes down entirely to its leaders. And as the saying goes, innovation moves only at the speed of trust.

GoodRx embodies how creative business models can improve healthcare access. By focusing on cost transparency, the company helps patients take a more proactive role in finding the best prices and thus brings down the overall cost of healthcare. Established healthcare players often have little incentive to solve these problems—especially when they profit from the very inefficiencies that creative solutions aim to eliminate.

Competitive Solutions

This last quadrant is all about innovating by competing in an existing market, outpacing established players on factors like brand, experience, quality, scale, or focused expertise. Although not groundbreaking at a global level, these solutions are incredibly important because pockets of healthcare still lag behind other industries in all of those qualities. It is no secret that there are still many unmet needs across healthcare. Competitive solutions highlight the opportunity of creating a better experience within a familiar framework.

Warby Parker, the popular eye care company, is a prime example.

- **Established product:** When Warby Parker entered the market in 2010, eyeglasses were already a well-established product. The company didn't invent new lens technology or frame materials. Instead, it took on the incumbents by making stylish, high-quality eyewear more accessible and affordable. By offering a curated selection of frames designed in-house, it simplified and modernized the process of choosing glasses.

- **Business model fit:** Warby Parker didn't reinvent the business model. It marketed directly to consumers and accepted both cash-pay and (later) vision insurance. Consumers were already buying glasses this way, and Warby Parker provided another, better option.
- **Differentiation:** Warby Parker competed in a market dominated by a few large players by addressing several pain points: high prices, limited selection, and an inconvenient buying process. By controlling the entire supply chain, from design to manufacturing to distribution, Warby Parker could offer prescription glasses at a fraction of the prevailing market price. Its "Home-Try-On" program, in which customers can select five frames to try for free, was a novel way to improve the buying process. So too was its mobile app, which allows customers to try on frames instantly through a "Virtual Try-On" feature. Warby Parker also positioned itself as a socially conscious brand by becoming carbon neutral and launching a "Buy a Pair, Give a Pair" program, which has distributed more than 20 million pairs of glasses to people living on less than $4 per day.[2]

Competitive solutions work great in sleepy markets, where incumbents have gotten comfortable with their position and haven't kept up with serving their customers' evolving needs. This leaves plenty of room for new entrants to shake things up. Warby Parker identified a market ripe for change and leveraged technology and customer-centric design to create a distinctly better experience within the familiar framework of buying eyeglasses.

Founders can pull many levers in this quadrant, and it all comes down to understanding unmet market needs. Innovation can focus on offering superior support, ease of use, lower cost, or a simplified process that competitors haven't streamlined.

Competitive solutions can also target underserved groups to whom no one is catering. By finding a niche, new entrants can capture a market hungry for a solution that finally feels like it was designed for them.

Competition is good. And competitive solutions help drive healthcare forward. When multiple players vie for customers' attention, they're forced to innovate on price, quality, and experience. This pressure to improve leads to better outcomes for everyone: Patients get more choices and better service, and companies are pushed to become more efficient and customer-focused. In healthcare, where many markets have become stagnant because of consolidation or regulation, I think we should welcome competition.

THE SSI CHECKLIST:
SUSTAINABLE, SCALABLE, IMPACTFUL

Now that we've reviewed the four innovation pathways, let me share the checklist I use to evaluate potential healthcare investments. The three buckets to consider—sustainability, scalability, and impact—aren't just helpful for investors; they also can be used to refine your own startup idea, evaluate job opportunities, or assess potential partnerships.

This checklist comes from my experiences as an investor, entrepreneur, and startup adviser. I hope it can be a starting point for you to build your own checklist.

✔ Sustainable: Built to Last

First, we need to ensure that new solutions are *sustainable*. Every organization should have the capacity to endure both financially and operationally. Put another way, they need to bring in more money than they spend.

Founders with startup funding—from a grant, their savings, venture capital, or another source—can put sustainability off for a bit. It's a *J-curve*, in which initial investments and losses are steep before potentially breaking through to profitability. External funding acts as oxygen while you're in the bottom of the J, but it doesn't last forever. Founders need a clear path to sustainability.

Here are the hard questions to ask about sustainability:

- Is there a clear and compelling business case? This means that the organization can stand on its own or, as some say in the business, that it's a "product, not a feature."
- Are the *unit economics* sound? A quick look at revenue and cost per unit of product or service can help evaluate profitability.
- Is there a path to profitability? Most companies aren't profitable in the early days, but is there a reasonable plan to get there?
- How will this company be funded, not just for launch but for the long haul?
- What's the plan for navigating changing market conditions, regulatory landscapes, and competitive pressures?

Sustainability requires a smart business model, a reliable revenue stream, and the agility to adapt both of these things in the face of an ever-evolving market. Sustainability is the foundation upon which everything else is built. Without it, even the most promising ideas will crumble.

✔ Scalable: Built to Grow

If sustainability is about longevity, scalability is about reach. A scalable solution has the capacity to grow and expand, serving an ever-wider population while ideally becoming more efficient.

If a new solution can be used only by a handful of people, its overall impact will be limited. Those that are built to grow, in contrast, have the potential to move the needle in healthcare.

You can't plant a forest overnight, but you can tell quickly if you're holding a seed or a stone. Successful companies generally start with a targeted audience, hypersatisfy this group with the highest expectations, and grow from there. This approach allows for refining the product or service, making it really good (and ideally more affordable) before scaling up to serve a larger market.

Scale is not the same thing as growth. *Growth* typically means adding resources (costs) at the same rate as revenue. It's linear.

Scaling, in contrast, means adding revenue faster than adding costs. As revenue grows, so does profitability. You'll often hear this referred to as *economies of scale,* meaning a company gets more efficient as it scales.

The challenges of scaling, however, are endless: long sales cycles, imbalanced cash flows, hiring and retention, and facing the incumbent blockade, to name just a few. But the opportunity for scale is enormous—in a $4.9 trillion industry, even narrow solutions can reach millions of people.[3]

When assessing a business's scalability, questions to ask include the following:

- What has your growth been so far, and how will you scale beyond the current users?
- What makes growth defensible over time? Is it based on network effects, data, intellectual property (IP), distribution partnerships, brand, or something else?
- How will economies of scale come into play as you grow? What aspects of your business model will become more efficient with increased scale? How do you expect your gross margins to change?
- Can the product or service be effectively implemented across different settings and contexts?
- Is the product compatible with existing systems and infrastructures?
- Are you stealing market share or creating a new market?
  - If stealing market share, how much of the market can you reasonably obtain? How will you differentiate your offering? How will the incumbents react?
  - If creating a new market, is there a clear pathway for widespread dissemination and implementation?

Market size also matters. Investors often evaluate this using Total Addressable Market (TAM), Serviceable Addressable Market (SAM), and Serviceable Obtainable Market (SOM). While the TAM reflects the full market opportunity, SAM narrows it to those you can realistically serve based on your offering, and SOM represents the slice you can likely capture in the near term. I tend to prefer a bottoms-up approach—estimating the number of target customers and revenue per customer. For example, if you're building a solution for postpartum depression (PPD), you might start with the number of annual births in the United States, the percent of those who experience PPD, and what you'd earn per customer. Regardless of the approach, the goal is the same: to understand the size and shape of the opportunity, and how it might expand over time.

Businesses built for scale tend to share certain characteristics. The products are simple and frictionless, with strong evidence demonstrating effectiveness across diverse populations. They integrate seamlessly into existing workflows and are adaptable to different care settings. For services businesses, a strong technology component can provide the competitive edge and operational efficiency needed to scale (we refer to this category of companies as *tech-enabled healthcare services*).

When an innovation is both sustainable and scalable, it has the potential to drive metamorphic change across all of healthcare. But there's one last thing to consider: impact.

✔ Impactful: Built to Make a Difference

Sustainability and scalability tell us how far something can go, but only impact can tell us if it's going in the right direction. Plenty of sustainable and scalable innovations don't improve healthcare. Avoid those at all costs. Build something that makes a meaningful, positive difference. Build something you can be proud of.

When it comes to assessing impact, here are some questions to ask:

- Does this innovation address a significant unmet need?
- Is there evidence to support its effectiveness?
- Can it meaningfully improve patient outcomes?
- Does it have the potential to bend the cost curve and improve value in healthcare?

- Can it help reduce healthcare disparities and advance health equity?
- How are they mitigating any trade-offs or negative externalities?

High-impact innovations share certain traits. They're focused on the most pressing healthcare challenges, where the status quo is miserable. They're grounded in a deep understanding of the needs and preferences of their stakeholders. The solution is rigorously tested and validated through clinical studies and real-world evidence. And they often "take a stand" by positioning themselves as advocates for change in their specific domain.

Mike Pykosz, who founded and ran value-based care startup Oak Street Health, which went public in 2020 and was acquired by CVS for $10.6 billion in 2023, spoke about their impact equation: "Our impact equation was how well we're taking care of every individual patient and then how many patients we were taking care of."[4] This approach—balancing the depth of care for each patient with the breadth of their reach—ensured that their growth was not only scalable but also impactful.

When we think about what innovation looks like in healthcare, I like to keep these three things in mind. Successful healthcare startups are sustainable over the long term, they are scalable to meet the needs of a large population, and they make a real, measurable impact.

LESS INNOVATION, MORE IMITATION?

Healthcare has a dissemination and implementation problem. We often know what to do and how to do it, but we don't do it consistently.

It's worth considering whether the industry needs to invest less in innovation and more in imitation. As Anna Roth and Thomas Lee suggested in the *Harvard Business Review*, perhaps we should anoint fewer chief innovation officers and more chief imitation officers—people who scour the world for effective innovations to bring home.[5]

Creative, upgrade, and competitive solutions all play a role in this regard. These pathways take proven business models or products and go one step further, adapting them to new contexts or enhancing them in meaningful ways. By building on existing solutions and tailoring them to specific needs, these approaches can drive improvements in outcomes.

When it comes to innovation versus imitation, the answer is that we need to invest in more of *both*. The status quo isn't working; we need new ways of doing things. Innovation can push the boundaries of what's possible and find new solutions to our most pressing challenges in healthcare. Breakthrough solutions, which involve both new technology and new business models, have the potential to make huge leaps forward.

At the same time, we must invest in solving healthcare's dissemination and implementation problems. Even the most groundbreaking innovations will have limited impact if they don't reach the patients and providers who need them most. This is where imitation comes in—by identifying and adapting proven solutions, we can accelerate the spread of best practices and ensure that more people have access to high-quality care.

THE ROAD AHEAD:
INNOVATION AS A NECESSITY

Throughout this chapter, I've shown that innovation is more about building something *better* than simply building something new. It's about addressing real needs and pain points in the healthcare system, whether the complexity of managing multiple medications (as PillPack does) or the opacity of drug pricing (as GoodRx tackles). It's about putting the patient at the center and designing solutions that improve the experience and health outcomes.

Knowing what meaningful innovation looks like is only half the battle. The other half is figuring out where these innovations come from in the first place. After all, breakthrough ideas and creative solutions don't just appear out of thin air. They come from smart, curious people—just like you. In the next chapter, we'll explore the genesis of change in healthcare.

TL;DR

- **Healthcare innovation takes many forms:** Often, technology is merely an enabler, not the innovation. Focus on solving problems to improve outcomes, lower costs, improve experience, and expand access.
- **There are four pathways to innovation:** They include breakthrough solutions, upgrade solutions, creative solutions, and competitive solutions.
- **Use the SSI checklist:** A truly innovative solution is sustainable over the long term, is scalable to meet the needs of a large population, and makes a real, measurable impact.
- **We need innovation and imitation:** We don't just need new solutions; we need to solve healthcare's dissemination and implementation problems. Even the most groundbreaking innovations will have limited impact if they don't reach the patients and providers who need them most.

5

WHERE DOES INNOVATION COME FROM?

You can't solve problems with the same thinking used to create them.

—ALBERT EINSTEIN

Innovation doesn't always come from where we expect it. No single group—not doctors, not tech companies, not the government— has a monopoly on the solutions healthcare needs. Sometimes innovation is driven by sheer necessity, fueled by the frustration of those who can no longer wait for someone else to solve the problem.

I was reminded of this early in the COVID-19 pandemic when cases were spiking but reliable information on infection rates was impossible to find.

My husband Jeff is a data scientist. He and I love spreadsheets. Many aspects of our personal lives, from travel to financial planning, take place in well-organized (and highly satisfying) Google Sheets. We had travel planned for the spring of 2020, and we wanted to understand the risk of infection. Were cases spiking at the locations we hoped to visit?

The Centers for Disease Control and Prevention (CDC) wasn't publishing the data. The responsibility of reporting had shifted to the fifty individual states. This created a patchwork of inconsistent data, making it impossible for Jeff and me, as well as everyone else, to grasp the scale of the crisis.

So on March 4, 2020, Jeff started collecting data on COVID-19 cases. He would visit every single state website and manually add the numbers in his spreadsheet. Then, at 5:00 p.m. each day, he would share the data on social media. That task done, he'd join us for dinner.

By happenstance, two days after Jeff got started, *Atlantic* reporter Alexis Madrigal published a story showing how very few people had been tested for COVID. Jeff, who knew Alexis from college, immediately reached out to see where he was getting his data. Perhaps Alexis had found an official source. But after realizing they were both collecting data as rogue citizen scientists, they decided to collaborate on a single spreadsheet. They thought they were providing a stop-gap solution to a temporary problem. Surely, the CDC would start publishing the data, at which point their homegrown effort could step aside. They figured they'd be at it for at most a few days.

It ended up being a yearlong endeavor. When the government failed to respond with transparent information, hundreds of volunteers rallied to help Jeff and Alexis create the COVID Tracking Project. They meticulously collected and published, for free, the most comprehensive data on COVID-19.

The data they collected was used in more than eighty thousand news reports and in thousands of academic articles.[1] Ironically, even federal agencies, including the CDC, cited data from the COVID Tracking Project. So too did both the Trump and Biden administrations. Because of their efforts, millions of Americans had access to usable data that they could rely on to make more informed decisions.

We did not end up traveling that spring. It wasn't just because Jeff was consumed with the project, but because the very data he was helping make public convinced us it was safer for our family to stay home.

Sometimes innovation emerges unexpectedly, driven by frustrated people who pursue solutions to pressing problems at the right moment and context. In this case, ensuring clear, accurate, and accessible health risk information became a valuable innovation when traditional sources fell short.

In answering the question of where innovation comes from, *where* matters most, because the answer—anywhere and everywhere—speaks to a truth about solving hard problems. In healthcare, solutions often arise when diverse perspectives are brought to bear on the problems. And oftentimes innovation comes not from those with the expected credentials but from those most willing to act.

In this chapter, we'll explore the four key ingredients of healthcare innovation:

- Diverse teams
- Relentlessly pursuing meaningful problems
- In the right place
- At the right time

By understanding where innovation comes from, you can better position yourself to shape it.

DIVERSE TEAMS

Diversity trumps like-mindedness. People with different skills and backgrounds have varying ways of looking at problems, which can spark creativity and reduce the risk of groupthink. A diverse team is more likely to challenge each other's viewpoints and generate better solutions.

There's science behind this. Studies show that diverse groups of problem solvers outperform even groups of the best experts.[2] Why? Diverse groups approach problems from multiple angles, considering a broader range of options. Uniform teams tend to think similarly; consequently, they all get stuck in the same places.

Although startup success has many factors, research consistently shows a notable performance edge for teams blending different backgrounds and skills. One academic study that tracked US startups found that companies whose founders had more diverse industry experiences grew faster than peers with more uniform backgrounds. They were also more likely to achieve outlier growth (top 1 percent).[3]

One of my portfolio companies, Cityblock Health (figure 5.1), exemplifies the benefits of diversity. Spun out of Sidewalk Labs, an urban planning and infrastructure subsidiary of Alphabet, Cityblock Health set out to address a critical gap in the US health-care system: providing comprehensive, high-quality care to under-served urban populations. With an understanding of the integral nature of city systems such as transportation and food access in affecting health, the team built a model that integrates healthcare

Figure 5.1 Cityblock Health team.

and social services. The founding team brought together diverse perspectives:

- **Dr. Toyin Ajayi**, CEO, a Harvard-trained physician with experience in caring for complex, high-need patients
- **Iyah Romm**, a healthcare policy expert who had previously worked on Medicaid transformation
- **Bay Gross**, a computer scientist who previously worked at Google

What these three, and their now one-thousand-plus-person team, have built has been remarkable. Cityblock has expanded beyond urban communities to serve more than one hundred thousand Medicaid and Medicare members across 15 markets in multiple states. Results have demonstrated significant improvements in health outcomes and reductions in costly and avoidable hospital admissions.

By combining clinical expertise with policy knowledge, technological innovation, and a deep understanding of community needs (nurtured partly by its origins in an urban planning incubator), Cityblock has created a model for improving care for underserved populations.

BOX 5.1.
Does Age Matter for Founder Success?

There's a long-standing debate over whether younger or older founders are more likely to succeed. Although we often associate innovation with youth—like Mark Zuckerberg starting Facebook in his college dorm room—data suggest that more experienced entrepreneurs actually have higher success rates.

An HBR analysis found that founders who started their companies between ages forty and fifty-nine create disproportionately high-growth companies. The authors said this: "Although there are many other factors that may explain the age advantage in entrepreneurship, we found that work experience plays a critical role. Relative to founders with no

---

relevant experience, those with at least three years of prior work experience in the same narrow industry as their startup were 85 percent more likely to launch a highly successful startup."[4]

This holds true in healthcare, where deep expertise and professional connections often take years to cultivate. In 2025, I analyzed sixty-one digital health companies that exited for more than $100 million or went public with a market cap of more than $1 billion. The median age of the CEO at the time of exit was forty-eight, with a range from twenty-five to sixty-eight years old.

Experience (more so than age) is what's valuable. The most successful founders bring industry knowledge, professional networks, and seasoned judgment to their ventures. Age itself isn't the determining factor, but the relevant experience that often comes with it can significantly increase your chances of success. That said, I was just twenty-seven when I founded Rock Health. Sometimes, you just have to be ready and willing.

RELENTLESSLY PURSUING MEANINGFUL PROBLEMS

It's not just about the *who* of innovation but the *what* and *why*. Truly impactful healthcare solutions begin with a laser focus on the right problems, the pain points that keep patients, caregivers, and providers up at night. This requires empathy for the lived experience of those the innovation is meant to serve.

We've already discussed the disparities in healthcare access that plague marginalized communities and the tragic fact that preventable diseases continue to claim far too many lives. These are the daily struggles of millions and addressing them requires *relentless* pursuit.

I emphasize the word relentless because succeeding requires a burning desire to understand the problem intimately—to obsess over it. It means embedding yourself in the quirky realities of healthcare, listening to patient stories, observing the challenges faced by clinicians, and educating yourself on the research that reveals where the system breaks down.

That is where innovation comes from.

Impatient people. Frustrated people. Those who refuse to accept the status quo. They're willing to wake up every day and push forward in what usually feels like s l o w m o t i o n. They understand that innovation, when focused on a critical unmet need, can create a cascade of positive impacts. This pursuit requires relentlessness—along with tenacity, resourcefulness, and a willingness to challenge entrenched, rigged systems.

BOX 5.2.
In the Trenches: Tidepool.org

Howard Look's mornings used to start with a tangle of cables and a frustrating ritual. Downloading data from his young child's insulin pump and then their glucose monitor (each with its proprietary software), he painstakingly tried to piece together a picture of his child's blood sugar levels. For a child with type 1 diabetes, those numbers were the difference between a good day and a dangerous one. But making the necessary real-time adjustments throughout the day felt more like guesswork than informed medical care.

Howard, a software engineer, refused to accept this limitation. It was a barrier to his child's health and a technological inconvenience. He envisioned a solution: an open platform that would unify data from different diabetes devices, putting patients and their doctors in control. It was a vision that grew out of a father's desperation and the confidence of someone who understood the opportunity for interoperability.

Thus, Tidepool was born. Under a nonprofit model, the team built a secure, open-source platform that aggregates data from insulin pumps, glucose monitors, and more, empowering patients and doctors with a complete picture of diabetes management. From there, they launched Tidepool Loop—an interoperable controller for automated insulin dosing, the result of open-source efforts by the diabetes patient community.

Tidepool's relentless advocacy pushed the entire medical device industry to evolve. Once fiercely protective of their data, major device

---

manufacturers began opening up, recognizing that integration and patient choice were necessary for better outcomes. Today, every single diabetes device maker partners with Tidepool.[5]

Howard Look's story illustrates how frustration can fuel relentless pursuit of change. What began as a caregiver's daily struggle became a mission that would transform diabetes care for millions, proving that the most powerful innovations often come from those who simply refuse to accept the status quo.

THE RIGHT PLACE

Diverse teams working on pressing problems also need to be in the right place, where ideas can take root and flourish. By "place," I don't mean a specific geographic location but rather the cultural ecosystem surrounding you—one that inspires innovation, rapid learning, and excellence.

A Culture That Learns Quickly

Innovation inherently involves venturing into the unknown. Going from zero to one requires a willingness to test new ideas, even when they're unlikely to succeed. But that is often at odds with the risk-averse culture of medicine, where the stakes are undeniably high.

To innovate, we must accept that most ideas will fail. So it becomes more about failing intelligently—minimizing harm, extracting valuable lessons, and using those lessons to move forward. A culture that learns quickly doesn't fear failure; it sees setbacks as opportunities for growth.

Learning quickly requires a detachment from the solution and a willingness to change your mind and pivot in the face of new data. It's about remaining obsessed with the problem, not stubbornly clinging to a single approach.

A Culture of Excellence

"Move fast and break things" may be the ethos in tech, but that motto doesn't work in healthcare. In fact, it's just the opposite. Successful innovation looks more like "move thoughtfully and build trust."

Sloppiness never wins in healthcare. The most successful organizations have high standards, accountability, and rigorous testing to ensure that new solutions are effective, safe, and equitable. Be thoughtful and careful, even while experimenting and iterating.

It's like that sign at Apple HQ that said, "Love Is in the Detail." A culture of excellence means paying meticulous attention to detail, recognizing that even the smallest aspects of a healthcare solution matter—from user experience to workflow integration to data privacy. Such a culture demands a commitment to continuous improvement, even after a solution is deployed, through ongoing monitoring, feedback, and refinement.

The key is ensuring that excellence doesn't slow down learning with unnecessary processes and that rapid learning doesn't lower the bar for excellence. The ultimate goal is to create an environment in which team members can learn and adapt quickly while still upholding the highest standards of quality, privacy, and patient safety.

Does Organizational Size Matter?

The story of innovation often pits startups against incumbents. David versus Goliath. On one side, established corporations bring deep expertise and even deeper pockets. On the other, nimble startups and passionate outsiders have little bureaucracy to stop them. I have worked for and with small and large organizations and can tell you that each has pros and cons.

Inside large and established organizations, enormous transformation is possible. They have the resources, customer base, and market power to launch major new initiatives or make significant acquisitions. But this scale also breeds inertia. It's incredibly difficult for a large company to pivot quickly, execute nimbly on small-scale projects, or disrupt their profitable revenue streams, even when it's the right long-term strategy. This can be demotivating to innovative employees.

Startups, in contrast, are unburdened by legacy infrastructure and entrenched revenue streams. These outsiders can design entirely new models and move at breakneck speed. Yet usually they lack the resources for massive, overnight transformations. Startup success hinges on doing thousands of small things right, creating a snowball effect over time. With a focus on continuous improvement and a willingness to experiment, startups can ultimately topple giants.

When founding Rock Health, we set about building a place where cross-sectional collaboration between newcomers and incumbents could flourish. What we have learned is that the most successful solutions often emerge from partnerships among different types of entities. Combining the strengths of each—agility, deep expertise, resources, and policymaking power—accelerates progress and creates more sustainable solutions.

Location, Location, Innovation?

My nine years living and working in San Francisco were transformative. The city gave me the intoxicating optimism to believe anything was possible. There, I met many colleagues, entrepreneurs, and even my now-husband—a community united by a drive to create positive change.

The serendipity of connecting with like-minded individuals at a random happy hour, the access to experts, and the sheer density of talent created the perfect launchpad for Rock Health. It's hard to imagine achieving the same success if I had lived elsewhere.

But today is different. A decade ago, many San Francisco–based investors (including us at Rock Health) wouldn't have even considered backing a company outside of Silicon Valley. There were enough companies to back locally, so why get on a plane?

Now, about one-third of employees with jobs that can be done remotely work from home, compared with less than 7 percent before the pandemic.[6] People are more accustomed to working and doing business virtually than ever before, and this is reflected in the changing distribution of venture funding.[7] In fact, investors are increasingly backing companies based in nonhub cities across the United States as dealmaking is becoming more decentralized. Before 2019, the median distance between a seed startup and its lead investor was less than 100 miles. By 2022, this median distance lengthened nearly sixfold to 591.3 miles.[8]

There's still great innovation coming out of San Francisco, but people there don't hold a monopoly on good ideas or great execution. Innovation hubs like Atlanta, Austin, Denver, Nashville, and Miami are flourishing all across the country, with existing hubs like Boston, Seattle, and New York continuing to thrive. This is a win for everyone, because it allows for greater diversity of thought and the emergence of solutions tailored to the needs of communities outside the wealthy tech bubble.

THE RIGHT TIME

Let's think about the typical phases of innovation in the market, sometimes overlapping or occurring in parallel:

- **Ideation and discovery:** the birth of new concepts and initial research
- **Proof of concept:** initial testing and prototyping to demonstrate feasibility
- **Validation:** formal testing of the product to build evidence
- **Regulatory approval:** any necessary approvals to go to market
- **Market introduction:** the initial launch and early adoption phase
- **Scaling:** expanding reach and adoption of the solution
- **Integration:** when the solution becomes part of standard practice
- **Evolution:** continuous improvement and adaptation based on real-world use and feedback

Of course, different innovations enter at various points, and the duration of each phase is unpredictable and heavily influenced by external factors.

Breakthrough solutions, which introduce both new products and business models, start at the earliest phases. Even if they sail through the first four phases and obtain regulatory approval, they may stall at market introduction. Even if they're ready to introduce their new product, the market may not be ready. Many breakthrough solutions die in this phase, unable to sustain themselves while waiting for customer adoption. I've been around long enough to see new ideas flop in the market, only to be reintroduced years later and succeed. Timing is everything.

Upgrade solutions, which bring new products into established models, might face validation and regulatory hurdles. Once approved, however, they often find it easier to scale as they work within familiar business frameworks and market dynamics.

Creative solutions apply new business models to existing technologies. They may skip early phases but encounter challenges in market introduction as they attempt to get stakeholders to buy into their new way of doing things. These solutions often require a shift in mindset, which can slow adoption even if the underlying technology is well established.

Competitive solutions typically enter in the scaling or integration phase, focusing on differentiation within established frameworks. Although they may have an easier time gaining initial traction, they can sometimes struggle to stand out in a crowded market.

How to Know If the Market Is Ready

An element of luck is involved in timing, as is skill. Successful innovators know their market so well they can see around the corner. They can sense upcoming *inflection points* where market demand, technological advances, and a favorable regulatory environment all align in their favor. When seized, these opportune moments can catapult an idea from obscurity to ubiquity.

What do these inflection points look like? Think of changing healthcare as all of us chipping away to reshape a mountain. We each have our tools—some might have hefty pickaxes, others just small chisels—but together, we all contribute to this gargantuan task.

Occasionally, a powerful avalanche alters things entirely, reshaping the mountain and revealing new pathways we couldn't see before. This can create casualties for some but can also clear the way for those in the right place with the right tools to go forward. These are inflection points. Opportune moments.

This is, for example, what happened with the COVID-19 pandemic: It forced adaptation, innovation, and rapid regulatory change. Emergency measures were passed that relaxed regulations and expanded telehealth reimbursement. Suddenly, telehealth, remote monitoring, and virtual clinical trials became necessities, pushing us to adopt new tools in months that would have otherwise taken years.

Let's look at the inflection points that have shaped where we are today. These can be bucketed into market drivers, regulatory drivers, and technological advances (figure 5.2).

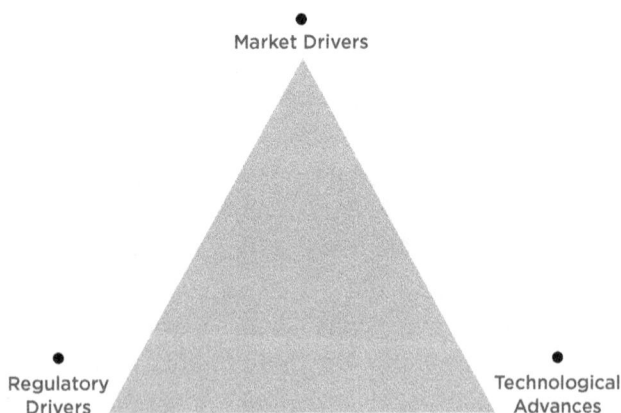

Figure 5.2 Inflection points can be bucketed into market drivers, regulatory drivers, and technological advances.

Market Drivers

Many factors are pushing the US healthcare system toward change. Although these challenges are significant, they also present opportunities for new solutions. The main market drivers include the following:

- **Rising costs:** Healthcare spending is unsustainable, outpacing inflation and economic growth. With healthcare expenditures topping a staggering $4.8 trillion in 2023—$14,423 per person—everyone from individuals to employers to the government is feeling squeezed.[9]
- **Provider shortages:** We face clinician shortages from physicians[10] to nurses[11] to pharmacists.[12] These widespread workforce gaps mean longer wait times, reduced access to care, and increased burnout among existing healthcare workers.
- **Consumer-driven demand:** As we discussed in chapter 3, today's patients are more informed and proactive and are demanding a say in healthcare. They expect convenient access, price transparency, and personalized care.
- **The shift to value-based care (VBC):** The adoption of VBC, which ties payment to patient outcomes rather than service volume, nearly doubled from 2015 to 2021. As of 2021, almost 60 percent of healthcare payments were tied to quality or value.[13] (More on VBC in chapter 9.)

Regulatory Drivers

It's wild to think that sometimes all it takes is the stroke of a pen in Washington, D.C., to make (or break) a generation of healthcare solutions. The following are regulations that have made a huge impact on healthcare innovation over the years:

- **Health Insurance Portability and Accountability Act (HIPAA) (1996):** Standardizing the handling of protected health information, HIPAA created a baseline of trust necessary for technology adoption and set the floor for standards so that new entrants have guidance on what is acceptable.

- **The Medicare Prescription Drug, Improvement, and Modernization Act (2003):** This legislation laid the groundwork for *e-prescribing*, the process of sending a prescription to a pharmacy electronically instead of on paper or fax, by requiring states to allow electronic prescribing of most prescription drugs. Adoption was accelerated through the 2008 Medicare Improvements for Patients and Providers Act, which authorized e-prescribing incentives for providers. E-prescribing hovered around 7 percent in 2008 and is near ubiquity today, with virtually all pharmacies able to accept e-prescriptions.[14]

- **Health Information Technology for Economic and Clinical Health Act (HITECH) (2009):** HITECH significantly shaped digital health by establishing financial incentives for "meaningful use" of electronic health records (EHRs) and fueling their widespread adoption.[15]

- **Affordable Care Act (ACA) (2010):** The ACA, also known as Obamacare, introduced significant reforms that changed many things about our healthcare system. Digital health grew at an unprecedented pace after the ACA was signed, partly because it included incentives for providers to implement new systems to increase efficiency. The ACA also established the Center for Medicare and Medicaid Innovation (CMMI), which has funded and tested numerous innovative value-based care programs, such as accountable care organizations (ACOs) and bundled payments. These programs have encouraged healthcare providers to adopt new technologies and care models to improve quality and reduce costs.

- **The Twenty-First Century Cures Act (Cures Act) (2016):** This act aimed to accelerate medical product development and innovation. It included provisions to streamline clinical trials, advance precision medicine, and promote interoperability. It spurred more investment in digital health and encouraged collaboration among researchers, technology companies, and healthcare providers. Most notably, its information-blocking provisions and interoperability requirements forced the healthcare industry to make patient health information more readily available.[16]

- **Coronavirus Aid, Relief, and Economic Security Act** (2020): Passed in response to the COVID-19 pandemic, this act included provisions that significantly expanded access to telehealth services. The act waived certain Medicare restrictions, allowing beneficiaries to receive telehealth services from their homes and expanding the types of providers that could offer these services. These changes facilitated the rapid adoption of telehealth during the public health emergency, demonstrating the potential for remote care delivery and paving the way for longer-term changes in healthcare delivery.

Technological Advances

The rapid advancement of technologies, from smartphones to artificial intelligence (AI), has impacted most industries, including healthcare.

- **The internet:** The World Wide Web was introduced in 1990, and by 2000, 52 percent of US adults were online.[17] Today, 96 percent of Americans use the internet, giving us widespread access to instant medical information, online health communities, telehealth, and more. Internet adoption has a strong correlation to better health outcomes, even after controlling for other confounding factors, such as education, income, and rurality.[18]
- **Smartphones:** The internet is no longer tethered to our computers. Mobile devices, owned by more than 90 percent of US adults, enable constant connectivity.[19] When it comes to healthcare, this means increasing access to health information, streamlining communication with providers, and enabling convenient self-management of health metrics like activity levels.
- **Modularization of healthcare technology:** It's now easier than ever for companies to access plug-and-play tools to build the organization's infrastructure. Instead of developing everything from scratch, companies can now instantly integrate pieces like insurance verification, claims processing, EHRs, and even back-end virtual care providers through APIs and third-party services. This modularization drastically reduces both

time-to-market and capital requirements. What once took years and millions to build can now be assembled in months for a fraction of the cost. The result is faster innovation and easier scaling of new solutions.

- **Artificial intelligence:** AI tools can analyze vast amounts of data to uncover patterns and insight that humans alone cannot. This capacity has applications across the board—from accelerating drug discovery to predicting disease risk and personalizing treatment plans. The ability to process and learn from millions of datapoints simultaneously means AI has the potential to scale expertise and improve care delivery in ways previously impossible.

- **DNA sequencing:** The cost of sequencing the entire human genome has dropped from about $10,000 in 2012 to $600 just a decade later, allowing for a better understanding of the human body.[20] This technology can reveal genetic predispositions to diseases, predict drug responses, and guide targeted therapies. Once limited to research settings, genetic insight is now being integrated into routine care through applications like noninvasive prenatal testing and cancer diagnostics.

- **Wearables:** Wearable sensors have gotten smaller, smarter, and more affordable. Some 44 percent of Americans now own wearable health tracking devices, which can provide continuous health data, including heart rate, blood pressure, blood glucose, body temperature, respiration rate, movement, and more.[21] This allows for early detection of anomalies, better disease management, and personalized feedback loops for behavior change in a way that was not possible before.

- **Robotics:** Surgical robots are already improving precision and reducing the invasiveness of procedures, leading to faster recovery times, lower risk of complications, and potentially lower costs. Beyond surgery, robots assist in rehabilitation, medication dispensing, and even providing companionship.

Good timing is knowing the inflection points that enable you to make change and scale your solution today. From technology to regulations to market demand, these forces create windows of opportunity during which previously impossible ideas can take hold. Your job is to spot these moments and be ready with the right solution when they arrive.

BOX 5.3.
In the Trenches: Circulation

If timing is everything, Dr. John Brownstein's story is a master class in seizing the moment. As the chief innovation officer at Boston Children's Hospital, he had a front-row seat to a persistent problem plaguing hospitals: getting patients, especially low-income and elderly ones, safely home after discharge.

For years, hospitals relied on an inefficient system of taxi vouchers that was expensive, unreliable, and frequently abused. Meanwhile, outside of healthcare, rideshare companies like Uber and Lyft were transforming transportation. Brownstein saw an opportunity to bridge these worlds.

His team started small, partnering with Uber in 2014 to support a flu vaccination campaign. Through this initiative, they arranged for registered nurses to deliver flu shots on-demand through the Uber app. The program's success in reaching underserved areas proved that rideshare partnerships could meaningfully improve healthcare access.

But Brownstein recognized that the bigger opportunity was in solving the broader patient transportation crisis. This led to the creation of Circulation, a platform designed to improve nonemergency medical transportation through technology.

Circulation replaced the old taxi voucher system with a streamlined, secure platform that let hospitals coordinate patient transport through rideshare services. The solution improved discharge efficiency, reduced costs, and increased patient satisfaction. More important, it helped ensure that patients, especially those from underserved communities, could reliably access the care they needed.

The timing was perfect. Rideshare services had become mainstream enough to be trusted, but healthcare-specific solutions hadn't yet emerged. By 2018, Circulation was acquired by Logisticare for $57.5 million.

Circulation's story shows how innovation often comes from recognizing when existing trends are ready to be applied to healthcare problems in new ways. But timing alone wasn't enough. Brownstein's deep understanding of the problem, gained from working within the system, allowed him to execute the idea in a way that worked for all stakeholders. He saw both the problem and the moment when a solution became possible.

INNOVATION BEGETS INNOVATION

The best education for innovators is work experience. Specifically, the get-your-hands-dirty, in-the-trenches, no-holds-barred kind of experience that you can get only from being on the front lines. It's the experience that throws you into the deep end and forces you to sink or swim.

When you're pushed out of your comfort zone and forced to think on your feet, the real learning happens. It's the same reason that quizzing yourself is a better way to study for a big test than just rereading the materials.[22] With practice tests, you better retain the lessons and develop resilience and resourcefulness that you can't get from simply reading a textbook.

This is why startups are a breeding ground for the next generation of healthcare entrepreneurs. Employees at these companies gain invaluable experience from both successes and failures. They learn what innovation looks like, how to navigate the healthcare stakeholders, and, ultimately, how to get the job done. Many of them go on to start their own companies, taking the lessons they've learned and applying them to new challenges.

For example, Athenahealth, a Boston-based company offering physician billing, practice management, and electronic health record software, was a massive launchpad for talented folks who have gone on to make their own mark in healthcare.

Out of Athenahealth have come innovators like brothers Todd and Ed Park (Todd was a cofounder and Ed's many roles included chief technology officer and chief operating officer). Todd went on to serve as US chief technology officer under President Obama. Then both brothers cofounded Devoted Health, a Medicare Advantage "payvider" providing virtual and in-home medical care for older Americans. Kyle Armbrester, Athenahealth's former chief product officer, became CEO of Signify Health (which went public, then sold to CVS for $8 billion) and is now the CEO of Datavant.[23] Ada Glover, another alumna, joined forces with Jonathan Bush, former Athenahealth CEO, to cofound Zus Health, aiming to build a national health data platform. These employees took their lessons learned from one startup, Athenahealth, to new endeavors, showing the multiplier effect of startups.

Plus, when a groundbreaking idea takes hold and proves its worth, it captures the imagination of other innovators, too. It shows what's possible and sparks new ideas for building on or adapting the original concept. Most important, it keeps companies competitive.

In the end, innovation begets innovation in countless ways. Innovation isn't just a one-time event; it's also a catalyst for all the creativity and progress that follows.

YOU, INNOVATOR

Innovation comes from expert teams relentlessly pursuing meaningful problems in the right place, at the right time. Most important, it comes from *you*.

Healthcare is too important to leave to others. The problems are too complicated, the stakes too high, and the potential for improvement too vast to assume someone else will solve them. The COVID Tracking Project and Tidepool remind us that innovation isn't limited to those who already have the job. You don't need an advanced degree to make a difference. You just need the will to make it happen.

Here's how you can leverage your unique skills:

- **Let your frustrations guide you:** What keeps you up at night when you think about healthcare? Is it making sure your aging parents understand their medication protocol? The opaque cost of prescription drugs? Navigating insurance paperwork? Use your experiences and concerns as a starting point for identifying areas ripe for change. Then become an expert in the problem that fires you up the most.
- **Use your transferable skills:** Your life experiences and expertise in other fields are an asset. Are you a caretaker who understands the patient

experience? A marketer with a talent for crafting compelling messages? A researcher who excels at gathering and synthesizing information? You can offer a fresh perspective that those steeped in the healthcare system might miss.

- **Find your people:** Certainly others care about the same problems as you, and it's time you find them. Share your thoughts and ideas with others in the community. Create a newsletter, share ideas on social media, or write a guest post for a news outlet. Begin positioning yourself as the thought leader you would like to be. It starts with listening and learning, then sharing as much as possible.
- **Just get started:** Don't feel like you have to build the next billion-dollar startup to be an innovator. Could you volunteer with a nonprofit? Pitch a new idea to your boss? Create a social media campaign to raise awareness about a specific health issue? Small actions build momentum for a bigger change.

No matter what role you play today or even tomorrow, you have an important part to play in making healthcare massively better.

The time for waiting is over. The tools for innovation are more accessible than ever, and the healthcare system desperately needs fresh perspectives. Share your ideas, find collaborators, and don't be afraid to start small. Every improvement you make, no matter the scale, is a meaningful contribution and a valuable step forward.

TL;DR

- **No single group has a monopoly on innovation:** Healthcare innovation comes from diverse teams relentlessly pursuing meaningful problems in the right place, at the right time.
- **Seismic shifts (e.g., COVID-19) can accelerate change:** Keep an eye on market drivers, regulatory changes, and technological advances that create a ripe environment for innovation.
- **Innovation isn't confined to Silicon Valley:** The "right place" for innovation isn't a dot on a map; it's a culture and mindset where great ideas can turn into something real.

- **Innovation begets innovation:** As companies succeed, they inspire others and seed the next wave of founders, ideas, and momentum.
- **You have a role to play:** Healthcare is too important to be left to someone else. Anyone with the passion and drive to make a difference can contribute to a healthier future.

6

HEALTHCARE IS HARD,
SO MAKE HARD YOUR MOAT

Not all hard things are valuable, but most valuable things are hard.

—VINOD KHOSLA

The lore of Silicon Valley thrives on stories of rapid growth and billion-dollar valuations achieved within just a few years. The gospel of disruption, built on the veneration of speed and scale, is a powerful and alluring tale.

I know this because I chased those companies—or rather, what I thought would become those companies. But what I learned, and what everyone innovating in healthcare eventually learns, is that healthcare is *hard*. It takes time, patience, and the will to navigate a whole host of challenges.

Although founders dream of instant disruption, healthcare isn't impressed. In fact, it resists transformation.

It's estimated that it takes an average of seventeen years for health research findings to translate into clinical practice.[1] Seventeen years! That's nearly two decades from the time a potentially lifesaving innovation is discovered to when it actually starts helping people.

This isn't necessarily a bad thing. Some of the difficulty of building in this sector helps keep us safe. It also acts as a barrier to entry for those not fully committed or prepared. This *moat*—a term used in business to describe a company's competitive advantage that protects it from rivals—not only guards against casual, fly-by-night entrants but also enhances the credibility and impact of those who do stick around.

So, yes, healthcare is hard. But no other sector today is more worthy of our time and energy.

In this chapter, we will explore why healthcare is so hard and how to turn that difficulty into a competitive advantage. I'll share the systemic barriers you may face, the slow pace of adoption in the industry, and the most common pitfalls. By the end, you'll understand why making hard your moat is your greatest opportunity.

THE MARKET WILL CHOOSE THE WINNERS AND LOSERS

A sign in our office at Rock Health read: "The market will choose the winners and losers." It was put up by Geoff Clapp, a healthcare veteran who often came by the office to support our founders. The message was a defiant response to the Cranky Old Guard (the C.O.G.), those who believed innovation had no hope and thought we should all just go home and stop trying.

Geoff understood the obstacles our founders faced. As an early tech leader in the space, he'd witnessed firsthand the system's aversion to change, seeing promising ideas wither under bureaucracy or get crushed by powerful incumbents. Yet he knew the healthcare market, with its endless need for value and efficiency, also held a sliver of hope. If solutions could prove their worth—not just in a polished pitch deck, but in the real world of patient outcomes and bottom lines—they had a fighting chance to break through.

That sign was our daily reminder. It pushed us to focus on creating real value and reminded us that our judges weren't the naysayers but the stakeholders who would ultimately use our solutions.

THE HARDEST THING(S)
ABOUT INNOVATING IN HEALTHCARE

We soon learned that the problem with the market choosing the winners and losers is that this market is completely rigged. Geoff's sign was right; it just needed a little disclaimer at the bottom.

The deck is stacked against healthcare innovators in several ways. The following are some of the major systemic barriers that make change so challenging:

- **The free-rider problem:** when multiple parties benefit from an innovation, but no one wants to be the first to foot the bill
- **Switchover disruptions:** the temporary drop in productivity and the potential for chaos when adopting a new technology
- **The time-horizon problem:** the disconnect between who pays for a solution and who benefits from it, especially when people stay in jobs or on health plans for just a few years
- **The patchwork payer problem:** the difficulty of coordinating and aligning incentives for population-wide initiatives when there are numerous fragmented payers
- **The incumbent blockade:** how established players in healthcare use their market power to resist change and stifle innovations that threaten their business models
- **Regulatory capture:** when regulations favor incumbents and create barriers for newcomers

Let's start with the *free-rider problem.* In their book *Why Not Better and Cheaper*, brothers James Rebitzer and Robert Rebitzer outline a great example: Imagine new software to notify physicians when they've ordered a duplicate test. This could make healthcare more efficient, but providers (at least those who make money by fee-for-service) likely wouldn't pay for software that actually lowers their revenue because they make money on each test.

So what about the payers? They would undoubtedly benefit economically. But if a single provider contracts with dozens of payers, and they each benefit, which one pays for it? The reality is that in these scenarios, usually no one wants to pay. Our healthcare system lacks a mechanism for shared investment in shared benefits. Nobody wants to be the first to foot the bill, even when the long-term returns are obvious.

The authors note, "The nature of competition in healthcare markets allows dominant incumbent firms to overlook potentially value-enhancing and cost-reducing innovations and inhibits disruption by more efficient new entrants."[2]

Even when a payer is willing to invest, *switchover disruptions* present another hurdle. A switchover disruption is an economic term referring to the temporary drop in productivity and the potential chaos when adopting a new technology or process. Think of the temporary strain when hospitals switched to electronic health records (EHRs)—training staff, integrating systems, and handling productivity dips while everyone adjusted. This is one reason why it took so long and required so many incentives to get the EHR to ubiquity.

Even with clear long-term benefits, the short-term pain can be a major deterrent for large incumbents. This reluctance slows down innovation, even when solutions have the potential to improve care and reduce costs in the long run.

This disconnect becomes especially pronounced with preventative health solutions. Although the downstream savings might be enormous, individual payers often have trouble justifying the upfront costs when the economic benefits will likely not directly accrue to them. Remember, most people are insured through their employers, and the median time at a job is just four years.[3] This is the *time-horizon problem*; it's easier for payers to pass the buck until it becomes Medicare's problem. This leaves potentially game-changing innovations, especially those focused on prevention, stranded without someone willing to invest.

Another challenge that arises when implementing population-wide prevention programs is the *patchwork payer problem*. Imagine rolling out a heart health program to a neighborhood where residents are covered by fifty different health plans through their employers, Medicaid, or Medicare. With such fragmented payers, it's challenging to coordinate partnerships for these types of broad initiatives. Even if the long-term benefits are clear, the logistical hurdles can be prohibitive when there's no single payer to take the lead.

Next up on the bingo card is what I call the *incumbent blockade*. Established players in healthcare—especially the large commercial

---

BOX 6.1.
In the Trenches: PillPack

PillPack faced the incumbent blockade just eighteen months into its operation (in 2016) when PBM Express Scripts threatened the startup's very existence.

Express Scripts, which controls a significant portion of the market and has its own competitive mail-order pharmacy, announced it would kick PillPack out of its network. This move threatened to cut PillPack off from a substantial portion of its fervently loyal customer base. With only twelve days before losing their contract, the team had to act fast.

In an impressive display of startup agility, they launched FixPharmacy.com in just days, gathering testimonials from more than two thousand customers, healthcare advocates, and even politicians. They orchestrated a massive media campaign that had forty-five press hits in the first twenty-four hours. This response (which would be nearly impossible for a larger organization to execute so quickly) paid off. Express Scripts reversed its decision just in the nick of time.

The incumbent blockade in healthcare is real. But startups can overcome it by doing what only startups can do: moving quickly and using their underdog narrative to change hearts and minds.

---

health plans and the pharmacy benefit managers (PBMs) they own—wield considerable market power. This power allows them to resist change, stifle competition, and sometimes even quash small competitors that threaten their business. These incumbents might use their clout to influence regulators, control access to data, or leverage existing relationships to lock out newcomers. They can also simply outspend startups in marketing or lobbying efforts.

Speaking of lobbying efforts, healthcare regulations can be confusing to newcomers. And these regulations can also be stacked against you. In a speech on regulation at the 2023 All-In Summit, venture capitalist Bill Gurley had the audience scream out loud: "Regulation is the friend of the incumbent!" (The speech's title, "2,851 Miles" referred to the distance between Silicon Valley and Washington, D.C.)[4]

What did he mean by that? It's called *regulatory capture*: when regulatory agencies favor the incumbents they are supposed to regulate rather than serving the public interest. It can happen for many reasons, including the following:

- Incumbents with deep pockets influence policy through lobbying.
- A "revolving door" of people move between industry and regulatory positions.
- Industry provides the information and expertise that regulators rely on.
- Close relationships are formed and favors are passed between regulators and industry representatives.

Certificate of Need (CON) laws, which exist in about two-thirds of US states, are an example. CON laws require healthcare providers to receive state approval before opening new facilities or expanding services.

CON laws seem designed to protect incumbents at every level. Existing providers often serve on the boards that review applications, giving them veto power over their competition. In most CON states, incumbent providers can object to competitors' applications, triggering expensive and time-consuming hearings. Regulators are required to deny applications that would "duplicate" (compete with) existing services, and large hospitals can block competitors simply by refusing to sign required transfer agreements. These laws can mean less competition, fewer options, and higher costs for patients.[5]

Regulation in healthcare is important, but some policies are biased toward incumbents and can stifle innovation. As Sergei Polevikov of AI Health Uncut aptly points out: "Policy, not innovation, drives American healthcare. And policy is dictated by corporate interests. Emotionally and psychologically, this is a hard pill to swallow for most of us in digital health. But this is an unfortunate reality."[6]

THE BIGGEST COMPETITOR TO INNOVATION

Usually, an innovation's biggest threat isn't a direct competitor or even the healthcare incumbents. It's the inertia of "how things have always been done." Change can be scary, especially when it feels like a threat to our livelihoods. Employees are usually inclined to favor the familiar, and new technologies or processes can be perceived as disrupting their flow—or worse, taking their jobs.

I always think about the tale of the first ATM appearing in London in the 1960s. Fearing the "robot cashiers" would cost them their jobs, some bank tellers decided to fight back. They covered the ATMs in honey, hoping to clog up the machines and save their livelihoods.

The honey-covered ATMs highlight a theme that's not unique to healthcare: the human resistance to change. *That* is usually your biggest competitor.

In most of healthcare, there's a resistance to change at every level. The medical field operates under the principle of "First, do no harm." Providers have a duty to protect patients, which naturally breeds a culture of caution when adopting new solutions. This culture means it takes time to gain widespread trust and acceptance, creating a high bar for entry that slows the pace of change.

New innovation doesn't just need to be better than the alternatives; it must be so compelling that it convinces users to ditch their familiar routines. This is where you must get creative not only in solving your customer's most pressing problem but also in change management and behavior design. You have to make it harder *not* to use your solution.

Healthcare stakeholders will likely be wary of the initial learning curve and disruptions a new approach may cause. While I was writing this book, hundreds of Kaiser Permanente nurses protested in downtown San Francisco against the use of artificial intelligence (AI) in their hospitals. Michelle Gutierrez Vo, president of the California Nurses Association, said: "All healthcare corporations need to make sure that the technology is tested, it's valid, and it's not harmful to patients. And before they deploy it, they need to sit down with nurses so that the nurses can review and make sure it's congruent with patient safety."[7]

Read that last line again. A successful product involves the stakeholders in its development. It includes user feedback, training, onboarding, and ongoing support baked into the plan from day one. Having internal champions, like nurses, makes adoption far easier.

You must also understand the end user's workflow, pain points, and motivations. The product should plug seamlessly into existing workflows or offer such an extraordinary value proposition that the effort of change is outweighed.

In banking, customer-centric innovation eventually won out. ATMs didn't make bank tellers obsolete (in fact, the number of teller jobs actually increased as ATMs made it cheaper to open more branches), but they did enable extended hours and convenience that traditional banking couldn't match. Mobile banking followed suit, allowing customers to manage their accounts from anywhere. The focus wasn't on replacing people but on empowering customers and making banking services more accessible. Healthcare can follow a similar trajectory.

BOX 6.2.

In the Trenches: Johnson & Johnson's Sedasys

The Sedasys machine was approved by the US Food and Drug Administration (FDA) in 2013 and promised to revolutionize anesthesia administration. It automated the sedation process for certain procedures, meaning only a nurse and not an anesthesiologist would need to be present.[8]

The machine was initially hailed as a disruptive innovation that could improve safety and lower the costs of procedures requiring anesthesia. But anesthesiologists—some of the highest-paid specialists in healthcare—lobbied against it, arguing that replacing human expertise posed safety risks.[9] In an effort to appease them, Johnson & Johnson, Sedasys' manufacturer, agreed to limit the machine's use to specific procedures like colonoscopies and to have an anesthesiologist or nurse on call in case of emergencies.

With the compromised offering, Sedasys struggled to gain widespread adoption and was pulled from the market.[10] Resistance from the anesthesiologist community undoubtedly played a role, as providers were reluctant to accept a technology seen as a direct threat to their profession.

Even when a technology shows clear potential, overcoming entrenched interests can derail even the most promising, well-funded innovations.

SOMETIMES YOU HAVE TO PUT UP A GOOD FIGHT

Sometimes you have to adapt to the healthcare system's confines; other times, you must actively work to reshape the system. This means fighting to change policies, reimbursement models, and even hearts and minds.

Healthcare's resistance to change isn't always a passive force. Sometimes it's an active, entrenched resistance that requires you to advocate for your vision. This can take many forms—forming coalitions, engaging in strategic litigation to challenge unfair practices, working with payers to demonstrate value, or launching media and public awareness campaigns.

It's a fight that requires patience and persistence. Changing healthcare doesn't happen overnight. It's a long game that requires sustained effort, often over years or even decades. Be prepared for setbacks, resistance, and a slow pace of change.

But it's a fight worth fighting. Those who are willing to put in the work to reshape healthcare are the ones who will ultimately drive systemic change. They're the ones who will break down barriers, open up new possibilities, and create a system that works better for everyone.

I think back to when Omada Health introduced its digital health programs for chronic disease prevention and management. The team's innovative approach faced a pretty big hurdle: how to get paid. At the time, there was no billing infrastructure to file claims for its value-based pricing model. Much of healthcare was still stuck in a fee-for-service world.

Sean Duffy, Omada's founder and CEO, quickly realized that the company would have to actively work to change the healthcare billing infrastructure. This meant engaging in advocacy, education, and collaboration at the highest levels of healthcare policy.

The company took on the challenge of adapting its value-based pricing model to fit within the existing fee-for-service billing system. To enable this, Omada went directly to the American Medical Association (AMA) with its clinical trial results and made the case for the creation of a new Current Procedural Terminology (CPT) code specific to a digital intervention for the prevention of type 2 diabetes.

Their persistence paid off. The AMA issued the first-ever digital-specific CPT code, creating billing infrastructure not just for Omada but for the entire digital health market delivering diabetes prevention, giving us a great example of what it means to put up a good fight.

DON'T FALL IN THESE TRAPS

If you hang around long enough, you start to see founders fall into the same traps. They've got a brilliant idea and the drive to make a difference, but they get blindsided by one of these common hurdles that could've been avoided. Here are a few common traps, and how to avoid them.

Trap 1: Death by Pilot

The opportunity to pilot with a big-name organization can be exciting and even game-changing. But more often, it becomes a time-consuming and costly distraction that drains resources and leads nowhere.

I see it all the time: weeks turn into months, and after endless meetings and deployments, you're still stuck in unpaid pilot mode.

Pilots *can* be useful, but don't let them become black holes. Set clear goals and make sure you're working with key decisionmakers, those who can actually make decisions and write checks. Outline specific time-based milestones that determine when and if you'll convert to a paid relationship.

Trap 2: Focusing on the Hammer, Not the Nail

It's easy to fall head over heels for your solution. But if you haven't spent serious time digging into your stakeholders' actual pain points, you might be building the answer to a problem no one really has.

You have to be ruthlessly objective in discerning if your product or service is truly valued. You may like the solution, but will customers? Are there enough people willing to switch to your product—and *pay* for it—to turn it into a sustainable, scalable business?

Talk to people. Don't just theorize from your office. Shadow clinicians, administrators, and patients. Interview the folks who make purchasing decisions. Understand their daily frustrations, wish lists, and hurdles. Then, and only then, go out and find a solution that cures their headaches.

Trap 3: Ignoring the Regulatory Beast

I already talked about the burden of regulatory capture. If you're working in healthcare, you must understand how the game is played. Ignoring the regulators can seriously derail your best-laid plans and destroy your reputation. Founders sometimes think they can wing it or worse, ask for forgiveness and not permission.

Get familiar with the regulations that apply to you (e.g., HIPAA) and the government agencies that will be watching (e.g., FDA, Federal Trade Commission, Office of the National Coordinator for Health Information Technology). Budget for regulatory experts early; a good expert is worth their weight in gold.

Then, go one step further. Know who the incumbents are, the special interest groups they back, who is lobbying on their behalf, who and what they're trying to influence, and how it might block you from succeeding.

Trap 4: Only Selling Once

Congratulations, you closed the deal! The customer is on board, the contract is signed, and you're popping bottles of champagne to celebrate. Enjoy the moment but remember: In healthcare, you often have to sell your product *twice*. Why? Because the person paying for it isn't usually the person using it. This is the difference between *covered lives* (the number of people you *can* reach through a payer deal) and *utilization* (the number of their members or employees who *actually* use your product).

Just because Janet in human resources (HR) agreed to pay for employees to use your new telehealth app doesn't mean she also has the interest or capacity to get employees to sign up.

You can't always count on HR to spread the good word. Make sure to invest in that last mile of getting members onboarded:

- Make it easy for Janet to include your product in employee newsletters (and ensure onboarding is dead simple).
- Ask if you can get an employee email list for marketing, then use it wisely.
- Send company swag for Janet to distribute at new-employee orientation.
- Run ads on LinkedIn by using the "company targeting" feature, which allows you to select specific companies.
- Offer on-site enrollment events or "office hours" during which employees can learn about and sign up for the service in person.
- Offer incentives for early adopters or referrals to drive initial uptake.
- Create seasonal or topical campaigns tied to health observances or company events.

If the employees actually use and fall in love with your product, Janet is more likely to renew your contract in a year.

SLOWER, BETTER BUSINESS

Healthcare may demand a Herculean level of patience, but the rewards are enormous for those able and willing to invest the time and resources. The long sales cycles, regulatory hurdles, and high switching costs all contribute to your competitive advantage. Once in place, the solutions that solve real healthcare problems gain exceptional staying power. That's how you build truly successful and impactful change in this industry.

This isn't just my anecdotal observation. A report by Bessemer Venture Partners found that while contracts take twice as long to close in healthcare than in other industries, they have lifetime value/customer acquisition cost (LTV/CAC) ratios that are almost double those of tech companies.[11] This means that despite the initial investment in time and effort, healthcare customers deliver significant returns over their lifespan.

Why is "slower, better" an okay approach? The challenges of building in healthcare weed out less-committed ventures. Those who successfully navigate the obstacles earn stakeholder trust and create a formidable barrier to entry, allowing them to solidify their position in the market.

Healthcare solutions that address pain points and improve outcomes tend to be deeply embedded into an organization's systems and protocols. This integration makes switching costs high for customers, reducing churn and increasing long-term revenue streams.

Although other industries may prioritize speed, healthcare transformation tends to be steadier and more incremental. This "slower, better" model may not fit the Silicon Valley archetype of explosive growth, but it's the reality of innovating in healthcare today. By accepting the challenges inherent in the industry and committing to delivering true value over time, you can build an enduring business.

HARD IS YOUR ADVANTAGE

I don't need easy. I just need possible.

—BETHANY HAMILTON

Healthcare being hard can be your competitive advantage. Your commitment to enduring the marathon, not just the sprint, ensures that fewer competitors make it to the finish line. In a sector dominated by the inertia of the familiar, embracing a long-game mindset puts you miles ahead.

Be aware of healthcare's resistance to change, sluggish adoption cycles, and myriad complexities—but don't let them discourage you. These very challenges can help establish your moat; it's the barrier to entry your competitors will try and fail to overcome. And within the confines of that hard-won moat, you'll develop sustainable growth, healthier margins, and, ultimately, the satisfaction of creating lasting contributions to our healthcare system.

Let the get-rich-quick opportunists play in other sandboxes. Healthcare offers those who endure the rewarding task of making a tangible difference in countless lives. That sign in our old office rings true today, tomorrow, and for all the years to come: The market will indeed choose the winners and losers. Those winners won't just be the clever or the lucky. They'll be the ones who never gave up.

By making hard your moat, you're not just adapting to healthcare's quirks; you're leveraging its very quirkiness to your advantage. Accept the challenge, persist through the difficulties, and let your endurance become your greatest asset.

TL;DR

- **Make healthcare's challenge your advantage:** The difficulty of innovating in healthcare can be your competitive moat. Those who commit to the long game will find fewer competitors and greater potential for enduring impact.
- **The market chooses the winners, but don't forget that it is rigged:** Founders who take the time to understand healthcare's pain points have a better chance of breaking through. But sometimes we must simply acknowledge that the market is rigged and irrational.
- **Healthcare plays by different rules:** Understand factors that slow healthcare innovation and adapt your strategies accordingly to navigate this quirky industry.
- **Patience is rewarded:** The "slower, better" approach, while less glamorous, leads to more sustainable businesses and higher customer satisfaction. Focus on building products that deliver tangible, long-term value.
- **Avoid common traps:** Learn from others' mistakes. Don't get stuck in endless pilots. Make sure you're solving a real problem. Understand the regulatory landscape. And remember: selling in healthcare often means selling twice (to payers *and* users).

7

WHEN INNOVATION FAILS

It takes 20 years to build a reputation and five minutes to ruin it.
If you think about that, you'll do things differently.
—WARREN BUFFETT

The year was 2012, and two earnest scientists-turned-entrepreneurs sat across from us in the Rock Health office, pitching their direct-to-consumer microbiome testing startup, uBiome. The concept was intriguing: analyze a customer's gut bacteria through a home-collected stool sample and provide them with personalized health insight.

Were consumers ready for collecting and shipping their poop at scale? We decided they weren't and passed on investing.

It turns out they didn't need our investment or support. They went on to join the tech incubator Y Combinator and raised more than $100 million in venture funding.[1] The founder was featured on Forbes's "30 Under 30" list and made Fast Company's roster of The World's Most Innovative Companies.[2] I often saw the CEO, Jessica, at healthcare conferences where we exchanged polite hellos.

Had we missed out on the next big thing in healthcare?

Then, we heard rumblings of a Federal Bureau of Investigation (FBI) raid of their San Francisco offices, not too far from ours. It turns out they were moving too fast and breaking too many things. The company was growing; but to get there, it had allegedly been defrauding insurance companies, billing patients without consent, and pressuring doctors to approve tests without oversight.

A federal grand jury handed down a thirty-three-page indictment charging the cofounders with multiple federal crimes, including conspiracy to commit securities fraud, conspiracy to commit health-care fraud, and money laundering. For example, they allegedly wrote doctor notes that falsified an encounter between a patient and a doctor to justify ordering a test.[3]

In 2019, uBiome filed for bankruptcy and shut down. The found-ers, one of whom held German citizenship, quickly got married and fled to Germany, where both are now citizens.[4] German citizens are not extradited to the United States. Since 2021, the FBI has consid-ered them fugitives.

As investors, we dodged a bullet. But scandals are disappointing for everyone. The blast radius is *huge*, casting a long shadow over our sector. The public loses trust in healthcare innovation. Inves-tors become more risk-averse. Potential partners, like health plans or providers, slow down the adoption of potentially beneficial tech-nologies. Everyone loses.

In this chapter, we'll unpack failure. I'll share scandals that have shaken the industry and explore the more common, less sensational reasons why most healthcare startups don't make it. We'll dive into the pressures that can lead founders astray and discuss the three things that need to be true to prevent misbehavior. All with the goal of creat-ing a stronger and more resilient healthcare innovation ecosystem.

WHEN HEALTHCARE STARTUPS FAIL SPECTACULARLY

Ninety percent of all startups fail, and healthcare startups—despite our noble ambitions—are not immune to this harsh reality.[5] Even the most well-funded, well-intentioned, star-studded startups can find themselves going in the wrong direction. Some founders, under immense pressure to succeed, make horrible decisions that sink the company and make things more difficult for the rest of us.

In my class, I often share cautionary tales for my students to discuss.

We talk about Outcome Health, which managed video screens in doctors' offices and waiting rooms. The company sold advertising space that didn't exist, yet billed clients as though it had fulfilled its contractual obligations. Executives and employees hid their underperformance, inflating engagement metrics and manipulating third-party reports to maintain the illusion of success. They reportedly misrepresented the situation to auditors and investors, perpetuating the scheme until it eventually unraveled. The founders were sentenced for a $1 billion corporate fraud scheme and are currently serving time in prison.[6]

And mental health startup Cerebral, where nurse practitioners alleged they were pressured to prescribe unnecessary attention-deficit/hyperactivity disorder (ADHD) medications and a former executive filed a lawsuit claiming the company prioritized profits over safety.[7] The tragic death of a twenty-one-year-old who obtained ADHD medication from Cerebral without a previous diagnosis amplified concerns about its prescribing practices.[8] The US Drug Enforcement Administration launched an investigation, and the company agreed to pay more than $3.65 million in connection with business practices that "encouraged the unauthorized distribution of controlled substances." But it didn't end there. Separately, the FTC filed a proposed order for the company to pay more than $7 million for allegedly disclosing consumers' sensitive personal health information to third parties and failing to honor its easy cancellation promises.[9] The company ultimately stopped prescribing most controlled substances, and the founder and CEO was removed.[10] The founder later told reporters that his investors pushed the company to prescribe more stimulants, and then used him as a "scapegoat" when investigators caught on.[11]

Then there's the story of Done, another startup offering ADHD medication. Attorney General Merrick B. Garland said the company "exploited the COVID-19 pandemic to develop and carry out a $100 million scheme to defraud taxpayers and provide easy access to Adderall and other stimulants for no legitimate medical purpose." Among other things, Done allegedly engaged in deceptive advertisements on social media, instructed its clinicians to pre-scribe stimulants even if the customer did not qualify, and paid clinicians based on the number of patients who received prescriptions. The CEO and clinical president were arrested and charged with fraud by federal authorities.[12]

Of course, most of my students already know about Theranos and Elizabeth Holmes's story (a bestselling book! An HBO documentary! A podcast!). Initially hailed as a revolutionary startup promising faster, cheaper, painless blood testing, Holmes built a company on a mountain of lies. The core technology didn't work, yet elaborate schemes were put in place to create the illusion of success. The potential harm of inaccurate medical tests, combined with the scale of the deception, make Theranos an extreme but tragically real example of outright fraud.

WHY GOOD PEOPLE MAKE BAD DECISIONS

Although inexcusable, these founders' actions don't exist in a vacuum. Systemic pressures and cultural norms within the broader world of startups and venture capital play a role. The intense pressure to succeed, driven by the need to justify massive company valuations, can lead to a mentality in which scaling eclipses all else. Founders may be tempted to cut corners, embellish results, and blur ethical lines to pursue rapid growth.

The Milgram Experiment in the 1960s revealed something surprising about human behavior: Ordinary people could be pushed to take actions they would normally consider unethical, simply because an authority figure told them to continue. In the study, participants were instructed to administer what they believed were increasingly painful electric shocks to another person. Despite hearing cries of pain (which were actually recordings), 65 percent of participants continued to the maximum voltage as the experimenter calmly insisted, "The experiment must continue."[13]

This is an extreme example. But I do think otherwise well-intentioned healthcare founders can end up making increasingly questionable decisions under heightened business pressure. When expectations are for high growth above all else, founders might find themselves crossing lines they never thought they would.

Fraud and unethical behavior aren't unique to healthcare. The difference in healthcare is the stakes. Making a misleading marketing claim for a gaming app is one thing; doing the same in digital health introduces a whole different level of risk. With lives at stake, the consequences are far more severe.

When the primary metric of success becomes funding rounds and ever-increasing valuations, a dangerous mindset can emerge during which "fake it till you make it" stops being an optimistic mantra and crosses into harmful territory. It becomes easy to rationalize questionable decisions as simply "hustling." Add to this the slow, grinding pace of healthcare—regulations, reimbursement, the incumbent blockade—and the temptation to find shortcuts increases.

But as you can probably guess, there are no good shortcuts in healthcare.

PREVENTING MISBEHAVIOR

How do we prevent well-intentioned founders from sliding down this slippery slope? How do we build companies that can withstand the intense pressure to grow at all costs?

Based on my experience working with healthcare founders, I've found that three things need to be true.

First, you have to be genuinely okay with failure—with the idea that your startup may never work out (remember, most don't). The moment you become so afraid of failing that you can't accept it as a possible outcome is the moment you become vulnerable to making compromised decisions in "survival mode."

Second, you need to be hyperaware of the pressures that could compromise decision-making or subtly reward deception, whether they come from investors, market conditions, or your own ambitions. Call them out and stand up to them.

Finally, you must be willing to walk away from venture capital and Wall Street investors if their growth expectations don't align with your values. I realize this is easier said than done, but it is possible to build a successful business without investors. Just look at electronic health record company Epic, which never took outside investment and still built one of the largest healthcare companies ever, reaching $4.9 billion in revenue in 2023.[14]

DUE DILIGENCE

The most permanent feature of a new startup is its founder,
followed by its market, and then finally, its product.
—TERRENCE ROHAN

The fallout from scandals forces us to take a hard look at how healthcare innovation is supported and evaluated. I think people can be both enamored by bold ideas and charismatic founders, and also cautious about how it could play out. Investors, advisers, partners, and employees play a role in safeguarding the integrity of the ecosystem. This starts with better due diligence.

Due diligence, the upfront research you perform before a business transaction, mitigates risk by uncovering potential red flags. It comes after and is separate from the SSI checklist, which considers the sustainability, scalability, and impact of a new solution. Due diligence is about thoroughly vetting both the promise and the reality of what's being presented.

- **Look deeper:** Understand how the product will be developed and brought to market. Does the team have the operational depth and track record to execute? Do their projections match their capabilities?

- **Ask the experts:** Connect with subject matter experts who understand the nuances of the technology or the specific area of healthcare the solution touches.
- **Verify:** You'll want to verify claims, projections, contracts, and any scientific data behind the pitch. I've been in situations where founders claimed they had major customers on board, only to discover during diligence that nothing had been signed.
- **Do your homework:** Test the product yourself. Read user reviews and talk to customers to compare the company's public narrative with how it's actually perceived. This kind of surface-level digging can reveal inconsistencies or reinforce confidence.
- **Don't just talk to the CEO:** Although founders are usually the most passionate and compelling, make sure to also speak with other team members (past and present). These conversations can provide insight into the day-to-day realities of the business.
- **Think about the patients:** Understand how patient data will be handled, how consent will be managed, and what safeguards are in place to protect health information, particularly for vulnerable populations.

The earlier the stage of the company you are evaluating, the harder this is. With a shorter track record, there are fewer red flags to catch in the first place. Take the uBiome founder, for instance. After high school, she started and sold a company, went to Stanford for her undergraduate education (she studied interdisciplinary engineering), and then to Oxford for graduate school. She was working toward her doctorate in computational social science when she started uBiome, and she brought on medical advisers from Harvard and University of California–San Francisco. On paper, the team was impressive. Even our initial reluctance to invest based on the practicalities of stool shipping feels minor considering the transgressions the company would later commit.

Maybe we need to look beyond improved due diligence and create environments in which corners simply cannot be so easily cut. This could involve better benchmarks for healthcare startups and rethinking how we measure success, shifting focus away from mere growth metrics and more toward impact.

MOST FAILURES ARE NOT SCANDALS

Now that we've covered the worst of the worst cases, let's look at the more common reason for failure in healthcare. Most of the time, across every single industry, startups simply don't work out.

The good news is that very few failures in healthcare innovation are rooted in fraud or intentional deception, although those that are get outsized media coverage. The challenges of building in healthcare, combined with bad timing and bad luck, can lead to solutions that don't succeed, even if undertaken with the best of intentions and ideas.

Startups are built upon dozens, if not hundreds, of assumptions about how the future will unfold. Founders assume that a product will work as envisioned, that acquiring customers will be economically feasible, that somebody will pay for the product or service, that competitors will respond in a certain way, that the regulatory environment will remain favorable, and that investors will fund them—the list goes on and on. When a startup fails, it's generally because one of the core assumptions did not pan out.

For example, Pear Therapeutics raised more than $400 million and even went public.[15] The company built FDA cleared apps—*digital therapeutics*—for conditions like insomnia and substance use disorder. There were a lot of assumptions made, including that the products would work at least as well as existing interventions, that patients would want to use these apps, and that payers would start reimbursing for apps (something they had not done previously). Unfortunately, many of those assumptions proved incorrect, and Pear Therapeutics failed to obtain widespread adoption. The CEO shared on LinkedIn: "We've shown that our products can truly help patients and their clinicians. But that isn't enough. Payers have the ability to deny payment for therapies that are clinically necessary, effective, and cost-saving."[16] The price was probably a sticking point, too—use of the app was priced at an average of $1,300 for three months, higher than many prescription meds.[17]

Or take Haven, a high-profile joint venture by Amazon, Berkshire Hathaway, and JPMorgan Chase that aimed to deliver simplified, high-quality, and affordable healthcare to their respective employees. Despite hiring renowned surgeon, writer, and public health leader Dr. Atul Gawande as CEO, and despite the parent companies' combined 1.2 million employee base, Haven still lacked sufficient market power to negotiate lower prices with increasingly consolidated health systems.[18] The timing was also not on their side: The pandemic shifted providers' focus and stalled consideration for new, risk-bearing models. It is a humble reminder that healthcare is hard for even the most well-connected and resourced teams.

These examples of honest failure, while disappointing, are completely expected. As I've discussed, building in healthcare is hard. Some startups fail because their vision was far ahead of its time, either technologically or in terms of market readiness. They might have attempted to solve a problem with no viable technical solution, or they targeted patient behavior change that even the best design couldn't address.

Here are the three most common reasons I see healthcare startups fail:

- **Unrealistic product assumptions:** The technology doesn't work as hoped, or stakeholders don't find it solves a problem well enough to justify changing their current workflow.
- **Payer problems:** No reimbursement pathway exists, or no one wants to pay for the product. Think back to the free-rider problem and the time-horizon problem we discussed in chapter 6.
- **Underestimating the incumbent blockade:** Misjudging the balance of power in the market (like Haven assuming they could force better prices from providers) and not strategizing around it sooner.

Most of the time, however, startups simply run out of money. They fail to raise (enough) funding, or they burn through their cash too quickly in an industry in which adoption and results take time. Less than half of tech companies that take outside funding ever raise a second round.[19] This means their first round of financing, usually led by angel investors, is all the money they ever get to build their business.

Failure in healthcare innovation is inevitable, but it doesn't have to be catastrophic. By learning from both honest missteps and egregious misconduct, we can build a more resilient, ethical, and ultimately successful ecosystem.

We can't avoid failure entirely, but we can learn to fail forward—learning, adapting, and always keeping patient welfare at the forefront of our efforts.

TL;DR

- **Scandals damage the entire sector:** Fraudulent startups hurt themselves and cast a shadow on healthcare innovation, eroding trust and making it harder for legitimate companies to thrive.
- **Pressure fuels bad decisions:** The drive for growth and sky-high valuations can tempt founders to cut corners or even cross ethical lines, but that's not an excuse.
- **Due diligence must go deeper:** Validate the team's ability to execute, pressure-test their claims, talk to people who've worked with them, and evaluate both the tech and its impact on patients.
- **Metrics should emphasize impact, not just financial growth:** Develop metrics that will disincentivize risky or deceptive practices.
- **Most failures are honest attempts:** Startups often fail as a result of market forces, timing, or unrealistic assumptions, not malicious intent. Learning openly from these failures can help us progress.

PART III

THE NEW RULES OF BUILDING MASSIVELY BETTER HEALTHCARE

8

RULE 1

Work from the Inside Out, Not the Outside In

Fall in love with the problem, not the solution.

—URI LEVINE

Not long after the first Oculus Rift virtual reality (VR) headset was released, two young entrepreneurs walked into our office to pitch their healthcare startup. VR was still in its infancy then, with more promise than practice, but San Francisco was all over the hype.

These two founders, just a few years out of college, had that familiar mix of nervousness and excitement as they set up their bulky VR headsets. Their startup's mission? To create a VR-driven virtual world for lung cancer patients.

As they began their presentation, I found myself both intrigued and skeptical. "Imagine," one of them started, his voice full of conviction despite the slight tremor, "a world where lung cancer patients can escape the isolation of their diagnosis and connect with others facing similar challenges, all from their beds."

It was an earnest pitch. The founders described a vision of immersive environments, virtual support groups, and educational games for people with lung cancer. The demo was rudimentary—blocky graphics and laggy movements—but you could see the potential. It was ambitious, especially given how new VR tech was at the time.

When we asked why they picked lung cancer, they didn't have a great answer, just that it was a diagnosis riddled with stigma. True. It's an important population to serve, no doubt. But it felt like they were trying to squeeze the shiny new object of VR headsets into a healthcare context instead of considering all the potential solutions to the core problem they were trying to solve. Unfortunately, the company never gained traction.

Technology has, and will continue to have, an outsized impact on healthcare. Healthcare innovation, however, shouldn't begin with technology. Technology-first, outside-in approaches create something similar to a hammer looking for a nail: You fall in love with a technology—blockchain, artificial intelligence (AI), VR—and then scramble to find an interesting medical problem it can help address. Sure, you might find some uses, but you end up building solutions in search of problems.

Instead, the first rule of massively better healthcare encourages us to work from the inside out. It calls for us to become experts in the problem we're trying to solve first and *then* work on the solution. Put simply, we have to understand the world before we try to change it.

Think of yourself as an anthropologist of healthcare, focusing on the corner of healthcare you want to tackle, and with a curiosity for that corner's interconnectedness to the full ecosystem. Immerse yourself in the daily struggles of stakeholders—every part of the system a solution may touch. Observe where things break down, where communication falters, where frustration festers. This is how you get an accurate picture of what needs mending and where new solutions can actually bring tangible results and not just add complexity and cost.

These contrasting approaches—inside-out versus outside-in—shape everything about how we build solutions in healthcare (table 8.1).

Although the outside-in approach might seem more exciting at first, the inside-out approach consistently leads to more meaningful

Table 8.1
Inside-Out Versus Outside-In Approaches

Inside-Out Approach	Outside-In Approach
Anthropological approach	Explorer approach
Problem oriented	Solution oriented
Needs first	Ideas first
Go slow to go fast	Fast to start, more likely to fizzle out
Flexible about the journey, inflexible about the destination	Fixed on the path; ignores warning signs
Better chance innovation will be valued by stakeholders	Risk of investing in solutions that don't address real needs

and lasting impact. Let's explore exactly how to put this approach into practice in seven steps:

1. Become an expert in your problem
2. Study noncustomers
3. Remember: "nothing about us, without us"
4. Go slow to go fast
5. Meet people where they are
6. Date your ideas; don't marry them
7. Learn collectively

BECOME AN EXPERT IN YOUR PROBLEM

Getting advice from industry experts is overrated (yes, I realize the irony of writing this in a book in which I'm positioned as one). And I still think you can talk to experts—just don't let their constraints become yours. As venture capitalist (VC) Vinod Khosla has pointed out, "Experts are experts in a previous version of the world, not the world you're trying to create."[1] Relying too heavily on their opinions can lead to conservative, incremental solutions rather than the big ideas we need.

Instead, become an expert yourself. Build empathy for those the problem affects. Understand their struggles, work-arounds, and frustrations firsthand—not through a messenger.

Here's how to do this:

- **Identify your stakeholders:** Get to know the perspectives of the payer (a.k.a. key decisionmaker) and the user—these are often separate people. Also, think through any indirect stakeholders who may be affected.
- **Talk to them:** Don't go in with assumptions. Or if you have assumptions, don't go in believing they are always right. Engage in meaningful, open-ended conversations with folks from each stakeholder group.
- **Survey them:** If one of your stakeholders is consumers, it's relatively easy to conduct a large-scale survey by running ads or using a tool like Qualtrics. When we founded Cofertility—a company I helped start and am on the board of—we wanted to solve the problem of the accessibility and affordability of egg freezing. One idea we had was to enable women to freeze their eggs *for free* by donating a portion of the eggs retrieved to a family that could not otherwise conceive (think: gay couples, women facing infertility, cancer survivors). But would women do it? We ran an eight-hundred-person survey and got our answer: a resounding yes. This gave us the confidence to begin building this new model of egg sharing.
- **Walk in their shoes:** Observe how stakeholders interact directly with the problem. Watch their struggles, work-arounds, and frustrations. Try to understand how stakeholders are already trying to solve the problem. Have they tried five things, and nothing worked? Where have existing solutions run into problems?
- **Study their problem:** Understand the problem your stakeholder is facing at a population level. Great resources for healthcare research include the Commonwealth Fund, KFF.org, Rock Health, the Cochrane Library, and the RAND Corporation, along with medical journals specific to your area of focus.

- **Keep learning and relearning:** Needs change, and so does willingness to try new things. You'll always want to have your ear to the ground, listening (and responding) to the needs of your stakeholders. Be willing to change your mind in the face of new data.

BOX 8.1.

In the Trenches: Maven Clinic

Kate Ryder, founder of Maven Clinic, was frustrated with the shortcomings of women's healthcare. Wanting to do something, she didn't just rely on market reports or theoretical analyses. Instead, Kate became an embedded observer within the system she sought to reshape.

Kate's initial research revealed a woefully inadequate market for women juggling careers, family, and their own well-being. Fertility treatments posed financial and logistical barriers; postpartum support felt nonexistent; even basic telemedicine options seemed catered to men's health or pediatric concerns. But these findings were just a jumping-off point.

To break through the surface-level limitations and identify hidden pain points, Kate immersed herself in the lives of everyday women. She went to coworking spaces where expectant and new mothers shared stories of appointment struggles and isolation. She joined parenting groups online and offline, absorbing the unspoken hurdles women faced seeking everything from mental health support to lactation specialists.

Instead of solely relying on formal interviews or surveys, Kate—a former journalist at the *Economist*—became a participant in the day-to-day experiences of her target population. She observed not just the lack of available solutions but also the emotional toll, the constant mental load, and the discouragement women felt as they tried to navigate a system not designed by or for them.

As Maven Clinic expanded into new markets, particularly Medicaid (which covers 42 percent of births in the United States), Kate recognized the need to deepen her understanding of a broader spectrum

---

(continued on next page)

(*continued from previous page*)

of experiences. She conducted roundtables with Medicaid moms in Iowa and New York City, acknowledging that many of the women she initially interviewed weren't on Medicaid. These conversations revealed that for low-income women, giving birth in the United States is a deeply unsupported experience with its own distinct set of challenges and barriers to care.

It was within these real-world spaces, away from conference rooms and spreadsheets, that Kate sharpened the vision for Maven Clinic. She recognized that "women's health" couldn't be relegated to a once-a-year wellness exam. It was continuous, evolving, and intrinsically linked to a woman's productivity, her sense of self, and her role within a family and broader community.

Maven Clinic, now a leader in women's health valued at more than $1.7 billion, stemmed directly from Kate's commitment to understanding the daily lived experience of its potential users. This grassroots-level immersion equipped her with insight unmatched by conventional market research. It enabled her to design a care model that resonated with users because it genuinely addressed the nuanced realities of women's lives.

All this said, sometimes being an expert in the problem means envisioning solutions your stakeholders might not yet be able to articulate. Use market research as your foundation, but don't let it constrain your thinking. Trust your instincts.

John Mackey, the founder of Whole Foods, told me he never did market research. But then he described what can only be called *informal* market research—he was always in the stores and close to the customers so he could meet their needs. This allowed him to stay attuned to shifting consumer preferences and market trends even without a formal market research process.

You may have heard the famous Henry Ford quote about selling the first cars: "If I had asked people what they wanted, they would have said faster horses." Turns out, Ford didn't actually say this.[2] What he did say, however, is even better: "If there is any one secret of success, it lies in the ability to get the other person's point of view and see things from that person's angle as well as from your own."[3]

Let empathy be your edge.

STUDY NONCUSTOMERS

Peter Drucker, the father of modern management theory, famously stressed the importance of studying "noncustomers." He argued that the seeds of fundamental change rarely sprout within the walls of your organization or among your existing customers. Instead, they lie in the choices of those who opt *not* to use your product or service.

In healthcare, noncustomers often include the most vulnerable among us, those whose needs are ignored or whose circumstances make accessing care a struggle. I think about my uncle, who did not have health insurance or a regular doctor despite being, by definition, a patient in desperate need of care.

By understanding why people like him choose not to engage with the healthcare system or are unable to, we can gain insight into unmet needs and even latent desires they may not be fully aware of. Perhaps the cost is prohibitive, the system is too confusing to navigate, or existing solutions don't cater to their specific circumstances. Maybe it's a matter of mistrust, fear, cultural barriers, or a lack of awareness. Understanding noncustomers can help us design better, more inclusive, and more effective products and services. We can break down the barriers perpetuating health disparities and serve more people.

Studying noncustomers can also help us anticipate the future. As Drucker reminds us, every innovation eventually becomes obsolete. Markets shift, technologies evolve, and regulations change. By continuously studying noncustomers, we gain insight into developing trends and new opportunities.

"NOTHING ABOUT US, WITHOUT US"

The phrase "nothing about us, without us" has roots in social justice movements, particularly disability rights advocacy. It's a call for self-determination, demanding that those most affected by policies and decisions have a seat at the table.

Representation matters at every level of healthcare innovation, from the initial concept to design, development, testing, and implementation. When the very stakeholders a solution intends to serve are left out, the consequences can range from embarrassing oversights to life-threatening errors.

I remember when Apple launched HealthKit in 2014. Despite offering the ability to track numerous health metrics like weight, blood alcohol content, sodium intake, and even asthma inhaler usage, it notably excluded menstrual cycles—a biometric half of all humans have tracked for millennia. At the time, 70 percent of the company's employees were male.[4] It's unclear whether there were any women on the HealthKit team, even though women are more likely to track their health and fitness.[5] This oversight wasn't corrected until a full year later, after significant public outcry and pressure from women's health advocates, including myself.

Even more concerning was the case of pulse oximeters, a standard medical device used to measure blood oxygen levels. These devices worked less effectively on people with darker skin because melanin interferes with light absorption. A 2020 University of Michigan study revealed that Black patients were three times more likely than white patients to have hidden hypoxia (undetected dangerously low oxygen levels).[6]

This inaccuracy led to serious consequences: Patients with darker skin received less supplemental oxygen during intensive care unit stays and were more likely to have a delay in life-saving treatment.[7] As it turns out, the FDA's premarket guidance for pulse oximeter developers recommended only a minimum of two darkly pigmented subjects or 15 percent of the study group in clinical studies—a number far too low to predict real-world performance across diverse populations.

Representation matters at every stage of healthcare innovation:

- **Concept and design:** Having team members who represent the target user base ensures that real needs and pain points are identified and addressed from the outset.
- **Development:** When the development team includes individuals who share experiences with the end users, they can anticipate potential issues and create solutions that resonate with the target audience.
- **Testing:** Involving a test group that accurately represents the intended users is a must for uncovering how a product performs in real-world scenarios for those it's meant to serve.
- **Implementation:** Representation in leadership and decision-making roles helps ensure that products and services are deployed in ways that are accessible and beneficial to the intended user base.
- **Feedback and iteration:** Creating channels for ongoing feedback from the user base allows for continuous improvement that directly addresses their needs and experiences.

Teams should reflect the diversity of the people they aim to serve. Employees, advisers, investors, and even the board should reflect the life experiences, values, and perspectives of the communities they affect.

GO SLOW TO GO FAST

There's a Navy SEAL mantra, "slow is smooth, smooth is fast," which espouses the benefits of a controlled, consistent pace. The idea is that by slowing down and not rushing, you can:

- Develop systems and processes that scale
- Minimize errors and mistakes
- Thoughtfully make high-impact decisions

- Save time in the long run by getting it right the first time
- Maintain a steady pace, preventing burnout

Going slow to go fast means taking time up front to build the infrastructure and expertise to tackle billing, clinical workflow, regulatory, and all the other details of your healthcare business. You'll want to map out your strategy in crazy detail, from end to end, so you don't get trapped in a corner later on. Building a solid foundation upfront can save your future self from countless cycles of wasted effort.

It's tempting to be fast out of the gate when getting started. The slow and steady mindset can feel at odds with the rapid-fire pace of startups in other sectors. This pressure to move quickly often comes from comparing healthcare startups to tech companies, but it's a dangerous parallel to draw.

Far too often, I hear from remorseful founders who took funding from a technology VC who expected the sort of hockey-stick growth you see in software companies. The VC, not fully understanding healthcare, has expectations that push exponential top-line growth at all costs. Investors focused on quick financial returns can sink your business and leave everyone disappointed. Instead, align yourself with folks who understand the patience required to work in healthcare.

MEET PEOPLE WHERE THEY ARE

Sometimes the future we envision isn't ready to happen today. And although it would be nice to just skip to the good part, you have to build a bridge between where we are and where we want to be. This often means being *backward compatible*—creating solutions that work within existing systems and workflows while simultaneously laying the foundation for future innovation.

The urge to completely blow up and remake broken systems is real. But attempting to force radical change often leads to resistance, rejection, and failure. Find ways to meet stakeholders where they are, solving immediate problems while building toward a better future.

BOX 8.2.

In the Trenches: Doximity

Doximity began with a mission to empower physicians with tools to enhance productivity and improve patient care.

When it was founded in 2010, healthcare still relied heavily on outdated tools like fax machines because of strict security requirements (even today, 90 percent of providers still use fax machines).[8] The Doximity team recognized that although the healthcare system might be stuck in the past, physicians themselves were digitally savvy, carrying advanced technology—their smartphones—in their pockets.

Instead of trying to eliminate faxes entirely, they focused on being backward compatible: creating tools that met physicians where they were, and working within existing systems, while laying the foundation for a more connected, digital future. As CEO Jeff Tangney explained, "Digital health companies have great visions for the future—but we also have to solve the problems that doctors still have today."

In 2013, Doximity launched a Health Insurance Portability and Accountability Act (HIPAA)-compliant digital fax service, allowing physicians to send, receive, and manage faxes directly from their smartphones. Over a decade later, that digital fax tool remains one of the company's most trusted services. Now it's integrated with its generative AI tools, which help doctors write and send prior authorization and appeals letters to insurance companies.

By aligning solutions with physicians' existing workflows rather than forcing them to adopt entirely new ones, Doximity, now a publicly traded company, has become the largest network of US medical professionals. Its platform now connects more than two million members, including more than 80 percent of US physicians.

DATE YOUR IDEAS; DON'T MARRY THEM

By now, you understand that building massively better healthcare starts with a deep and empathetic understanding of the problem you're trying to solve. With that groundwork laid, you're ready to evaluate potential solutions—whether new products, business models, or a creative hybrid of both—to find the best way to solve the problem.

This process is easier said than done. Many products require significant groundwork before you even bring on your first user. FDA clearance, becoming "in network," or establishing a management services organization (MSO) structure for hiring providers can all be time and capital intensive.

Still, avoid getting trapped by the *sunk cost fallacy*—the urge to cling to an idea simply because you've already invested time, money, and energy. The most successful founders are flexible. This allows them to pivot when needed, stay ahead of evolving market dynamics, and constantly improve alignment with stakeholder needs. Remember, Netflix started by sending DVDs . . . by mail.

In the early stages, treat your solutions like a promising first date, not a lifelong commitment. Although you should put your best effort into your minimum viable product (MVP) based on stakeholder insights, the market *will* give you excellent feedback. Be ready to add features, explore new channels, or pivot altogether. Being agile is one of the few (and best!) advantages of being a startup, so use that card.

At this stage, it's not about having all the answers instantly. It's about the speed of learning. Your goal should be to learn and implement those learnings faster than your competitors. Build something, put it out into the world, and use the feedback loop to inform continued improvements.

LEARN COLLECTIVELY

Making healthcare massively better is a cumulative process. We build on what works and learn from our failures to avoid repeating them. We need to do this within our organizations and across the industry.

BOX 8.3.
In the Trenches: Brightside Health

When I invested in Brightside Health in 2017, it was a cash-pay virtual mental health service staffed by experienced primary care physicians (PCPs) who had a track record of prescribing antidepressants. It seemed like a solid strategy—after all, PCPs historically wrote about 80 percent of antidepressant prescriptions.

But when Brightside gained enough scale to pursue payer contracts, the company hit a wall. The behavioral health arms of payers wouldn't credential PCPs, insisting that only behavioral health specialists could be credentialed and, therefore, paid by the insurance company. This model ultimately blocked Brightside from working with payers.

Cofounder and CEO Brad Kittredge's first instinct was to fight the system. "My logic told me that surely payers would see that it was a silly rule, that they'd see that PCPs were qualified to do this work as they were doing most of it already," he recalls. But he quickly realized this was a losing battle. "Payers are so complex and policy-driven that nobody internally felt empowered or inclined to make an exception or change a policy."

Ultimately, Kittredge recognized the need to throw out the entire network strategy and start over. "I realized that there are certain things we can change, and others that we just need to accept," he told me. "Some things are foolish to try to change and we need to work around and within them."

Brightside completely rebuilt its prescriber network, replacing PCPs with psychiatric nurse practitioners (NPs) supervised by psychiatrists. This new approach aligned with payer requirements, allowing Brightside to secure contracts and rapidly expand its reach.

Today, the product is available to more than two hundred million people. Kittredge acknowledged, "If we had continued our network and contracting strategy, I think we'd still be waiting today for that exception to the rule."

The takeaway is this: Be nimble, recognize when you're butting heads with immovable objects and find creative ways to work within the existing system even as you try to change it. Sometimes the best move is knowing when to let go of your original strategy and go in a new direction.

This means moving away from exclusion and secrecy and toward inclusion and transparency. In healthcare, learning collectively manifests in several ways:

- **Openly sharing our successes:** Research has consistently shown that knowledge sharing and openness lead to greater creativity, innovation, and improved performance and commitment at all levels—individual, team, and organizational.[9]
- **Openly sharing our failures:** Society often views success as the only path to progress. But equally important to sharing wins is sharing and learning from what *doesn't* work as we had expected. Failures should also be shared or published, studied, and understood so they are not repeated elsewhere.
- **Collaborating across organizations:** Collective learning includes partnering across the industry, even with unlikely partners.

Our shared goal is to improve human health—a mission that inherently calls for collaboration, not division. Your real competitor isn't other healthcare organizations, but the status quo. This includes ingrained health disparities, systemic inefficiencies, and the barriers that hinder better care.

Viewed in this light, another organization committed to your cause should be considered a potential ally, not a competitor. This shift in thinking can encourage an environment in which successes are shared, and challenges are addressed collectively—all in the name of better healthcare.

If that's not convincing enough, think about it this way: Your career in healthcare will last much longer than your job today. It will span decades, most likely outlasting your current organization and role. By sharing knowledge and learning collectively, you're also building a network, reputation, and knowledge base that will serve you throughout your entire career. The connections you make, the insight you share, and the collaborative spirit you embody will open doors and create opportunities far into the future.

THE DANGERS OF OUTSIDER THINKING

I witnessed an embarrassing embodiment of outsider thinking when Pinky Gloves burst onto (and then quickly out of) the scene in 2021. Featured on the German version of Shark Tank, this product—developed by three men—was pitched to solve menstrual hygiene "problems" that don't actually exist. Pinky Gloves sold pink (of course), disposable gloves for removing tampons, packaged in a cutesy box that completely missed the mark of actual user needs. (I recommend pausing for a quick Google image search.)

But as any tampon user could tell you, tampons already have strings for easy removal. Bathrooms have toilet paper, trash cans, soap, and running water. Tampon removal is not an actual problem. After public outcry and ridicule, the founders apologized on Instagram and said they would better consider the stigmatization of menstruation.

We can't fix healthcare *without* outsiders. We need new perspectives and talents to help us right this enormous ship. But being an outsider doesn't mean you must act like one.

Here's how outsider thinking goes wrong:

- **Alienating stakeholders:** A founder thinks they know more than the stakeholders and ignores or dismisses their voices.
- **Impatience:** They rush to launch, executing sloppily.
- **Overconfidence:** An inflated sense of their solution's potential leads to overpromising and underdelivering, setting impossibly high expectations that the product or service ultimately fails to meet.
- **Contextually unaware:** Applying traditional tech mindsets without calibrating them to healthcare leads to disappointment.
- **Surrounded by yes-men:** The founder builds a team that only reinforces their ideas, avoiding necessary feedback.

One telltale sign of outsider thinking is the overuse of the now cliched term "disruption." This word has been thrown around so much in the healthcare startup world that it's become almost meaningless, and it's often associated with giant messes like Theranos. One corporate executive told me, "We've seen plenty of wrecking balls. Build a bridge and help people cross it." Instead of focusing on "disrupting" the healthcare system, we have to meet people where they are.

THE INSIDE-OUT ADVANTAGE

By contrast, the inside-out approach works better precisely because it understands the system it aims to improve. It means eagerly and earnestly learning and understanding healthcare's peculiarities. Then, finding a healthy balance between accepting the industry's realities and challenging the status quo.

Working from the inside out has nothing to do with how long you've been working in healthcare. It has everything to do with your approach.

There's a Zen Buddhism concept called *shoshin* that encourages you to cultivate a "beginner's mind"—an attitude of openness, eagerness, and lack of preconceptions when approaching a problem, even if you've spent years learning about it. They say in the beginner's mind, there are many possibilities, but in the expert's mind, there are few.

This is a great approach to our work in healthcare. Expertise and curiosity aren't mutually exclusive. We can simultaneously hold deep knowledge and remain open to new possibilities. Embody this duality: understand the system's byzantine ways but refuse to be imprisoned by them. Learn to recognize the difference between necessary constraints and artificial barriers, between rules that protect patients and rules that merely protect the status quo. In doing so, you will maintain the fresh eyes needed to spot opportunities that others, perhaps too immersed in "the way things are," might miss entirely.

Here's how the inside-out approach goes right:

- **Deep stakeholder empathy:** Instead of rushing to solutions, you take time to understand the daily struggles, workarounds, and frustrations of everyone your solution might touch.

- **Looking beyond obvious users:** You seek to understand why some people opt out or can't access care, revealing opportunities others miss.
- **Representative thinking:** Your team reflects the people you aim to serve, leading to better solutions and fewer blind spots.
- **Patient persistence:** You recognize that healthcare requires a marathon mindset, not a sprint. Like Doximity's approach to faxing, you meet the industry where it is while building foundations for lasting change.
- **Flexible focus:** You stay committed to solving the core problem while remaining open to different paths to get there. As Brightside Health showed us, sometimes the best move is knowing when to adapt your strategy.
- **A balanced perspective:** You combine insider knowledge with outsider optimism—understanding which constraints protect patients and which ones just protect the status quo.

These principles of the inside-out approach might seem simple, but they're surprisingly hard to maintain when you're in the thick of building a company. It's tempting to rush ahead with solutions, to brush aside feedback that doesn't fit your vision, or to get frustrated with healthcare's glacial pace. Building massively better healthcare requires a commitment to "walking the halls" of healthcare. We can't merely be spectators of its problems; we must immerse ourselves in them.

BE AN ANTHROPOLOGIST

Innovation rarely starts with a solution in search of a problem. Instead, it comes from curious innovators who become experts in a problem by building empathy for the people living with it every day.

Don't be a hammer looking for a nail. Be an anthropologist, taking time to understand the people and systems you hope to help. Then, find the best tool possible to solve their problem.

TL;DR

- **Become a student of the system:** Ground yourself in healthcare expertise first. Immerse yourself in the healthcare problem you aim to solve and understand the nuances and complexities *before* seeking a solution.
- **Look beyond the obvious:** Study those who opt out of or can't access current solutions—their challenges often reveal the biggest opportunities for impact.
- **Prioritize representation:** Ensure your team reflects the diversity of people you aim to serve. "Nothing about us, without us" should be a guiding principle.
- **"Go slow to go fast":** Take time to get the infrastructure, compliance, and partnerships right. Find investors who understand healthcare's timelines. The stakes are too high to "move fast and break things."
- **Meet people where they are:** Create solutions that work within existing systems while laying the groundwork for future innovation. Success often means being backward compatible.
- **Stay nimble:** Date your ideas, don't marry them. Treat your initial solutions as experiments and be willing to change course based on data and feedback. Be flexible and prioritize the speed of learning.
- **Share the journey:** Healthcare innovation is a cumulative process. Share both successes and failures openly, fostering collaboration across the industry.

9

RULE 2

Align the Margin and the Mission

Show me the incentive and I will show you the outcome.
—CHARLIE MUNGER

My son was six years old when my husband and I finally decided to stop trying for another child using in vitro fertilization (IVF). Years of procedures and more than a dozen miscarriages had left us physically and emotionally exhausted. Each of the four fertility specialists we saw over the years had instilled hope that our baby was just around the corner. But the corner never seemed to arrive.

Although I believe our doctors genuinely wanted to help us, at the end of the day, their clinics profited *more* because they did not. The awful reality is that the most profitable fertility patients are those who require years of tests and procedures, including IVF, which costs upward of $20,000 per cycle. The least profitable are those whose goal of having a child is achieved more quickly, with fewer billable treatments.

This happens all over the place in healthcare, and perhaps you, too, have a story about how the system profited from your pain and suffering. Maybe it was an invasive procedure you didn't need (researchers found knee surgery to be inappropriate in 34 percent of cases), leaving you with a lengthy recovery period, lingering pain, and feelings of defeat.[1] Or perhaps it was a prolonged diagnostic odyssey, bouncing from specialist to specialist, undergoing countless tests and scans, all while your condition worsened and medical bills piled up.

Of course, financial incentives aren't the only driving force for providers; most come to medicine with the authentic desire to help and make a positive impact. But good intentions can be warped by a system full of misaligned incentives. In many ways, healthcare providers are trapped, unable to fully realize their potential to deliver the best possible care. As author James Clear said, "You do not rise to the level of your goals, you fall to the level of your systems."[2]

The path toward massively better healthcare must begin with fundamentally restructuring the misaligned incentives that plague our healthcare system. It must ensure that the margin and the mission become two sides of the same virtuous cycle. Only when the financial sustainability of a healthcare organization is rooted in its ability to improve lives can we begin to heal a system that has for too long been compromised by perverse incentives.

This is the second rule of massively better healthcare: align the margin and the mission. This principle cuts across every industry dimension. It is a rallying cry for a new era of healthcare innovation that doesn't settle for a zero-sum game between profits and impact but instead forges a link between the two.

In this chapter, I'll explain what aligning the margin and the mission means. We'll discuss the business of healthcare, examining the types of customers and the influence of different payment structures. You'll learn how each of the four main business models in healthcare—D2C, B2C2B, B2B, and B2B2C—presents distinct challenges and opportunities for aligning profit with purpose. We'll also discuss the concept of the *sweet spot*, at which financial success and positive health impact become two sides of the same coin, and how to avoid the *icky zone*, in which profit motives directly conflict with patient well-being. By the end of this chapter, you'll understand why creating a virtuous cycle between margin and mission is a strategic necessity.

WHAT IS THE MARGIN? WHAT IS THE MISSION?

Aligning the margin and the mission means creating a business model in which financial sustainability (the margin) and impact

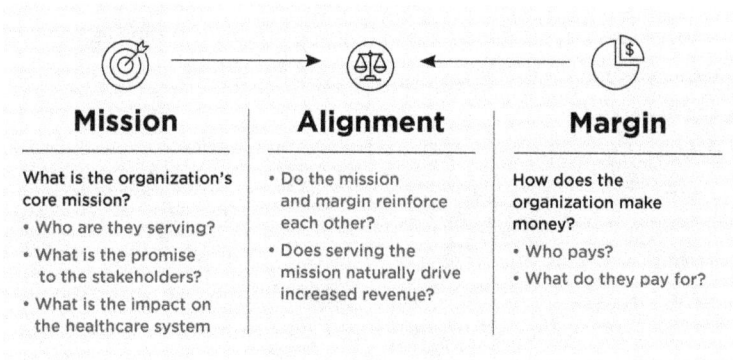

Mission	Alignment	Margin
What is the organization's core mission?	• Do the mission and margin reinforce each other?	How does the organization make money?
• Who are they serving?	• Does serving the mission naturally drive increased revenue?	• Who pays?
• What is the promise to the stakeholders?		• What do they pay for?
• What is the impact on the healthcare system		

Figure 9.1 Aligning the margin and mission reinforces and amplifies the other.

(the mission) reinforce each other. It's about building sustainable and scalable companies *because* they contribute to better healthcare.

Money-making and mission-advancing do not have to be at odds. In the best business models, monetary success and societal mission are inextricably linked. They form a virtuous cycle in which delivering meaningful impact drives revenue, enabling scaling to an ever-broader population.

Rather than pitting margin against mission, aim to align the two so that investing in one perpetually reinforces and amplifies the other (figure 9.1). This intrinsic alignment can help your organization realize its full potential to move the needle on entrenched health issues while also building a lasting enterprise.

So what do I mean by these terms?

- **Mission:** The mission cuts to the heart of the organization's promise to stakeholders. It should be a clear, impact-driven mission focused on serving specific groups of people or communities. The mission should also positively affect healthcare by improving outcomes, lowering costs, improving experience, or increasing access. If an organization lacks that lucid core purpose, it becomes rudderless—prone to drifting off course when financial pressures mount. Defining the "who" is also critical, as misaligned incentives often stem from a disconnect between those an organization claims to serve and those it must please to keep the lights on.

- **Margin:** Every organization needs to bring in money to cover expenses, so the question turns to *how* the organization brings in revenue. The business model (more on this shortly) inevitably shapes an organization's behavior, creating incentives that either reinforce or undermine the mission. Payments directly linked to the successful delivery of the core impact align motivations. Revenue for services disconnected from positive outcomes, however, can get messy. Understanding who holds the financial responsibility—and what they receive in return—helps us understand whether profit motives align with positive impact.
- **Alignment:** Examining what prompts an inflection in an organization's growth curve reveals whether money-making and mission-advancing are connected. Does serving the mission naturally drive increased revenue? If not, it's time to rethink the business model.

Now, let's go a step deeper.

FOLLOW THE MONEY

To understand where the margin is coming from, we need to answer three questions:

- Who pays?
- What is the business model?
- Do customers pay for volume or outcomes?

The answers to these questions help us understand a healthcare company's incentives, its priorities, and, ultimately, its ability to drive meaningful, sustainable impact.

WHO PAYS?

The question of who pays for a company's product or service is a core determinant of its ability to align its margin with its mission. The entity writing the checks wields significant influence over a company's priorities, decision-making, and, ultimately, its impact.

As the saying goes, "He who pays the piper calls the tune." When a company's revenue is tied to a particular stakeholder—be it patients, providers, payers, or employers—that inevitably influences its focus and direction. Don't let anyone tell you otherwise. The paying customer's needs, preferences, and pain points become a force behind product development, service delivery, and business strategy.

Let's take a look at five types of customers and their motivations (table 9.1).

I often meet founders who are confused about who really pays. When venture capital (VC) is funding your operations, it's easy to lose sight of your true customer. You'll hear founders say they're "customer-obsessed" while burning millions in VC money without a clear path to getting actual customers to pay for their solution.

Dr. Rushika Fernandopulle, cofounder and former CEO of Iora Health, said this: "You can hide a lot of sins by throwing VC money at things and not being responsive to customers and not getting product market fit. But when all of your income comes from the people who are your customers, you better get product market fit pretty quickly, or you go away."[3]

Iora Health lived this philosophy. They built a technology-powered primary care model focused on delivering care for adults sixty-five and older who were enrolled in Medicare Advantage and other at-risk reimbursement models. Their platform combined a custom-built electronic health record (EHR) with team-based care, health coaches, and behavioral health support to deliver better outcomes at lower costs.

TABLE 9.1
Customer Types and Motivations

Customer	Motivations
Patients	- Improve health outcomes and quality of life - Reduce out-of-pocket costs - Increase convenience and accessibility of care - Gain a sense of control and autonomy over their health
Employers	- Reduce healthcare expenses - Improve employee health, productivity, and job satisfaction - Attract and retain top talent with competitive benefits packages - Comply with employer mandates and regulations - Enhance corporate social responsibility and brand reputation - Reduce distractions from core business
Commercial health plans	- Improve cost-effectiveness during the time period when a member is on their health plan - Increase member satisfaction and retention - Comply with government regulations and quality standards - Gain market share and competitive advantage
Government	- Improve population health outcomes - Protect public health and safety - Control healthcare spending and ensure cost-effectiveness - Ensure organizations follow laws, regulations, and quality standards - Enhance public trust and political support
Technical buyers (e.g., providers, health plans, biopharma)	- Improve operational efficiency and productivity - Enhance clinical decision-making and care coordination - Reduce administrative burdens and streamline workflows - Comply with regulatory requirements and quality standards - Increase revenue and financial performance - Gain a competitive edge in the market

Iora Health bootstrapped for seven years. They grew slowly and more methodically, but their disciplined focus on their actual paying customers paid off big-time. One Medical acquired the company in a $2.1 billion all-stock deal in 2021.

WHAT IS THE BUSINESS MODEL?

This is where the choice of business model comes into play. The four main archetypes—D2C, B2C2B, B2B, and B2B2C—each represent a different approach to creating, delivering, and capturing value (table 9.2). The decision of which model to pursue is intrinsically linked to the question of "who pays," as it determines the primary stakeholder the company must serve and satisfy to generate revenue and stay afloat.

Let's look at these four business models in more detail, each with advantages and challenges when it comes to aligning profits with purpose.

TABLE 9.2

Business Models

	D2C	B2C2B	B2B	B2B2C
Who is the user of the product or service?	Healthcare consumers		Employees of the enterprise customer	Healthcare consumers
Who distributes the product to the user?	The company selling the solution		The enterprise customer	
Who pays for the product?	Healthcare consumers	The enterprise customer		
Example	Hims & Hers	Talkspace	Veeva	Collective Health

D2C (Direct-to-Consumer)

In the D2C model:

- Healthcare consumers are the end user.
- The company selling the solution distributes it directly to the end user.
- The healthcare consumer pays for the solution.

Think about Hims & Hers, an $10 billion publicly traded digital health company. Patients visit the Hims & Hers website, fill out an intake form that a clinician reviews, and, if approved, get access to medications like Tretinoin (for acne) or Viagra® (for erectile dysfunction) without ever visiting a clinic or pharmacy. Hims & Hers now has more than two million subscribers, who pay the company out of pocket for medications.[4]

D2C gives companies the most direct control over the user experience and the clearest line of sight to consumer needs. It also means, however, that the company's financial success depends entirely on its ability to acquire and retain users willing to pay out of pocket.

Over the last decade, an increase in high-deductible health plans has exposed healthcare consumers to more of the cost of care, making them more willing to pay out of pocket for healthcare products and services. At the same time, people are becoming increasingly more comfortable with digital health tools like wearables and telehealth.[5] Because of these drivers, D2C business models have proliferated, and more than a third of digital health funding now goes to D2C companies.[6]

Companies selling directly to healthcare consumers must ensure that the marketing costs to acquire a user (often called CAC or *customer acquisition cost*) are substantially lower than the total amount a user will spend (known as LTV or *lifetime value*) to be sustainable. So these companies not only have to deliver value that patients feel is worth paying for but also have to find these patients in an economically efficient way.

B2C2B (Business-to-Consumer-to-Business)

B2C2B can be thought of as a subcategory of D2C, with a key distinction: Although the healthcare consumer remains the end user, the company's revenue comes from a third-party payer.

In the B2C2B model:

- Healthcare consumers are the end user.
- The company acquires the user.
- A third-party is the payer.

Many care delivery models operate this way: They market to the consumer and get reimbursed by that person's health plan. Talkspace, which offers virtual talk therapy, and Midi Health, which provides virtual menopause care, are B2C2B examples that market directly to patients but are covered by many health plans.

This strategy lowers the cost barrier for patients with coverage, who are more likely to try to stick with the solution because their out-of-pocket costs are lower. Plus, insurance coverage can signal legitimacy and quality to consumers, particularly for newer solutions.

If you decide to go this route, you'll have to figure out *reimbursement*, which is the process by which insurers pay for healthcare. This includes understanding *medical codes*—the unique identifiers for diagnoses, procedures, and services used for billing and claims processing.[7] These differ from *diagnostic codes*, such as the International Classification of Diseases (ICD-10) codes, which describe the diagnosis or condition.

To accept reimbursement, you'll need to establish payer contracts. This takes time and money, as you have to go state by state, and plan by plan. Then you must build the infrastructure for your claims to be processed and paid. (The Digital Medicine Society (DiMe) has excellent resources for virtual first care companies, including their Payment and Coding Toolkit.) Because of these

hurdles, many companies start by going D2C, and add reimbursement later to scale.

While health plans are a common third-party payer in B2C2B
models, they aren't the only ones. Companies like Picnic Health,
which helps patients aggregate their medical records, and Evida-
tion Health, which rewards users for healthy behaviors, market
to consumers but generate revenue from life science companies
and researchers who value the data and insights these engaged
users provide.

B2C2B models offer the advantage of leveraging consumer
demand to drive adoption, but they also require the heavy lift of
building out either reimbursement capabilities or other business
customer relationships. Success requires delivering value to both
sides of the equation—enough user value to keep healthcare consumers engaged and enough business value to justify the third
party's investment.

B2B (Business-to-Business)

In the B2B model:

- An enterprise customer (technical buyer) pays for the product or service.
- An employee of that enterprise customer is the end user.

This model is common for products and services operating in
the background of healthcare delivery or life sciences, such as clinical decision support tools, clinical trial software, and population
health management platforms—what I referred to earlier as healthcare's "power grid."

An example of a B2B company in healthcare is Veeva, a publicly
traded company that generated more than $2 billion in revenue
in 2024. Veeva provides cloud-based software for the life sciences
industry—pharmaceutical, biotechnology, and medical device
companies—to help them work more effectively from development to go-to-market. This includes improving how biopharmas

run clinical trials, manage regulatory submissions and drug safety reporting, drive quality management, and communicate with doctors about various treatments across sales and marketing. Although Veeva's customers are life sciences companies (and users are their employees), their software ultimately affects patients by helping bring new treatments to market faster.

The B2B model offers a couple of advantages. Contracts are larger and more stable than consumer-facing models. Sales cycles may be longer, but once a customer is acquired, the relationship can last for years, especially if there's a high *switching cost*, which refers to the time, money, and effort required to transition from one product or service to another. In healthcare, switching costs can be high because of data integration, staff training, and contract terms. As one hospital executive told me: "To actually rip something out and replace it with something else isn't just a financial commitment but an emotional one. It has to be 10 times better for me to justify that. Marginal improvement is not enough."[8]

Once an organization has invested in integrating a solution into its workflows and has trained its staff on using it, the cost and disruption of switching to a new system can be incredibly high. This creates a strong incentive for the customer to stick with their current solution, even if a marginally better option comes along. They need to be certain that the new offering is worth any transition costs and will deliver significant long-term value.

For B2B healthcare companies, this is both a challenge and an opportunity. Although the initial sale may take longer, the lifetime value of a customer can be substantial if you continue to deliver value and support over time.

If you choose a B2B business model, it helps to have deep industry ties and exceptional sales skills as you'll *always* be selling. You'll need to cater to a wide range of stakeholders, from clinicians to IT staff to executive leadership, and continually demonstrate the value of your solution on metrics like efficiency, cost savings, and quality of care.

B2B2C (Business-to-Business-to-Consumer)

B2B2C can be thought of as a subcategory of B2B, with a key distinction: the end user is a healthcare consumer. In the B2B2C model:

- Healthcare consumers are the end user.
- The enterprise customer distributes the solution to the end user.
- The enterprise customer pays for the solution.

This looks like a company selling its offering directly to a payer, such as an employer, provider, or health plan, which then distributes the product to the end user. B2B2C offers the potential for more stable enterprise revenue streams and faster scaling because one enterprise contract can reach thousands of users at once.

For example, Collective Health helps people get more from their employer-sponsored health benefits through care navigation, health screening suggestions, appointment reminders, and claims tracking. Although the end user is the healthcare consumer, the customer is the employer who pays for it all. Employers (the customer) benefit from increased health engagement and lower costs, while employees (the users) enjoy a better health benefits experience.

One challenge with the B2B2C model is the degree of separation between the company and the end user, which means the company must rely on its business partners to drive adoption and engagement. This is where the concept of utilization comes into play. Selling to an employer or health plan is just the first step—it's the difference between *covered lives* (the number of people the company can potentially reach through the deal) and actual *utilization* (the number of employees or members who end up using the product).

I've seen countless companies celebrate signing a big contract, only to find months later that utilization never materialized. Often, this comes down to the payer's lack of bandwidth, incentives, or priority to effectively communicate and promote the product to employees or members. Without solid utilization, the chances of that contract being renewed are slim. In the case of Collective Health, we're able to get high utilization because the product is how employees access their health plans—talk about making your solution indispensable.

B2B2C companies must work closely with their clients to educate and engage potential users. This might mean providing plug-and-play communication materials, hosting lunch-and-learns, or finding creative ways to incentivize sign-ups. The goal is to make it as easy as possible for champions within the organization to spread the word.

This, of course, is on top of investing in making the user experience as seamless and compelling as possible while also showing the customer that the product delivers measurable improvements in health outcomes and cost savings.

DO CUSTOMERS PAY FOR VOLUME OR OUTCOMES?

Now that we have an idea of who pays for healthcare solutions and the various healthcare business models (which, by the way, are not mutually exclusive), let's discuss what customers pay for.

The way healthcare payments are structured has enormous implications for the behaviors and results we incentivize. At a high level, we can divide healthcare payment models into two broad categories: paying for *volume* or paying for *outcomes* (table 9.3).

Paying for Volume

Paying for how much you consume (volume) is how most of our economy works. We buy groceries by the item, pay for haircuts per visit, and purchase movie tickets per showing. This is how healthcare has traditionally worked, too.

Paying for a specific service in healthcare can look like:

- **Fee-for-service (FFS):** FFS is a payment model in which customers pay for each unit of service they receive, such as a provider visit, test, or procedure.

175

TABLE 9.3
Paying for Volume Versus Paying for Outcomes

	Paying for Volume	Paying for Outcomes
Pros	- Straightforward and transparent pricing - Easy to understand and administer - More predictable revenue stream for companies	- Incentivizes companies to deliver on their promises to customers to improve outcomes or lower costs - Lowers financial risk for customers, as they only pay if the desired outcomes are achieved
Cons	- Incentivizes volume over value - Can create opportunity for waste and fraud through overutilization of services or *upcoding* (billing for more complex care than provided) - Doesn't inherently incentivize better health outcomes or lower costs	- Involves higher level of financial risk for organizations - Can be more complex to administer and negotiate - Requires a more challenging implementation and billing process - Opportunity for fraud by data manipulation - Can create opportunity for cost-cutting and rationing of care
Most Suitable for	- Discrete, easily quantifiable products or services - Situations in which the value proposition is more transactional - Circumstances in which the focus is on access to services rather than outcomes	- Contexts in which the "outcome(s)" can be clearly defined, measured, and attributed - Situations in which preventive care, care coordination, and efficiency can save lives or lower costs - Companies that can confidently deliver on promised outcomes and manage associated risks - Circumstances in which cost savings are easily measurable

- **Software-as-a-service (SaaS) subscription:** With a SaaS model, technical customers (such as providers, payers, or life science companies) pay a recurring subscription fee to access a software platform. Pricing is often tiered based on features, number of users, or volume of data.
- **Per member per month (PMPM):** With PMPM, an organization pays a fixed amount for each member enrolled, regardless of the services utilized by that member.

Paying for volume makes sense in many cases, such as a virtual therapy app charging per session, an artificial intelligence (AI) scribe tool charging per clinician user, or a mobile pharmacy charging for each vaccine administered. These discrete services are easily quantifiable and have a clear value proposition for the buyer, making it a straightforward and transparent way to determine fair pricing.

For other areas of healthcare, like primary or specialty care, FFS has been criticized for driving up costs and encouraging overutilization of services because providers are incentivized to increase volume. This misalignment of incentives has contributed to the ballooning costs and inefficiencies in the US healthcare system.

Paying for Outcomes

Paying for outcomes is how we wish more of our economy worked. Wouldn't it be great if we only had to pay for the workout program if it helped us gain muscle, or the test prep app that actually improved our test scores? This approach ties payments to achieving specific outcomes, aligning financial incentives around the results that matter most for stakeholders.

Much of the innovation in outcome-based payments has been led by the Centers for Medicare and Medicaid Services Innovation Center, which was founded in 2010 to improve healthcare quality, reduce costs, and transition the US healthcare system to value-based care by developing, testing, and evaluating new *alternative payment models* (APMs).

Today, APMs have gained traction beyond Medicare and Medicaid, with private insurers, employers, digital health startups, and even health systems increasingly adopting and adapting new approaches to getting paid. Driven by demand for alternatives to the traditional FFS approach, stakeholders across healthcare are seeking more effective ways to control costs while improving care quality and patient outcomes.

Outcome-based payment models include the following:

- **Value-based care (VBC):** VBC, sometimes called value-based payment, is a broad term used to describe any model that ties payment amounts to the results delivered.[9]
- **Shared savings:** In a shared savings model, providers are incentivized to reduce healthcare spending for a defined patient population while maintaining or improving quality. If the providers can lower costs below a set benchmark, they share in a portion of the savings achieved. This model encourages providers to prioritize preventative care, care coordination, and efficiency.[10]
- **Risk-sharing:** In a risk-sharing arrangement, providers and payers share the financial risk associated with patient outcomes. If costs are higher than expected, the provider may bear some of that burden. If costs are lower and quality is maintained, the provider shares in the savings.
- **Outcome-based pricing:** In the B2B space, companies may tie their pricing to the achievement of specific customer outcomes, such as reducing hospital readmissions or improving medication adherence.

These models have one thing in common: They facilitate getting paid for results and not just the volume of services provided, incentivizing organizations to deliver on promises while keeping down costs.

Outcome-based payment models are particularly well-suited for chronic conditions that require ongoing management, such as diabetes or heart disease, in which solutions can have a significant impact through preventive care, patient education, and care coordination.

Outcome-based payment models, however, aren't always appropriate or feasible. They work best when the outcomes are clearly defined and measurable and can be reasonably attributed to the actions of the organization. Because they involve a higher level of risk for the organization providing the service, some may be hesitant to take on this risk, especially if outcomes are influenced by factors outside their direct control.

Outcome-based models also face the challenge of determining the appropriate time frame in which to measure success. People and organizations need to get paid for the work they do *today*, but health outcomes often unfold over years or even decades. Although some interventions provide immediate returns—like reducing hospital readmissions within thirty days—other interventions take much longer to demonstrate their value. Unfortunately, in our system, healthcare is an annual enrollment.

As Dr. Sachin Jain, CEO of the Scan Health Plan told me: "I think one of the failures of the value-based care movement over the last several years was measuring value in one-year increments. Healthcare value is produced in much longer time frames than I think most people acknowledge."[11]

There's also been concern around the word "value" in value-based care. Research from Intermountain Health, a large nonprofit healthcare system, found that "value" was sometimes misinterpreted as "cheap." As a pioneer in the space, Intermountain continues to do the same work but has swapped the term "VBC" for "proactive care."[12]

In practice, many payment models blend service-based and outcome-based payment elements. For example, a primary care practice might receive a capitated payment to cover all necessary services for a patient population (outcome-based) *and* receive FFS payments for specific procedures (volume-based).

Ultimately, the goal is to create a system where healthcare companies are financially successful when they deliver real value to patients and society.

BOX 9.1.

In the Trenches: Zocdoc

When Zocdoc launched its platform to help people find and book medical appointments, the company faced a challenge aligning its business model with regulatory requirements and market realities. The Zocdoc founders knew they wanted to make the product free for healthcare consumers while charging providers. But *how* to charge providers was unclear. Because ambiguity in pre-internet-era state regulations regarding provider payments to third parties, the company wasn't sure if it could charge providers for each booking made on the platform.

Playing it safe, Zocdoc initially charged every provider on the platform the same monthly subscription fee to be listed on its marketplace. But this one-size-fits-all approach created a fundamental misalignment. As founder and CEO Oliver Kharraz, MD, observed, there's a reason no other marketplace—whether it's Priceline for travel or OpenTable for restaurants—charges its supply-side customers a flat fee: The price is almost always wrong. For doctors who receive a high volume of new patient bookings through Zocdoc, the flat fee was a bargain, while for those who did not, it was prohibitively expensive. As a result, doctors were leaving the platform faster than Zocdoc could sign up new ones.

By 2017, the company realized that proper alignment between its margin (subscription revenue) and mission (connecting patients with care) required charging providers based on the number of new patient appointments booked through Zocdoc's marketplace. It then had to spend years securing permission from regulators to transition to this new pricing model.

The multiyear effort to restructure the business model, which Kharraz pointedly referred to as "open-heart surgery," nearly killed the company. But Zocdoc emerged stronger, with a pricing model that better aligned incentives. The new pricing model skyrocketed the number of providers on Zocdoc, enabling the company to sustainably fulfill its mission of helping people find and book healthcare providers who are right for them.

Finding the right business model in healthcare often requires carefully balancing regulatory requirements, market dynamics, and mission alignment—and the patience to get it right.

A Third Option

Even if an FFS pricing model makes the most sense for your organization, you can align the margin and the mission by offering a money-back guarantee to show customers you stand behind your results. Although more common in direct-to-consumer health products (think Peloton's thirty-day money-back guarantee), providers, pharma, and medical device companies are now adopting this model, too.

Geisinger Health, a Pennsylvania-based health system, made waves by offering full refunds for certain procedures if patients weren't satisfied—no questions asked. In the first two years of the program, Geisinger refunded nearly $1 million to patients for procedures like lumbar back surgery and gastric bypass surgery. They had to hire staff to run the program, but Geisinger found that the improvements in their processes and patient experience more than made up for these costs.[13]

In the pharmaceutical world, Pfizer launched its Pledge Warranty Program to remove the financial risk of treatment failure for patients. The program refunds eligible patients' out-of-pocket costs if they need to discontinue certain medications, like PAN-ZYGA® (for chronic inflammatory demyelinating polyneuropathy) or XALKORI® (for lung cancer), for clinical reasons.[14]

Medical device company Stryker developed the SurgiCount system to prevent surgical sponges from being left inside patients—a surprisingly common occurrence that happens about a dozen times daily in US operating rooms. Under their "SurgiCount Promise," Stryker covers up to $5 million in legal costs if a retained sponge incident occurs while their system is being properly used, plus they refund the cost of implementation if the system fails catastrophically.[15]

FIND THE SWEET SPOT

As you've seen, who pays for your product and what they pay for can incentivize your organization's behaviors and outcomes. The goal, then, is to find the "sweet spot"—business models that align your organization's growth and success with the achievement of its mission, assuming that the mission is genuinely about improving health outcomes and creating value for the healthcare system as a whole (figure 9.2).

In this sweet spot, a company grows as it achieves better outcomes for patients and populations. The more effectively it improves health, reduces costs, and enhances the patient experience, the more financially successful it becomes. This creates a virtuous cycle in which the pursuit of the mission drives the margin, and the margin, in turn, enables the mission to sustain itself and scale.

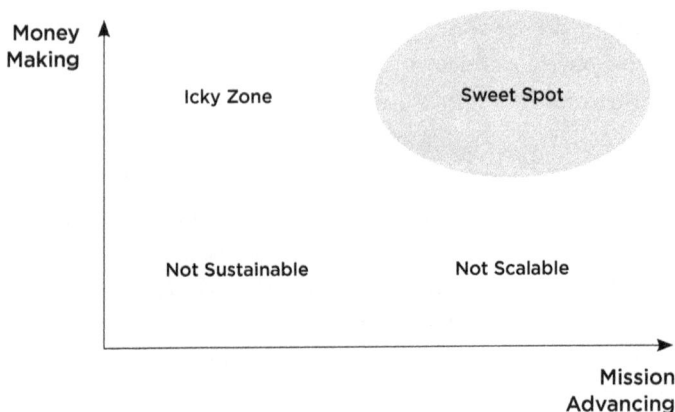

Figure 9.2 Finding the sweet spot in which your business model aligns growth and success to achieve the mission.

In the Trenches: Omada Health

I first met the Omada Health team in 2011 when they were part of the inaugural class of startups at Rock Health (figure 9.3). They set up shop in our San Francisco office, brimming with an energy and passion I've only seen in founders. CEO Sean Duffy, a medical school dropout, wanted to tackle the growing epidemic of chronic diseases like diabetes—not with pills or procedures, but with behavior change and software.

I was immediately drawn to their vision and their passion for accomplishing it. They were rethinking how we approach chronic disease prevention and management and also how we pay for it. They were building a platform that would empower individuals to make sustainable lifestyle changes, guided by personalized coaching, evidence-based programs, and the power of community.

What truly set Omada apart, however, was the team's commitment to aligning their business model with their mission. They believed that traditional revenue models, either FFS or blanket charges across whole populations regardless of utilization, didn't leave incentives aligned toward impact and shared success. Omada took a different approach, partnering with health plans, employers, and health systems to offer its programs with more performance-based pricing. This meant the

Figure 9.3 The Omada Team's setup in the Rock Health coworking office, September 2011.

(*continued on next page*)

(*continued from previous page*)

company only got paid when members signed up, engaged, and achieved clinically meaningful results, such as weight loss.

This performance-based pricing was a bold move, and also a brilliant one. It better aligned Omada's financial success with the success of its members, creating a clear incentive to deliver high-quality, effective programs that genuinely made a difference in people's lives. And it worked.

Over the years, I've watched with pride as Omada has grown from a scrappy startup into a publicly traded company. It has expanded its reach, its programs, and its impact, helping more than a million individuals improve their health and well-being. But Omada has never lost sight of its original mission: to empower people to live healthier lives. It found the sweet spot.

AVOID THE ICKY ZONE

In 2015, two Stanford design students (and former cigarette smokers) set out to disrupt the tobacco industry by developing a less harmful alternative to cigarettes to help smokers quit. They launched Juul, an e-cigarette company that would grow to dominate the market and become valued at $38 billion in just three years.[16]

But a disturbing trend emerged as Juul's sleek devices and candy-flavored pods gained popularity. The company's marketing tactics, including ads that a Stanford report called "patently youth oriented," attracted a new demographic: Teenagers who had never before smoked.[17] Suddenly, a generation that might have avoided nicotine addiction altogether was getting hooked on Juul.[18] Instead of serving as a smoking cessation tool, the company's product had become a gateway to tobacco use.

The rapid growth and skyrocketing profits from e-cigarettes came at a devastating cost to public health. By 2020, 19.6 percent of high school students and 4.7 percent of middle school students reported using e-cigarettes, with Juul being the overwhelmingly popular brand.[19] The mission of helping adult smokers quit had been overshadowed by the creation of a new money-making public health crisis.

This is the anti–sweet spot—an *icky zone* where making money directly conflicts with public health. It's a disconnect that should be utterly unacceptable in an industry dedicated to healing.

Juul did eventually stop selling its candy-flavored pods in the United States in 2019,[20] and the CEO apologized to parents of children addicted to Juul's vaping products.[21] Despite paying $255 million for a class action settlement in 2024, today Juul is the second-largest e-cigarette company in the United States, earning nearly a third of all e-cigarette revenue.[22]

This misalignment is everywhere in healthcare, even if it's not always intentional or malicious. When an organization profits from denying lifesaving care, delivering unnecessary treatments, keeping patients sick, or exploiting medical desperation, it's operating in the icky zone.

Physicians report that 21 percent of medical care is unnecessary, including 22 percent of prescribed medication, 25 percent of tests, and 11 percent of procedures—no doubt partly because organizations in our FFS system get paid more for doing more, regardless of the outcomes.[23]

I don't think most doctors are trying to take advantage of patients, but they're stuck in an antiquated model in which basic economic incentives just aren't aligned. We're long overdue for change.

In healthcare, the ultimate mission should be improving the health and well-being of patients and communities. Don't ever settle for a zero-sum game between profits and impact; instead, forge an inextricable link between the two.

TL;DR

- **Align the margin and the mission:** Money-making and mission-advancing do not have to be at odds. Aligning the margin and the mission creates a virtuous cycle in which delivering meaningful impact drives revenue, enabling scaling to an ever-broader population.
- **Understand the money trail:** Who pays for a product or service will tell us who can influence a company's priorities and decision-making. The paying customer's needs, preferences, and pain points become a force behind product development, service delivery, and business strategy.
- **What gets paid gets done:** *What* customers pay for—a specific service or outcome—has enormous implications for the behaviors and results we incentivize.
- **Consider different business models:** Understand the four main business models in healthcare—D2C, B2C2B, B2B, and B2B2C—each with its own advantages and challenges.
- **Aim for the sweet spot:** Build a model in which financial success and positive health impact are two sides of the same coin.
- **Avoid the icky zone:** Avoid models in which you profit from making healthcare worse.
- **Don't be afraid to break the mold:** Challenge outdated models that are misaligned. Explore innovative payment structures that align incentives with better outcomes.

10

RULE 3

Be a Good Steward of Health Data

Today we can analyze health data with massive computing power, including
using AI in new ways to address health inequities or find cures for rare
diseases—but only if people trust what we're doing with it.

—LUCIA SAVAGE

It was the night of the Rock Health launch party in 2011, and
there was a buzz of excitement in San Francisco's Chinatown
neighborhood. But my mind was elsewhere. One of my childhood
best friends, Erica, was receiving outpatient treatment for what we
thought was a benign brain tumor at Stanford University Medical
Center, one of the world's leading medical institutions.

She was supposed to join the party, but Erica didn't wake up that
morning. An ambulance rushed her to a nearby hospital, the University of California, San Francisco (UCSF), another top-tier hospital in the heart of Silicon Valley, where she would stay in a coma
for weeks.

UCSF had recently spent $160 million on a new electronic health
record (EHR) system with Epic, the same vendor Stanford Hospital
had used since 2008. Surely, with all this expertise and technology,
her care would be seamless.

I couldn't have been more wrong. For four days, including the
entire weekend, UCSF couldn't get Erica's critical health records
from Stanford. Merely thirty-five miles separated these hospitals
(the same stretch of land housing giants like Google, Facebook,
and Netflix). Yet there was no system for sharing her lifesaving

information—medical history, scans, anything. UCSF had to repeat those expensive tests, delaying Erica's care and adding unnecessary costs.

This dichotomy—the excitement about innovation swirling at the party versus the frustrations of moving health information thirty-five miles—explains why healthcare innovation isn't really about the technology.

The technology to electronically store medical records existed. But interoperability—the capacity for these two systems to talk to each other—did not. Policies requiring seamless sharing in emergencies were missing. The motivation for even two of the world's greatest hospitals, a stone's throw away from each other, to collaborate was absent. Incentives were entirely misaligned, and neither hospital loses financially when this happens. In fact, hospitals can even profit from this inefficiency.

Erica's story is a good reminder that our industry needs to be better stewards of health data—enabling it to be safely and easily exchanged for the greater good.

In an age when you can instantly access your bank account from your phone or stream any movie ever made, why is it still so hard to get your medical records? Why are we still struggling to get different hospital systems to talk to each other? At the same time, why have one in three Americans had their personal health information stolen by cybercriminals?[1]

Data stewardship is a concept with roots in the science and practice of data collection, sharing, and analysis.[2] In the context of healthcare, it refers to the responsibility to realize the greatest possible benefit from the effective and appropriate use of health data while minimizing the risk of harm.[3]

In this chapter, I share the third rule of massively better healthcare: being a good health data steward. I examine the current state of healthcare data, the need for interoperability, data protection, and regulatory compliance, and the steps we can take to build a culture of responsible healthcare data management.

THE STATE OF HEALTHCARE DATA

The healthcare industry is a massive data generator, accounting for 30 percent of the world's total data volume.[4] Think about that for a minute. If you compiled every byte of data ever created across every single industry—social media, telecommunications, education, retail, automotive, finance, and everything else—nearly a third of it would be from healthcare.

A few decades ago, your medical history might have fit in a single doctor's file folder. Today, your health record alone typically generates up to eighty megabytes a year.[5] That's equivalent to roughly forty thousand text messages. And that doesn't include any data created outside the formal healthcare system, from wearables, genetic tests, or at-home diagnostics.

Despite this wealth of data, we face a paradoxical situation:

Most Health Data Is Inaccessible

Some estimate that up to 97 percent of healthcare data remains untapped.[6] It's trapped in isolated, unstructured networks and closed ecosystems, limiting the potential for benefits across the healthcare value chain and hindering patient trust and engagement.

The vast majority of our health data remains unused because our default in healthcare is closed, not open. It's a culture problem. Some even say it's an integrity problem.[7]

Many business models are built on the premise of withholding data, while a lack of trust among stakeholders makes it worse.[8] Data ownership remains a contentious issue, with no clear consensus on who has the ultimate rights to this valuable information, even though we all know the patient *should* be the rightful owner.

Concerns about privacy and control also contribute to the hesitancy to share. Moreover, in the academic world, the "publish or perish" culture encourages researchers to hoard data, viewing it as their intellectual property rather than a resource for others to build on. These factors combine to create a siloed system in which valuable healthcare data remains locked away, hindering progress and limiting the potential for improved care and outcomes.

Health Data Is Vulnerable to Cyberattacks

At the same time, the healthcare sector has become a prime target for cybercriminals.

Several factors contribute to the healthcare sector's vulnerability. First and most shockingly, a medical record is fifty times more valuable on the dark web than a credit card number.[9]

The allure of this data is compounded by the outdated security measures in place at many healthcare institutions. These organizations still rely on legacy systems that lack modern security features, making them easier targets for cyberattacks.[10] A shortage of cybersecurity professionals leaves leaders at a loss for what to do.[11]

While I was writing this book, UnitedHealth, the largest health plan in the country, paid $22 million in bitcoin ransom to Russia-based cybercriminals after their cyberattack shut down operations at partner clinics and pharmacies for over a week.[12] The entire saga ended up costing the company more than $2 billion.[13] The stolen data—including highly sensitive information like medical records, names, and Social Security numbers belonging to more than a third of Americans—is still out there.

Cyberattacks also have deadly consequences for patient care. Studies show that patients admitted to the hospital during ransomware attacks face higher mortality rates, and the disruption extends beyond just the targeted hospital.[14] At nearby emergency departments, patient volume surges 15.1 percent, and under this strain, the number of patients leaving without being seen jumps by 127.8 percent—leading researchers to argue that we ought to treat these attacks as we do natural disasters requiring coordinated emergency response.[15]

This combination—of data being underused *and* misused—creates a worst-of-both-worlds scenario: Data that's simultaneously unavailable to those who need it most while being all too easily available to cybercriminals.

BALANCING ACCESS AND PROTECTION

> We think of ourselves not as owners of health data but as custodians.
> Every piece of information represents someone's personal health journey,
> and we have to honor that through how we protect and use it.
> —CHRISTINE LEMKE

If you work in healthcare, there's a good chance you or other people in your organization handle individually identifiable health information.[16] This comes with both opportunity and responsibility. Leveraging this data at scale can help create better patient experiences and drive healthcare forward. But you must also be its staunch protector. This is what it means to be a good steward of health data. It's the moral responsibility to protect every piece of health information in your care, ensure that patients have full access and control, and—when possible—use the data to benefit everyone.

The opportunities for utilizing health data are enormous:

- **Improved patient care:** When health data is accessible to the right people at the right time, it leads to better-informed decisions and more coordinated care. For patients like Erica, this could mean the difference between timely treatment and dangerous delays.
- **Consumer empowerment:** Access to their health data empowers healthcare consumers to take an active role in their care. It allows them to make more informed decisions, seek second opinions, and ensure the accuracy of their medical records.
- **Accelerated research:** Data can be shared and combined with other data to fuel research. When scientists can analyze real-world data to form real-world evidence, the time to breakthroughs shortens.

These benefits depend on our comfort level with *open data*—the degree to which health information can be accessed, shared, and used by authorized parties. But the risk-benefit ratio of data openness varies significantly across different individuals, communities, and contexts.

For some, such as those managing a rare disease or those training for a marathon, increased openness can be tremendously beneficial. The potential for personalized insight and accelerated research likely outweighs any perceived risks.

In contrast, communities that have historically been exploited or underserved by our healthcare system may perceive far greater risks in data sharing.[17] These groups might have valid concerns about privacy, discrimination, or misuse of their information.[18] Their risk-benefit calculation may tilt away from openness, prioritizing privacy above all else.

As good health data stewards, we should understand and respect these differing perspectives. This requires knowing the diverse needs, concerns, and historical contexts of the individuals and communities you serve. It may also involve developing flexible data sharing and protection strategies that can be adjusted based on individual preferences.

The goal is not to make all health data public but to create secure, standardized ways to share and use health data that benefit everyone while respecting privacy and preventing misuse.

MAKE INTEROPERABILITY A REALITY

Interoperability is the smooth, secure flow of health information across healthcare. It can help reduce unnecessary delays, dangerous medication conflicts, and costly duplicate tests. It's the difference between an emergency medical technician knowing your life-threatening allergies, or not. It's a new specialist, seeing you have had three MRIs this year and not ordering a redundant one. Even in routine care, interoperability translates to more efficient, data-driven care and better outcomes.

Virtually all physicians (96 percent) agree that easier access to critical information could help save someone's life; 95 percent believe increased data interoperability will ultimately help improve patient outcomes, and 86 percent believe it will significantly cut time to diagnosis.[19] Yet only 8 percent say it's actually easy to use information from different EHR systems.[20]

So why haven't we achieved seamless interoperability yet?

It's not a technical barrier. Just think about the financial services industry, in which different banks and merchants exchange information freely to facilitate purchases, ATM withdrawals, and wire transfers from anywhere in the world. Interoperability in healthcare is *technically* feasible.

It's also not a regulatory issue. While some may blame the Health Insurance Portability and Accountability Act of 1996 (HIPAA) for hindering interoperability, it's not the primary obstacle. HIPAA was designed to "support information sharing" while creating guardrails for data privacy.[21] More recently, the Twenty-First Century Cures Act (with information-blocking provisions) and the Trusted Exchange Framework and Common Agreement (TEFCA) have set the stage for greater data sharing and interoperability.[22] Federal mandates and incentives aim to speed up this movement to enable secure, nationwide health information exchange.

Here's the real problem: Proprietary software, with its closed systems and high switching costs, incentivizes vendors to maintain control over their data and customers. Simply put, there isn't a strong business case for vendors or providers to invest in being interoperable. And this comes at the expense of patient experience and outcomes.

I have heard it said that we don't have "big data" in healthcare; we have a large amount of "small data." When health data lives in isolated silos and incompatible systems, it makes data difficult to exchange, process, and interpret. The industry has long lacked the will (and incentives) to enforce common data standards, leaving fragmented systems in which data sharing is more of a hurdle than a given.

Another issue is semantic interoperability, meaning that data doesn't just need to be shared across different systems—this information needs to be understood using standardized terminology and codes.[23]

For those not old enough to remember the early days of cell phones, sending emojis from your iPhone to a friend using Android or Blackberry (RIP) would show up for them looking something like this: []. Each company had its own emojis, so sending a smiley face could result in a completely different image on the other end. It wasn't until the Unicode Consortium created a standardized system for emojis that communication across platforms became smooth and consistent.

In healthcare, we have something similar to the Unicode Consortium: Health Level Seven International (HL7). This nonprofit organization sets standards for exchanging, integrating, sharing, and retrieving electronic health information. HL7's Fast Healthcare Interoperability Resources (FHIR) is a newer standard using modern web technologies to facilitate easier data exchange. The Digital Imaging and Communications in Medicine (DICOM) standard, commonly used for medical imaging, plays a similar role in ensuring interoperability.

To fulfill the potential of health data, we need innovators to commit to interoperability, whether they choose to adopt a certified EHR or build their own system. Although many successful startups opt to build custom solutions that better fit their needs, budget, and vision, interoperability should always be on the road map.

Finally, we need health data standards that are intuitive, efficient, and so beneficial that adopting them is a no-brainer for every organization, creating a regulatory and market environment that rewards collaboration and data sharing, rather than hoarding and siloing. These standards should evolve and adapt, incorporating emerging technologies and addressing the broader context of patient care, including social determinants of health.

In the Trenches: OHDSI

The healthcare industry is awash in data but bringing it together to improve patient outcomes has been a long-standing challenge. Researchers worldwide struggle to make sense of information scattered across disparate systems with varying structures. The Observational Health Data Sciences and Informatics (OHDSI, pronounced "Odyssey") initiative was started as a response to this problem.

Founded in 2014, OHDSI united a community of researchers, clinicians, and data scientists, all committed to the idea of open health data. They maintain the Observational Medical Outcomes Partnership (OMOP) Common Data Model (CDM), a standardized format for organizing diverse health data. This allows researchers to integrate and analyze data from different sources, regardless of their original structure, effectively creating a "universal translator" for healthcare information.

Plus, by making all its tools and software freely available, the initiative promotes transparency and encourages its community of contributors to build on and enhance existing resources, accelerating the pace of innovation.

While prioritizing patient privacy, OHDSI also established a distributed network for collaborative research, enabling researchers to analyze standardized data securely within their own environments and sharing only the aggregate results of analyses without sharing any patient-level data. This approach ensures data security while fostering a collaborative spirit in which insight can be shared and validated across institutions and borders.

OHDSI has been instrumental in identifying drug safety issues, comparing the effectiveness of different treatments, and rapidly generating evidence during the COVID-19 pandemic. OHDSI has helped accelerate research, improve evidence generation, and ultimately, contribute to better patient care. It serves as a great example of using health data for good.

PROTECT HEALTH DATA LIKE IT'S YOUR OWN

We talked about balancing access with protection. But what do I mean by protection? Protecting health data means implementing safeguards to ensure the privacy, security, and integrity of the health information entrusted to your organization.

The first step in protecting health data is thoroughly assessing your risk.[24] This involves identifying what types of data you're handling, where it's stored, who has access to it, and what potential vulnerabilities exist in your systems. A risk assessment will help you understand where to focus your protection efforts and resources.

Many organizations, especially those just starting out, use third-party cloud providers who build systems for HIPAA compliance at scale. These vendors have already invested heavily in security infrastructure and compliance, which can save you significant time and resources. This doesn't automatically make your entire operation HIPAA-compliant, as you're still responsible for how you use and manage the data within that system. But it does improve your risk profile.

Last, I highly recommend engaging with experienced data privacy lawyers. These professionals can advise you on best practices for data protection because "we didn't know" is not an acceptable excuse.

Data breaches have far-reaching consequences. They can damage businesses, potentially resulting in fines, legal action, and remediation costs. They can also destroy reputations, making it difficult to retain existing customers or attract new ones.

But perhaps the most significant impact of data breaches is on the patients. A health data breach can lead to identity theft, financial fraud, or even blackmail. It can cause stress and anxiety for affected individuals, knowing that their most personal information has been exposed. This erosion of trust can make patients rightfully more reluctant to share information or seek care, ultimately compromising health outcomes.

Protecting health data means honoring the trust that patients place in us when they share their most sensitive information.

Behind every data point is a real person, with genuine concerns and vulnerabilities. We have a responsibility to be worthy of their trust.

So, as you build your systems and processes, ask yourself: "Would I be comfortable with my health data being handled this way?" If the answer is anything less than a resounding "yes," it's time to strengthen your protections.

GET TO KNOW HIPAA

Any organization that is considered a "covered entity" or "business associate" must comply with the rules of HIPAA.[25]

- A *covered entity* is a healthcare provider, health plan, or healthcare clearinghouse that handles PHI. For example, a telehealth startup that provides virtual psychiatry and maintains health records for patients would be considered a covered entity.
- A *business associate* is an entity that performs certain activities that involve the use or disclosure of PHI on behalf of, or provides services to, a covered entity. For example, a startup that provides transcription services to a physician is a business associate.

You'll need to know how your organization is categorized, because this category determines your specific legal obligations. The US Department of Health and Human Services (HHS) offers a Covered Entity Decision Tool on HHS.gov to help clarify which category applies to you. These obligations fall under three main components of HIPAA:

- **Privacy Rule:** Restricts the use of PHI unless it's permitted under the privacy rule or the patient has given authorization.
- **Security Rule:** Requires organizations to meet a national set of security standards for protecting certain health information that is held or transferred in electronic form.

- **Health Breach Notification Rule:** Requires covered entities to notify patients and the government after any data breaches. Breaches involving 500 or more individuals must also be reported to the media.[26]

Although the HHS Office for Civil Rights (OCR) is responsible for managing and enforcing HIPAA, the Federal Trade Commission (FTC) also plays a role in protecting consumers when it comes to health data privacy.

If you are building a product that will access, collect, share, use, or maintain information related to a user's health, the FTC will be watching. The FTC regulates digital health companies under its broader consumer protection mandate, particularly regarding unfair or deceptive practices.

For example, BetterHelp, an online therapy app, used and disclosed consumers' email addresses, IP addresses, and health questionnaire information to Facebook, Snapchat, and Pinterest for retargeting ads (you know, those ads that follow you around on the internet after you visit a website), despite promising consumers that it would only use or disclose personal health data for limited purposes.[27] The company ultimately had to pay a $7.8 million fine, the first FTC action requiring the return of funds to consumers whose health data was compromised. This is just one example of about 450 open investigations and 130 joint letters from the OCR and FTC to hospital systems and telehealth providers.[28]

GOOD DATA STEWARDSHIP

If you're working to improve healthcare, there's a good chance you're using health data to achieve your mission. Being a responsible health data steward means building a culture of respect for the health information entrusted to you. It means striking a balance between making data accessible for better care *while* protecting it from misuse.

Imagine if Erica's experience had been different. If responsible health data stewardship were the norm, her records would have been instantly available to her care team at UCSF, securely transferred, and protected. Her treatment could have started immediately without repeated tests or delays.

We are making progress. According to the Office of the National Coordinator for Health Information Technology, the routine use of interoperable exchange among nonfederal acute care hospitals increased from 28 percent in 2018 to 43 percent in 2023.[29]

The Twenty-First Century Cures Act and recent HHS regulations have also pushed for greater interoperability, but challenges remain. Some stakeholders argue that the current standards don't encompass the full scope of patient information, excluding things like non-medication substances, food allergies, physical activity assessments, and notes on medication instructions.[30]

Regardless, we need to shift our thinking about health information. We need to move from a data-hoarding culture to one of responsible sharing and protection. We must prioritize patient empowerment and collaborative research over proprietary interests.

This future is within our grasp and one that individuals like Erica, who faced the consequences of a closed system, are actively involved in creating. Thankfully, she is now fully recovered, tumor free, and working in healthcare to help make it better for everyone.

TL;DR

- **Understand the health data paradox:** Healthcare data is simultaneously underused and misused. Although most healthcare data remains untapped due to siloed systems, it's also increasingly vulnerable to cyberattacks.
- **Make interoperability a reality:** Commit to building interoperability into your products and culture from day one. Push for standardization and challenge the status quo of siloed systems that hinder the patient experience.

- **Protect health data like it's your own:** Implement safeguards, assess risks regularly, and create a culture of data respect. Use HIPAA-compliant services and engage privacy lawyers to stay ahead of regulations.
- **Get to know the regulatory landscape:** Know your obligations under HIPAA and FTC guidelines. Ignorance is not an excuse; compliance is important for maintaining patient trust and avoiding legal issues.

11

RULE 4

Invest in Evidence

Don't build confidence. Build evidence. Confidence comes as a result
of evidence. Not the other way around.
—ALEX HORMOZI

I first met Sami Inkinen, the cofounder of Trulia and an Ironman
competitor, soon after he was diagnosed with prediabetes. He
was shocked by the diagnosis; despite being a competitive triathlete
training more than ten hours a week, Sami had developed prediabetes from eating the typical low-fat diet that was, in reality, a high-·
carbohydrate, sugar-infused processed food trap.

Sami began hanging around our office and diving deep into the
science of nutrition, specifically how it related to type 2 diabetes
(T2D), which he might develop if he didn't reverse this new diagnosis. His research led him to nutrition experts Dr. Stephen Phinney
and Jeff Volek, PhD, RD, two pioneers in metabolic health. Under
their guidance, Sami began practicing nutritional ketosis, a metabolic state triggered by a low-carbohydrate diet, in which the body
burns fat and ketones instead of glucose, to improve his health and
prevent the onset of T2D.

Then Sami did something that surprised us all. In 2014, he and
his wife, neither of whom had really rowed before, rowed 2,400
miles from San Francisco to Hawaii on a twenty-foot-long, five-
foot-wide engineless vessel. Their goal was to raise awareness about
the harmful effects of sugar in our diets. They completed this task
and set a record, arriving in forty-five days and raising more than

$300,000 for the Institute for Responsible Nutrition. This was all while adhering to the ketogenic diet Sami had adopted to combat his prediabetes.

This voyage was his n-of-2 real-world experiment in the power of nutrition. Their provisions read like a low-carb manifesto: nuts, seeds, coconut butter, dehydrated fish and beef, select fruits, and olive oil. Every mile rowed, every day at sea, every record broken proved that this diet could reverse his prediabetes and fuel extraordinary physical achievements. It was this curiosity and commitment that would power Sami's next venture, too.

After the race, Sami convinced Volek and Phinney to join him in founding Virta Health to reverse T2D in patients by combining nutrition-based treatment and virtual coaching. From the outset, the founders recognized the need for long-term studies on the efficacy of their approach, particularly for T2D patients on insulin. So, in 2015, they used their seed funding to launch a clinical trial, a decision central to the company's success.

Their first study, conducted in partnership with Indiana University Health, was a nonrandomized controlled clinical trial following participants using the Virta app. It included telemedicine, educational resources, and biomarker-tracking tools to achieve and sustain nutritional ketosis.

The results were impressive. After two years, a majority of Virta participants achieved diabetes reversal. Participants cut back on diabetes medication, too—67 percent of prescriptions were discontinued, including most insulin and all sulfonylureas. The study also reported improvements in cardiovascular risk factors, liver health markers, and inflammation.[1]

The positive study results gave the team, and ultimately potential customers, evidence that the program worked. By 2025, Virta had published dozens of additional studies, secured deals with more than five hundred employer and health plan customers, and helped more than one hundred thousand people with T2D and obesity. One very happy member even got a Virta logo tattoo after getting her A1c low enough to get a tattoo safely.

Even though Sami didn't have a traditional healthcare background, he was able to build a successful digital health company in part because he invested in evidence. He knew early on the importance of demonstrating a real, measurable impact on people's health. Sami positioned Virta to gain the trust of not just investors but also healthcare providers, payers, and, most important, patients.

In this chapter, I'll share what you need to know about building evidence in healthcare. I'll cover ways to identify your stakeholders and define clear objectives, methods for establishing meaningful measures of success, and strategies for gathering evidence. I will also explain the importance of considering trade-offs and unintended consequences and evaluating potential externalities and their broader impact. By the end, you'll have a simple framework for measuring success beyond business metrics to understand your impact on patients, providers, and the healthcare system.

MASSIVELY BETTER = MEASURABLY BETTER

As a product's clinical risk increases, so does the need for clinical validation. A fitness tracker measuring heart rate during workouts isn't subject to US Food and Drug Administration (FDA) oversight. But a wearable monitoring heart rate to detect arrhythmias needs FDA clearance, which requires the clinical data to prove it's safe and effective. Regardless, I can't think of a product that wouldn't benefit from evidence that it works.

A 2022 study by Rock Health looked at 224 companies selling digital health tools targeting the prevention, diagnosis, or treatment phases of the care continuum to see if their medical claims were backed by data—what we call *clinical robustness*.[2]

The study found that most digital health companies lack strong scientific evidence and don't share much information about how well their products work. In fact, almost half of the companies (44 percent) earned a clinical robustness score of 0. This is a huge missed opportunity.

Here's why evidence matters:

- **Fueling growth:** Strong evidence that your product works as advertised can help you sell it to customers. A PwC report found that evidence-backed digital health solutions are more likely to achieve scale.[3]
- **Building conviction:** Evidence is the best way to reinforce your mission. It can help you and your team withstand naysayers and move forward with confidence that you're on the right path.
- **Driving adoption and trust:** Healthcare providers and patients are more likely to use products with proven results. A commitment to evidence helps build trust and brand affinity.
- **Marketing that stands out:** Evidence-based marketing can help position your brand as trustworthy and effective in a crowded market.
- **Staying on the right side of regulators:** If you make claims about your product diagnosing, treating, or preventing diseases, you need data and regulatory filings to back them up. The FDA and Federal Trade Commission (FTC) take these claims seriously and can take action against companies making unsubstantiated medical claims. (Helpful resources for this include the FDA's Digital Health Center of Excellence, DiME's Digital Health Regulatory Pathways Toolkit, and the FTC's Mobile Health App Interactive Tool.)

Investing in evidence sets your company up for long-term success.

APPROACHES TO GENERATING EVIDENCE

Now that you're hopefully convinced of the need for evidence, you may be wondering how to gather this data. Here are a couple of approaches.

Stakeholder-Reported Data

The most direct way to understand the impact of your product is often the simplest: Ask the people using it.

For deeper insight, qualitative methods like interviews or focus group discussions provide a way for users to share their experiences in their own words.

For more quantitative data, embedding surveys within an app or after an appointment can help collect user experience and satisfaction data. You don't need to reinvent the wheel. You can use patient-reported outcome measures (PROMs) to capture patient perspectives on their health and well-being. These standardized questionnaires allow patients to report health measures like quality of life, daily functioning, and symptoms. Because they're standardized, they also allow you to compare outcomes with other interventions.

For example, the team at my portfolio company Tia (an integrated primary care practice for women) incorporated PROMs into their workflow to understand quality beyond traditional quality outcome measures such as cervical cancer screening rates or hypertension control. They wanted to understand not just if women were engaged in preventive care or if their chronic illnesses were well managed, but if they actually felt better and if Tia was having an impact on their overall quality of life. At various points throughout a patient's care journey, the team integrated the World Health Organization's quality-of-life (QOL) screening questions. By systematically collecting patient-reported data on QOL, they can understand how their patients' health is from the patients' point of view (how people feel about their health is, in many ways, just as important as objective markers). This has resulted in a consistent more than 70 percent improvement in QOL from baseline once patients are under Tia's care.

Thousands of validated PROM questionnaires exist online, covering various health-related domains, from social isolation to belly pain. Resources like HealthMeasures.net, funded by the National Institutes of Health, host a repository of these tools, making it easier to choose the most appropriate measures for your specific needs.

Clinical Research

There's a wealth of published research on the effectiveness of various interventions. Your first step should be to dig into any existing research. (PubMed.gov, a free search engine of more than thirty-seven million citations and abstracts of biomedical literature, is a great place to start.)

By building on established clinical knowledge, you can focus on improving areas like access, cost-efficiency, experience, or implementation of proven treatments. This approach is particularly helpful for tackling chronic diseases—we know a lot about managing them, but there's still plenty of room to make that management more adherent, affordable, and widely available.

Sometimes, however, you have to orchestrate your own studies, like Virta Health did. This can be time-consuming and resource-intensive, but it offers a more specific validation that secondary research cannot. You can conduct this research in-house or by partnering with an academic medical center or research institution to lend additional credibility and expertise. The output of such studies, typically a peer-reviewed publication, is a form of social proof and validation that can pave the way for things like reimbursement and broader adoption, not to mention adding to our collective knowledge.

Real-World Data

Randomized controlled trials (RCTs) remain the gold standard in clinical research for their methodological rigor. By randomly assigning participants to either a treatment group or a control group, RCTs effectively isolate the effects of an intervention, minimizing bias and confounding factors. This controlled environment improves the likelihood of evidence quality and reliability, which is particularly useful for establishing causality and initial efficacy of new interventions.

RCTs, however, face limitations. They are time-intensive and costly, and their strict participant criteria in controlled environments may not fully capture the diverse real-world patient population. With the increasing availability of health data in recent years, RCTs are no longer the only—and often not the best—answer to research needs. Enter: real-world data.

Real-world data (RWD) is the industry term referring to the information that is regularly gathered about a patient's health and the care they receive. This data comes from various places, including:

- Electronic health records (EHRs)
- Claims and billing activity
- Product and disease registries
- Wearables and other digital health technologies
- Health-related data from social media
- Patient-powered research networks
- Customer records and sales data

A single data point might offer insight into the impact of a solution on an individual's health, so you can imagine how aggregating data across many patients can provide incredible insight into the effects of a solution on a population.

RWD can help RCTs be more effective by providing deeper, richer data, and allow you to contemplate more variables. That is because RWD, especially from an EHR, usually contains more data from more diverse demographic groups than data collected in controlled settings.

Building evidence is an ongoing process that should evolve and grow with your organization. Say you're building a new telehealth platform. You might start by reviewing existing research on telemedicine to understand what works. As you build your product, focus groups could guide which features to prioritize to satisfy the unmet needs of your audience. Once launched, user satisfaction surveys help measure PROMs and compare your solution to others. To sell to employers, you might conduct cost-effectiveness studies using claims data. Each time you expand to new specialties or add features, you repeat parts of this process, constantly collecting and analyzing data to improve your product and prove its value.

BOX 11.1.
In the Trenches: Supernatural

When my portfolio company Within launched Supernatural, a virtual reality (VR) fitness platform, it didn't want to compete with fitness companies like Peloton. Founders Aaron Koblin and Chris Milk focused on "competing with the couch"—creating engaging workouts for people who otherwise would be sedentary. They wanted to make cardio fun and accessible for folks like Aaron's mom, who could never find a consistent exercise routine.

Although they weren't making medical claims, the team knew that proving their product's effectiveness would help set them apart.

Secondary research showed that VR users experienced reduced perception of time and pain, suggesting that VR could help people stick to fitness routines longer.[4]

Aaron and Chris knew it was time to invest in evidence when people kept asking, "Is this *really* a workout?" They partnered with the University of Victoria to conduct a small clinical study measuring energy expenditure during Supernatural workouts.[5]

The study found the average "medium intensity" Supernatural workout produced the exercise equivalent to running or swimming, qualifying as "vigorous" physical activity under US Department of Health and Human Services physical activity guidelines.

This validation cemented Supernatural's position in the market. The study was peer-reviewed and published, and the platform was added to the industry's leading reference for measuring physical activity—a recognition typically updated only once per decade.[6] This evidence-based approach contributed to Within's success. The company was acquired by Meta for $440 million in 2023.

The Supernatural story shows that even nonclinical products can benefit from rigorous proof of effectiveness, especially when combined with a clear understanding of user needs.

ASSESSING YOUR IMPACT

Fifteen years into my career, after founding and running Rock Health and creating and teaching the first MBA–level course on digital health, I decided to go back to school myself. I felt good about my ability to identify business opportunities, but something was missing. I didn't just want to be a good businessperson; I wanted to understand if and how my work as a healthcare investor was making a positive, meaningful impact.

Pursuing my master of public health (MPH) gave me a new lens with which to evaluate success. I learned about the importance of considering not just the immediate impact of a solution but also its long-term effects on population health, health equity, and the sustainability of the healthcare system as a whole.

If you've gotten this far in the book, then it's safe to say you also care deeply about making a positive impact in healthcare. The evidence you gather is a big piece of doing just that. But it's important to step back and consider the bigger picture of your impact on the healthcare system. Let's walk through the steps (figure 11.1).

Figure 11.1 A practical framework for thinking through the full impact of your healthcare innovation. Start by identifying who you're trying to help (and who else might be affected), clarify what you're trying to achieve, identify the evidence you'll need to gather, and watch out for unintended side effects that inevitably pop up along the way.

1. Identify

The first step is to identify your **direct stakeholders**. These are the folks in your immediate circle of influence, the buyers or users directly interacting with your product or service.

Once you've identified them, consider your **primary objectives** from their perspective. What core benefits are you promising them? (Hint: look at your marketing claims.) Does the service help patients get pregnant faster? Are providers able to deliver care more efficiently? Are caregivers finding support and relief?

2. Optimize

Ultimately, your objectives should contribute to the quadruple aim of healthcare innovation (figure 11.2).[7]:

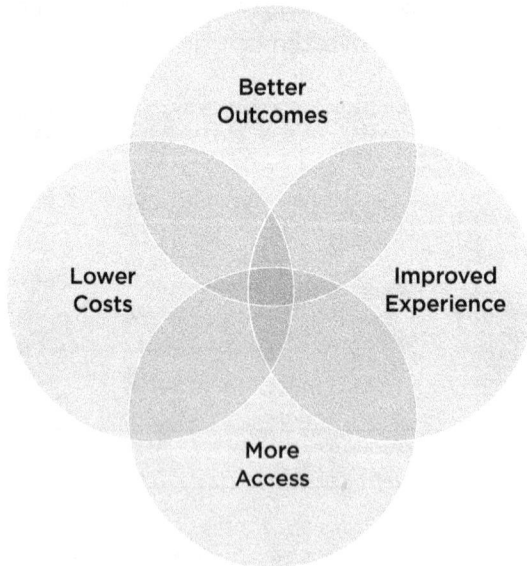

Figure 11.2 Quadruple aim of healthcare innovation.

- **Better outcomes:** Delivering safe and effective care that improves patient outcomes
- **Lower costs:** Making healthcare more affordable and sustainable for individuals and the system as a whole
- **More access:** Removing barriers that prevent people from obtaining the care they need
- **Improved experience:** Making the healthcare experience more satisfying for patients, families, and clinicians

Determine which key objectives you want to optimize with your product or service. It's unlikely you can pull all four levers at once, and that's okay. What matters is being intentional about where you're prioritizing, and why.

3. Measure

Once you know your big-picture objectives, you can start thinking about how you will measure them to build **evidence**. These indicators can help you quantify success, understand value, position the product to customers, recognize areas for improvement, and ensure that it ultimately benefits those it's designed to serve.

Outcome measures should be relevant to your objectives, measurable, time-bound, and actionable. You could get overwhelmed with the number of things you're trying to measure, so start with the ones that matter the most. Table 11.1 provides some examples.

Unfortunately, many solutions face the challenge of a long feedback loop. It may take years to understand the impact of an innovation, particularly its long-term clinical and financial return on investment. Remember when we talked about hard being your moat? This is where investing in research early, like Virta Health did, can set you apart from competitors and add credibility to your claims.

While some objectives can be backed by solid evidence today, others may fall short. These gaps in performance aren't necessarily failures—they're trade-offs you're making (for now), often in

TABLE 11.1
Objectives and Measures

Objective	Example Outcome Measures
Better outcomes	• Behavioral changes (e.g., medication adherence, steps walked) • Disease progression or prevention • Symptom reduction • Hospital readmission rate • Treatment adherence rates • Quality of life (e.g., quality-adjusted life years, or QALYs) • Clinical return on investment (ROI)
Lower costs	• Time saved on administrative tasks or data entry • Productivity metrics • Process improvement • Automation rate • Financial ROI
More access	• Coverage rates • Utilization rates by target population • Conversion rates • Willingness to use the solution • Balance of supply and demand • Time to treatment • Equitable dispersion • Adoption rates
Improved experience and satisfaction	• Net promoter score (NPS)—how likely a patient or clinician is to recommend the service or product • Overall experience rating • User satisfaction • Job satisfaction • Employee attrition • Engagement data

service of higher-priority goals. Acknowledging these trade-offs allows you to address them intentionally over time.

4. Mitigate

Finally, introducing new solutions involves balancing **trade-offs**. As mentioned, it's unlikely you can pull all four levers—quality, cost, access, and experience—at once. In fact, you may find you're nailing one or two of these aims but falling behind on another.

For instance, a new intervention with dramatic improvements in outcomes could be costly at first, making it inaccessible to patients who need it the most. The rise of glucagon-like peptide-1 (GLP-1) medications like Wegovy® is a good example. Although incredibly effective for weight loss and improving associated health outcomes, their initial high cost created a two-tiered system: Those with generous health insurance or the means to pay out of pocket had access, and the rest did not. This limited access despite the potential for these drugs to reduce long-term healthcare spending by preventing obesity-related complications like heart disease and T2D.

The good news is that initial trade-offs usually soften as the market matures and products scale. Over time, supply chain issues are resolved, competition increases, coverage expands, and economies of scale kick in, gradually improving accessibility and affordability.

Although most of your focus will be on the intended benefits of your solution, you'll also want to watch for and mitigate any secondary impacts and downstream effects—**SIDE effects**, as we'll call them—that can undermine the integrity of your work.

Unintended consequences are outcomes that were not anticipated when developing the solution. These typically affect direct stakeholders the users or buyers of your product or service. Although they can sometimes be positive, it's the negative ones you need to watch out for.

Continuing with the GLP-1 example, a negative unintended consequence may be the loss of muscle mass for patients on the drug, a condition known as sarcopenia. As muscle mass diminishes, patients may experience reduced strength, decreased stamina, and a lower resting metabolic rate. If not addressed, through activities like resistance training and eating a high-protein diet, a patient's overall health can be compromised, despite the weight loss benefits. Although sarcopenia is a risk in any rapid weight loss scenario and not unique to GLP-1 medications, it remains an unintended consequence that can and should be addressed.

(On the flip side, researchers are uncovering many positive unintended consequences of GLP-1 drugs, such as potential protection against dementia, reduced alcohol consumption, and lower risk of cardiovascular disease.)

Beyond the immediate circle of a solution's users and buyers, there's nearly always a wider group of **indirect stakeholders**—those who do not directly interact with the innovation but nonetheless experience its benefits and consequences. In economics, these benefits and consequences are called *externalities*, and they affect indirect stakeholders without being reflected in the cost.

Indirect stakeholders often have little power or influence over the innovation, yet they can be significantly affected. Their powerlessness means they frequently get overlooked, which is particularly problematic with *negative externalities*—that is, any unintended consequences that adversely affect them.

Understanding potential negative externalities can help you avoid building solutions that solve one problem while creating new ones. Without considering the needs and perspectives of indirect stakeholders, we risk exacerbating existing inequities.

Consider full-body MRI scans, which are becoming more popular in the United States. Several companies now offer full-body MRI scans that scan the body for abnormalities. Anyone who can afford to pay the high price can get one of these scans without *medical necessity* (meaning they have no symptoms or reason to believe something is wrong).

This kind of innovation got me super giddy when I was starting in healthcare. It felt like the obvious future we needed, a way to catch problems early and change the course of someone's health trajectory. And while I still see the potential, I've learned to approach such innovations with more cautious optimism. Understanding the externalities of an innovation like this is necessary for making healthcare massively better.[8]

Consider this: Although a true positive can be lifesaving, a false positive result can trigger a cascade of unnecessary and potentially harmful follow-up tests, invasive procedures, and emotional distress for the patient. The costs of these false alarms could be substantial for the individual and the entire healthcare system. Resources could be diverted away from those with genuine medical needs, potentially delaying diagnoses and straining an already overburdened system. What happens if there are more false positives than true positives? Is it still worth it?

Twenty years ago, I would have said, *so cool! Full-body scans for all!* Today I say, *so cool! How does this affect patients and the rest of healthcare?* And then I would ask questions:

- **The true-positive rate:** What percentage of these scans accurately detect a problem? Can we quantify years of life saved or overall medical costs saved by diagnosing the problem sooner?
- **The false-positive rate:** What percentage of these scans generate abnormal results that turn out *not* to be serious diseases?
- **Follow-up cost:** What's the average cost of follow-up tests, biopsies, and so on, triggered by a false-positive scan?
- **The emotional toll:** How does the anxiety and worry caused by a potential false diagnosis affect patients' quality of life? Are there studies to quantify this?

At best, full-body MRI scans for seemingly healthy people are the future of preventive health and early detection, improving healthcare outcomes for all. At worst, they contribute to rising healthcare costs and disparities, as unnecessary tests and procedures drive up spending without necessarily improving overall population health. The truth is probably somewhere in between, and the goal is to understand *where*.

If you're on the receiving end of these types of questions, your first reflex may be to become defensive. But if instead you prepare for these tough questions and even seek them out yourself, you're more likely to build trust and alliances.

BOX 11.2.
First, Do No Harm

Remember, *trade-offs* occur when new innovations improve one aim but sacrifice another. They result from a conscious decision to prioritize one goal over another because of limited resources or early inefficiencies. Trade-offs can and should soften over time.

Unintended consequences, in contrast, are unexpected outcomes that directly affect your primary stakeholders. They can be positive or negative; you'll want to anticipate and mitigate the negative ones.

Externalities are a spillover effect of an activity that affects an indirect stakeholder who did not participate. Externalities can be positive (the benefit of herd immunity on those not vaccinated) or negative (secondhand smoke).

Healthcare innovation is never black and white. The potential for impact is enormous, but so is the potential for harm. The longer you hang around, the better you get at asking tough questions about a solution's impact on the system. The trick is not to become a reflexive skeptic but to remain open-minded without losing sight of the broader implications.

USING INNOVATION TO SOLVE NEGATIVE EXTERNALITIES

Innovation can inadvertently create negative externalities, but we also have powerful mechanisms to identify, address, and mitigate them. Policymakers, for example, can implement public health programs to deal with unpriced negative externalities, including:

- **Regulations:** The Affordable Care Act (ACA), for example, made it illegal for health plans to deny coverage or charge higher premiums for people with preexisting conditions, leading to our current record-low uninsured rate.

- **Pigouvian taxes:** Imposing taxes on activities that generate negative externalities (e.g., cigarettes, sugary drinks) can incentivize reduced behavior while diverting revenue to education and prevention.
- **Public reporting:** Making data on hospital infection rates, readmission rates, and other quality measures transparent and publicly available can empower consumers to make more informed choices and incentivize providers to improve outcomes.
- **Labeling:** Requiring clear labeling of health risks (e.g., calorie counts on menus and warning labels on cigarettes) can help individuals make healthier choices.

The private sector can also help solve for negative externalities. For example, Progyny, a fertility benefits management company, has leveraged its market power to drive a significant reduction in medical costs associated with multiple births (i.e., twins, triplets), which are more than 400 percent higher than costs associated with a single childbirth.[9]

Fertility clinics historically were transferring multiple embryos during in vitro fertilization (IVF), often at the patients' request. Transferring multiple embryos at once, however, increases the risk of twin pregnancies, which are associated with increased health risks for both mothers and babies, including premature birth, low birth weight, and complications during delivery. But that's a problem for the obstetrician-gynecologist, the payer, and the patient—not for the fertility clinic.

To address this, Progyny developed a new model: partnering with employers to offer comprehensive fertility benefits that weren't traditionally covered by insurance. Through this approach, the company gained the market power needed to drive meaningful change in fertility care.

Because clinics wanted access to the growing number of patients covered by Progyny, they were incentivized to join its network and to adopt the company's evidence-based protocols. That included a requirement for IVF doctors to perform single-embryo transfers (instead of transferring multiple embryos), lowering the chances of having multiples and the associated medical risks and costs. Progyny meticulously tracked patient outcomes, and the results were quite impressive:[10]

- **Quicker time to pregnancy:** Progyny's IVF live birth rate per IVF transfer exceeded the national average by 17 percent.
- **More healthy babies:** Progyny achieved a 27 percent increase above the national live birth rate.
- **Fewer high-risk pregnancies:** Progyny patients had a higher single-embryo transfer rate, leading to 72 percent fewer multiple births—a significant win for families and the healthcare system.

The data tells a compelling story. The company helped enable better fertility care *and* smarter healthcare. With reduced complications and neonatal intensive care unit stays, Progyny's approach saved lives and money for everyone involved. It's the type of win-win I love to see.

MEASURING SUCCESS

If you take away one thing from this last rule, let it be that building evidence is an ongoing process of learning and growth. It requires a willingness to ask ourselves and others tough questions and to keep the bigger picture of massively better healthcare at the forefront of our efforts. But it really is possible to make positive change.

TL;DR

- **Invest in evidence:** Evidence can fuel your growth, build conviction, drive adoption, and keep you on the right side of regulators. There are many approaches to generating evidence, including stakeholder-reported data, clinical research, and RWD.

- **Consider product risk:** As the clinical risk of a product increases, so too does the need for clinical validation.
- **Evaluate your impact on the healthcare system's quadruple aim:** Ultimately, any measure of success should contribute to broader systemic change: improving quality, lowering costs, improving experience, and increasing access.
- **Beware of SIDE effects:** Think through any potential secondary impacts and downstream effects and mitigate anything that undermines the goal of massively better healthcare.
- **Commit to continuous learning:** Building evidence and assessing impact are ongoing processes. Be ready to ask tough questions and adapt as you learn.

12

GO FORTH AND FIX HEALTHCARE

The best way to predict the future is to create it.
—PETER DRUCKER

If you've made it this far, you may be feeling a mix of inspiration and intimidation. Good. That's exactly where you should be. Healthcare needs people like you—folks who see the problems, understand the challenges, and remain relentlessly committed to creating meaningful change.

Perhaps you're feeling "enlightened determination," the mindset that allows us to make meaningful, sustainable progress despite healthcare's myriad challenges. It's the drive to immerse ourselves in a problem, devise solutions, build evidence, forge strategic partnerships, and maintain focus, even when faced with inevitable setbacks and roadblocks.

Throughout this book, we've explored some of the challenges, opportunities, and strategies for creating meaningful change in one of our society's most important (albeit quirky) sectors.

We've covered much ground—from the four innovation pathways to the common traps innovators fall into. We've talked about measuring success, going slow to go fast, and how to align the margin and the mission.

Now it's time to take all we've learned and put it into action.

YOU DON'T NEED PERMISSION TO BEGIN

I once saw a sign at an art fair that said, "You're still an artist even if you haven't been picked up by a gatekeeper," and I thought, *the same goes for healthcare innovators.* Too often, I meet people with incredible potential, waiting for some mythical stamp of approval before getting started. Forget the gatekeepers!

Your specific perspective, skills, and experiences are your assets. Don't wait for the old guard to validate your idea or give you permission to start. Find like-minded people and stay curious and open to learning. The country needs your unique contributions, and you have everything you need to begin making a positive impact right now.

You don't *need* venture capital to get started. You don't *have* to work for a big organization. You also don't need a business or medical degree (although if you have one, great!). All you really need is passion, a burning problem to solve, and the courage to take that first step.

Start small if you need to. Maybe it's suggesting a better shift handover process in your department. Maybe it's developing a newsletter to help people like you manage a chronic condition. Or perhaps it's lobbying for policy changes based on your healthcare experiences. Whatever it is, don't wait for someone to give you permission. The healthcare system is full of people waiting for solutions—be the one who starts creating them.

Some of the most impactful ideas have come from people with fresh perspectives, often from outside of healthcare, who recognized and sought to solve everyday problems:

- The Band-Aid® was invented by a cotton buyer whose wife was prone to slicing her fingers in the kitchen.[1]
- The at-home pregnancy test was the brainchild of Margaret Crane, a graphic designer who recognized the need for a simple, private way for women to test for pregnancy at home.[2]

- The Orphan Drug Act, which incentivized the development of treatments for rare diseases, was primarily driven by patients and families affected by these conditions.[3]
- The EpiPen was invented by a businessman whose daughter was allergic to bees. He had been working on a contract for the US military to develop injection technology for the antidote to nerve gas and thought to do the same for bee stings.[4]
- Even the creation of the US Food and Drug Administration was largely due to a novelist, Upton Sinclair. His 1906 novel *The Jungle*, an exposé of the meatpacking industry, led to sweeping food and drug reforms.[5]

Stop waiting to "feel ready" because ready is not actually a feeling. Ready is a decision.

FOCUS ON WHAT YOU CAN CHANGE

There's a parable that goes something like this: A man is walking along a beach after a storm. Thousands of starfish have washed ashore, stranded and dying in the morning sun. As he walks, he notices a child picking up starfish one by one and tossing them back into the ocean.

"What are you doing?" he asks.

"Saving the starfish," she replies, bending down to pick up another.

The man looks down the beach at countless starfish stretching for miles. "But there must be thousands of starfish. You can't possibly make a difference."

The girl looks at the starfish in her hand, tosses it into the waves, and says, "I made a difference to that one."

Then, presumably, he and everyone else on the beach were inspired to join in.

A single person cannot possibly fix the entire healthcare system, but one person can absolutely make a meaningful difference and inspire others to as well. Progress is made by those willing to act. Not by the critics on the sidelines.

FIND YOUR SMART SHOT

Remember: Healthcare innovation comes from diverse teams relentlessly pursuing meaningful problems, in the right place, at the right time.

If you have diabetes, then you know the unmet needs of people living with this disease. If you are an oncologist, then you probably have a good idea of what's holding cancer patients back from the best outcomes. But what if you are new to healthcare? Or what if you currently work in healthcare but want to move horizontally? I would suggest finding a "smart shot."

We all find out, sooner or later, that healthcare has no silver bullets. There are no miraculous cures.

Change is possible. But it rarely arrives in a single, dramatic leap. Progress usually happens incrementally, haphazardly, and sometimes so gradually you may not notice until you realize you're somewhere completely different from where you started.

Unbridled enthusiasm drives innovation, and we need all the brilliant minds we can get to tackle problems this size. But that ambition deserves to be matched with a realistic road map. Trying to force magical, easy solutions onto healthcare only guarantees wasted effort and burnout.

That's why we need more smart shots. Smart shots are when you find a wedge where:

- A genuine need exists.
- Technology or new care models can make a difference.
- The regulatory and incentive environment allows for change to take hold *today*.
- You can build something sustainable and scalable, where the margin and mission align.

Look for seismic shifts. Watch for upcoming inflection points where market demand, technological advances, and a favorable regulatory environment all align in your favor.

This is how you identify areas ripe for change and impact. Think of it like aiming in archery. Whereas silver bullets imply you can fire blindly and magically hit the target, smart shots require careful consideration of trajectory, wind resistance, and the constraints of your surroundings.

BUILD BRIDGES

Success shouldn't be a walled garden—it should be a public park.
The greatest leaders don't just climb higher; they build openness,
creating spaces where others can thrive too.

—OLIVER KHARRAZ, MD

In 1982, a shocking exposé on anesthesia errors aired on the ABC television program 20/20. The episode, titled "The Deep Sleep: 6,000 Will Die or Suffer Brain Damage," featured tragic stories of patients who had fallen victim to anesthesia mishaps. The narrator warned, "If you are going to go [under] anesthesia, you are going on a long trip and you should not do it if you can avoid it in any way."[6]

This watershed moment was a wake-up call for the anesthesiology community. Dr. Ellison C. Pierce, Jr., then vice president of the American Society of Anesthesiologists (ASA), recognized the need for transparency and collaboration in addressing patient safety issues. He collaborated with colleagues in Boston and the United Kingdom to plan the first International Symposium on Preventable Anesthesia Mortality and Morbidity.

Two groundbreaking initiatives emerged from this conference. First, the idea for the Anesthesia Patient Safety Foundation (APSF) was born. The APSF's mission is to disseminate safety information and fund research to prevent anesthesia-related harm, ensuring that knowledge is shared openly and widely to benefit patients everywhere.

Second, it was decided that adverse events should not be hidden but rather analyzed and discussed by leaders in the space. With this goal in mind, the organizers obtained ASA approval to start the Closed Claims Project, a structured evaluation of adverse anesthetic outcomes gleaned from malpractice insurance claims. By pooling data from multiple sources—hospital records, anesthetic records, narrative statements, expert reviews, and more—anesthesiologists were able to identify patterns and gain insights that otherwise would have remained hidden in silos. The project has become one of the world's most successful and sustained studies of anesthesia patient harm, leading to insight like the discovery of the link between spinal anesthesia and sudden cardiac arrest in young, healthy patients.

The impact of these initiatives has been nothing short of impressive. Today, anesthesia is incredibly safe. Mortality and catastrophic morbidity rates for healthy patients undergoing routine anesthetics have plummeted by a staggering ten- to twenty-fold.[7]

This is what we should do for all of healthcare. We have to break down walls and build bridges. The anesthesiologists faced their crisis head-on, put aside individual interests, and worked together to save lives. Now it's our turn. No matter what healthcare challenge you're tackling, no one organization can solve it alone. Progress happens when we step outside our silos and work together.

The term *coopetition* was coined in the 1980s by entrepreneur Ray Noorda, who recognized that software companies could benefit from collaborating with their so-called competitors.[8] Partnering with industry peers moves us from a *zero-sum game mindset*, in which one party's gain is another's loss, to a *plus-sum game mindset*, in which collaboration can create value for all.

For example, the Diabetes Advocacy Alliance (DAA) includes twenty-five member organizations like Noom, Omada Health, Teladoc, and WeightWatchers, who are typically competitors in the diabetes care and prevention market.[9] The DAA, which also includes traditional organizations like the American Medical Association, the American Diabetes Association, and the American Academy of Ophthalmology, was formed to advocate for consistent standards in virtual diabetes prevention programs that could benefit the entire industry. By pooling their advocacy efforts, their push for including virtual programs in Medicare has led to greater access to diabetes prevention care.

Coopetition in healthcare can take many forms:

- **Joining forces to better compete:** Smaller or newer healthcare companies might collaborate to challenge larger, established incumbents.
- **Attracting attention:** Companies might work together on high-profile projects or initiatives to draw attention to their sector of healthcare. A well-known example of this from a different industry is "Restaurant Week," during which local restaurants jointly advertise a week of fixed-price meals.
- **Setting industry-wide standards:** Collaboration among competitors can help establish consistent standards and best practices that benefit the entire industry and, ultimately, patients.
- **Developing interoperability:** Companies can work together to ensure their systems can communicate effectively, creating a more seamless experience for users.
- **Sharing resources:** Organizations might pool resources to share the cost of segments of the supply chain or fund common-pool services that benefit all competitors and their customers.

Although research on the benefits of coopetition in healthcare is still emerging, a study of digital health companies found that coopetition directly and positively affects growth performance.[10] This suggests that when we find ways to collaborate with our competitors, we can achieve better outcomes than we would by operating in isolation.

PREPARE FOR THE "MESSY MIDDLE"

Everyone loves inspiring beginnings and happy endings;
it is just the middles that involve hard work.
—ROSABETH MOSS KANTER

Kanter's Law, from Harvard Business School Professor Rosabeth Moss Kanter, asserts that everything looks and feels like failure when you're in the middle (figure 12.1).[11]

Figure 12.1 When you are in the middle, everything feels like a failure.

Your initial optimism is waning. The difficulty of healthcare is weighing on you. The finish line is nowhere in sight. Welcome to the messy middle of healthcare innovation.

The first time you experience this, you might think you're failing. Fear not! This is when the real work happens, when your solution gets battle-tested against reality, when you figure out if you've got something worth pursuing or if it's time to pivot.

So when you're working on fixing a massive problem in healthcare, remember Kanter's Law.

Be flexible about the journey and inflexible about the destination. Keep your eyes on the problem you're trying to solve. Stay connected to the people you're helping. And know that your feelings of doubt are normal. But also listen to the feedback you're getting. Which brings me to our next point . . .

KNOW WHEN TO FOLD 'EM

There's an often-overlooked skill just as important as persistence: knowing when to move on from something that simply won't work.

Instead of continuing to throw good money after bad, valuable time after wasted, sometimes the best thing we can do is walk away.

In Japanese, the character for "giving up" (諦) also means "to see clearly." Quitting isn't failure—it's clarity. It's making room for something new. It's reorienting your energy to something with a better shot at making an impact.

Recognizing when a project has run its course is a valuable skill that can save you time, resources, and emotional energy.

Folding doesn't mean you're giving up on making a difference in healthcare. It means you're seeing clearly and making room for something new. Every "failed" project is a learning experience that shapes your understanding and prepares you for future innovations.

No matter the outcome, it's infinitely better to attempt fixing healthcare than to not try at all. Plus, the market rewards entrepreneurs for trying, even if the startup didn't work out. In fact, founders whose companies fail still end up better off than peers who never started companies to begin with. A 2022 study from the National Bureau of Economic Research analyzed the career trajectories of nearly thirty thousand VC-backed founders and found that founders of failed VC-backed startups typically obtained jobs about three years more senior and with 5 percent higher wages than their nonfounder peers.[12]

Entrepreneurship is a valuable experience no matter the outcome.

BEWARE OF THE CRANKY OLD GUARD

Here's my final piece of advice. As you move forward, be prepared for challenges beyond just the systemic hurdles discussed in this book. This includes meeting the individuals I've called the C.O.G. (Cranky Old Guard).

The C.O.G. represents those entrenched in the healthcare system who resist change. Although their skepticism can sometimes be rooted in valid concerns, their approach tends to stifle progress and innovation.

The problem with the C.O.G. is their tendency to see obstacles rather than opportunities and fear rather than progress. Locked in their ways, they often lose sight of the fact that innovating in healthcare, by nature, is about navigating trade-offs—there's rarely a "perfect" solution. Instead of contributing constructively to discussions about what could be done to make healthcare better, they fixate on potential failures without offering viable alternatives for positive change.

The C.O.G. also has a habit of gatekeeping, making it harder for newcomers to break into the space. Their naysaying can dampen enthusiasm and erect barriers to progress, preventing potential new solutions from being explored. To them, I like to quote aviator Amelia Earhart: "Never interrupt someone doing what you said couldn't be done."

You *will* meet the C.O.G. on your journey. You will have naysayers.

But what if we made peace with their reality? What if we took the improv approach of "yes, and" to find some common ground? Admit we have blind spots, but reiterate our commitment to always doing the right thing? What if we found solutions to move through their concerns, tap into their wealth of knowledge, and . . . turn them from obstacles to allies?

GO FORTH AND FIX HEALTHCARE!

As you've seen throughout these pages, we're at a crossroads. I shared the story about my obese uncle chain-smoking in a mold-infested, power-flickering trailer—but this isn't about one guy unengaged with his health. The United States is uniquely bad at keeping people healthy, and not because Americans are somehow inherently less responsible than everyone else.

It's because we've built a society that makes being healthy a constant uphill battle. Our cities were designed for cars, not people. Fast food joints outnumber grocery stores in too many neighborhoods. And nearly one-third of citizens lack access to primary care.[13] This makes being unhealthy the easier choice, the cheaper choice, sometimes the *only* choice.

To top it all off, instead of addressing these root causes, we've cobbled together a sick care system. We pour hundreds of billions into treating preventable diseases and patching up problems that shouldn't exist in the first place. We can keep patching over these cracks, or we can roll up our sleeves for a wholesale transformation. The choice between these options affects all of us—and our children, and our children's children.

If you take anything from this book, I hope it's the realization that you can make a difference in healthcare, not despite your unique background and perspective, but because of it.

Our loyalty is not to the healthcare system we were handed. It's to the future we can build. One that catches people before they fall through the cracks. One in which money-making and mission-advancing are not at odds. One worthy of a country that claims to be the greatest in the world.

Will it be easy? Absolutely not. You'll likely face naysayers, setbacks, and moments of self-doubt. But I hope the stories and strategies I've shared have shown you that these hurdles are not insurmountable.

Never forget that you have a secret weapon: Your passion and unwavering belief that a better healthcare system is possible. We can overcome challenges by learning, adapting, and never losing sight of the prize—massively better healthcare for all.

ACKNOWLEDGMENTS

This book would not exist without the support, wisdom, and encouragement of many people.

First, I want to thank Brian C. Smith for immediately supporting my vision for this book and helping me get it to print. And to my Columbia Business School colleagues Carri Chan and Cliff Cramer for supporting my work in the classroom.

To my Rock Health family, especially Nate Gross, Malay Gandhi, Katie Drasser, Michael Esquivel, Ryan Panchadsaram, Geoff Clapp, Bill Evans, Megan Zweig, and the many others who shaped our journey together—thank you for being part of the story that led to this book.

I am deeply grateful to my peer reviewers and beta readers who provided invaluable feedback on every draft: Stuart Blitz, Dr. John Brownstein, Lowell Caulder, R. Martin Chavez, Susannah Fox, Alex Herzlinger, Chris Hogg, Ed Jen, Vinay Raj, Rosalind Robertson, Lucia Savage, Dr. Stanley Shah, Annie Valente, and David Vivero. Your detailed comments, candid critiques, and suggestions for improvement helped make this book clearer, stronger, and more useful.

To the healthcare innovators who shared their stories and insight with me—thank you for your candor and trust. Your experiences bring these pages to life. While not all your stories made it into these pages, they fundamentally shaped my understanding and perspective: Rebecca Adams, Leonard Achan, Dr. Toyin Ajayi, Julie Batille, Dr. Melinda Buntin, Julia Cheek, Ankita Desphande, Todd Dunn, Ali Diab, Sean Duffy, Sami Inkinen, Oliver Kharraz, Aaron Koblin, Brad Kittredge, Serrah Linares, Dr. Daniel E. Polsky, TJ Parker, Kate Ryder, Vineet Singal, and John Wilbanks.

To the women who opened doors and made introductions that helped bring this book to production—Christina Farr, Susannah Fox, Kasia Kalinowska, Dr. Liz Kwo, Dr. Geeta Nayyar, Leslie Proctor, Jane Sarasohn-Kahn, Leslie Schrock, and the Starlings—thank you for exemplifying how women can lift each other up.

To all the entrepreneurs I've had the privilege of working with— thank you for letting me be part of your journeys and teaching me so much along the way.

To my incredible students, your insight and perspectives have shaped my thinking in countless ways. Special thanks to my former teaching and research assistant Jillian Damaris for helping with this book early on, and to Layla Daniels for painstakingly formatting every citation.

Last, but certainly not least, to everyone I'm lucky enough to call family. I love you all so much.

Although these pages reflect countless contributions from others who have shaped my thinking, any errors or oversights are entirely my own.

NOTES

1. THE DIRE NEED FOR HEALTHCARE INNOVATION

1. Telesford Imani, Paul Hughes-Cromwick, Krutika Amin, and Cynthia Cox, "What Are the Recent Trends in Health Sector Employment?," Peterson-KFF Health System Tracker, March 27, 2024, https://www.healthsystemtracker.org/chart-collection/what-are-the-recent-trends-health-sector-employment.

2. Munira Z. Gunja, Evan D. Gumas, and Reginald D. Williams II, "US Health Care from a Global Perspective, 2022: Accelerating Spending, Worsening Outcomes," Commonwealth Fund, January 31, 2023, https://www.commonwealthfund.org/publications/issue-briefs/2023/jan/us-health-care-global-perspective-2022.

3. Gunja et al., "US Health Care from a Global Perspective, 2022."

4. Petrullo, Justina, "US Has Highest Infant, Maternal Mortality Rates Despite the Most Health Care Spending," *American Journal of Managed Care*, January 31, 2023, https://www.ajmc.com/view/us-has-highest-infant-maternal-mortality-rates-despite-the-most-health-care-spending.

5. Roosa Tikkanen, Katharine Fields, Reginald D. Williams II, and Melinda K. Abrams, "Mental Health Conditions and Substance Use: Comparing U.S. Needs and Treatment Capacity with Those in Other High-Income Countries," Commonwealth Fund, May 21, 2020, https://www.commonwealthfund.org/publications/issue-briefs/2020/may/mental-health-conditions-substance-use-comparing-us-other-countries.

6. Daniel Gillison and Keller Andy, "2020 Devastated US Mental Health—Healing Must Be a Priority," *The Hill*, February 23, 2021, https://thehill.com/opinion/healthcare/539925-2020-devastated-us-mental-health-healing-must-be-a-priority.

7. David Himmelstein, "A Comparison of Hospital Administrative Costs in Eight Nations: U.S. Costs Exceed All Others by Far," *Health Affairs* 33, no. 9 (2014), https://doi.org/10.26099/87pf-1r65.

8. Ani Turner, George Miller, and Elise Lowry, "High U.S. Health Care Spending: Where Is It All Going?," Commonwealth Fund, October 4, 2023, https://www.commonwealthfund.org/publications/issue-briefs/2023/oct/high-us-health-care-spending-where-is-it-all-going.

9. Matthew McGough, Gary Claxton, Krutika Amin, and Cynthia Cox, "How Do Health Expenditures Vary Across the Population?," Peterson-KFF Health System Tracker, January 4, 2024, https://www.healthsystemtracker.org/chart-collection/health-expenditures-vary-across-population.

10. John Cawley, Adam Biener, Chad Meyerhoefer, Yuchen Ding, Tracy Zvenyach, B. Gabriel Smolarz, and Abhilasha Ramasamy, "Direct Medical Costs of Obesity in the United States and the Most Populous States," *Journal of Managed Care and Specialty Pharmacy*, no. 3 (2021): 354–66, https://doi.org/10.18553/jmcp.2021.20410.

11. Centers for Disease Control and Prevention, "About Obesity," January 23, 2024, https://www.cdc.gov/obesity/php/about.

12. Michelle M. Mello, Amitabh Chandra, Atul A. Gawande, and David M. Studdert, "National Costs of the Medical Liability System," *Health Affairs* 29, no. 9 (September 29, 2010): 1569–77, https://doi.org/10.1377/hlthaff.2009.0807.

13. Gianfranco Pischedda, Ludovico Marinò, and Katia Corsi, "Defensive Medicine Through the Lens of the Managerial Perspective: A Literature Review," *BMC Health Services Research* 23, no. 1 (2023), https://doi.org/10.1186/s12913-023-10089-3.

14. Consumer Financial Protection Bureau, "Have Medical Debt? Anything Already Paid or Under $500 Should No Longer Be on Your Credit Report," May 8, 2023, https://www.consumerfinance.gov/about-us/blog/medical-debt-anything-already-paid-or-under-500-should-no-longer-be-on-your-credit-report.

15. David U. Himmelstein, Robert M. Lawless, Deborah Thorne, Pamela Foohey, and Steffie Woolhandler, "Medical Bankruptcy: Still Common despite the Affordable Care Act," *American Journal of Public Health* 109, no. 3 (February 6, 2019): 431–33, https://doi.org/10.2105/ajph.2018.304901.

16. Nathan Place, "GoFundMe as Health Insurance: Why So Many Americans Turn to Crowdfunding for Medical Care," *The Independent*, May 10, 2022, https://www.independent.co.uk/news/world/americas/americans-gofundme-healthcare-crowdfunding-medical-b2071472.html.

17. In 2023, following pressure from the Consumer Finance Protection Bureau (CFPB), the three nationwide credit reporting companies–Equifax, Experian, and TransUnion—removed all medical debts that are paid, under one year overdue, or under $500 from consumer credit reports. In 2025, CFPB finalized a rule to ban almost any medical debt from appearing on credit

reports and to end "coercive debt collection practices that weaponize the credit reporting system." CFPD, "CFPB Finalizes Rule to Remove Medical Bills from Credit Reports," January 7, 2025, https://www.consumerfinance.gov/about-us /newsroom/cfpb-finalizes-rule-to-remove-medical-bills-from-credit-reports.

18. Undue Medical Debt, "Undue Medical Debt—Donor-Powered Medical Debt Relief, Liberating Everyday People," accessed January 15, 2025, https:// unduemedicaldebt.org.

19. Eric Young, "New Survey Finds Large Number of People Skipping Necessary Medical Care Because of Cost," National Opinion Research Center, March 26, 2018, https://www.norc.org/research/library/new-survey-finds-large -number-of-people-skipping-necessary-medic.html.

20. Lunna Lopes, Alex Montero, Marley Presiado, and Liz Hamel, "Americans' Challenges with Health Care Costs," Kaiser Family Foundation, March 1, 2024, https://www.kff.org/health-costs/issue-brief/americans-challenges-with -health-care-costs.

21. Megan Burns, Mary Beth Dyer, and Michael Bailit, "Reducing Overuse and Misuse: State Strategies to Improve Quality and Cost of Health Care," Robert Wood Johnson Foundation, January 2014, https://www.shvs.org/wp -content/uploads/2014/11/RWJF_SHVS_ReducingOveruseMisuse.pdf.

22. Peter S. Hussey, Samuel Wertheimer, and Ateev Mehrotra, "The Association Between Health Care Quality and Cost," *Annals of Internal Medicine* 158, no. 1 (January 1, 2013): 27–34, https://doi.org/10.7326/0003-4819-158-1-201301010-00006.

23. Martin Makary and Michael Daniel, "Medical Error—The Third Leading Cause of Death in the US," *British Medical Journal* 353 (2016): i2139, https://doi .org/10.1136/bmj.i2139.

24. Clayton M. Christensen, Jerome H. Grossman, and Jason Hwang, *The Innovator's Prescription: A Disruptive Solution for Health Care* (McGraw-Hill, 2009).

25. Marilyn J. Field and Christine K Cassel, *A Profile of Death and Dying in America*, NIH.gov, National Academies Press, 1997, https://www.ncbi.nlm.nih .gov/books/NBK233601.

26. Karen Hacker, "The Burden of Chronic Disease," *Mayo Clinic Proceedings: Innovations, Quality and Outcomes* 8, no. 1 (January 20, 2024): 112–19, https://doi .org/10.1016/j.mayocpiqo.2023.08.005.

27. World Health Organization, "Noncommunicable Diseases," September 16, 2023, https://www.who.int/news-room/fact-sheets/detail/noncommunicable -diseases.

28. Centers for Medicare and Medicaid Services, "Care Coordination," August 14, 2023, https://www.cms.gov/priorities/innovation/key-concepts/care -coordination.

29. Harvard Chan School of Public Health, "Zip Code Better Predictor of Health Than Genetic Code," August 4, 2014, https://hsph.harvard.edu/news /zip-code-better-predictor-of-health-than-genetic-code.

30. On air pollution, see American Lung Association, "Disparities in the Impact of Air Pollution," November 2, 2023, https://www.lung.org/clean-air/outdoors/who-is-at-risk/disparities. On asthma, see U.S. Department of Health and Human Services, Office of Minority Health, "Asthma and African Americans," accessed January 16, 2025, https://minorityhealth.hhs.gov/asthma-and-african-americans. On COPD, see Rui-Rui Duan, Ke Hao, and Ting Yang, "Air Pollution and Chronic Obstructive Pulmonary Disease," *Chronic Diseases and Translational Medicine* 6, no. 4 (July 11, 2020): 260–69, https://doi.org/10.1016/j.cdtm.2020.05.004.

31. Kulleni Gebreyes, Jay Bhatt, David Rabinowitz, Michelle A. Williams, Mani Keita, and Wendy Gerhardt, "The $2.8 Trillion Opportunity: How Better Health for All Can Drive US Economic Growth," Deloitte Center for Health Solutions, September 24, 2024, https://www2.deloitte.com/us/en/insights/industry/health-care/health-equity-economic-impact.html.

32. Sirikan Rojanasarot, Samir K. Bhattacharyya, and Natalie Edwards, "Productivity Loss and Productivity Loss Costs to United States Employers Due to Priority Conditions: A Systematic Review," *Journal of Medical Economics* 26, no. 1 (February 14, 2023): 262–70, https://doi.org/10.1080/13696998.2023.2172282.

33. Gebreyes et al., "The $2.8 Trillion Opportunity."

2. HEALTHCARE'S NOT-SO-SIMPLE FOOD CHAIN

1. Stephanie Miceli, "High-Quality Primary Care Should Be Available to Every Individual in the U.S., Says New Report; Payment Reform, Telehealth Expansion, State and Federal Policy Changes Recommended," National Academies of Sciences, Engineering, and Medicine, May 4, 2021, https://www.nationalacademies.org/news/2021/05/high-quality-primary-care-should-be-available-to-every-individual-in-the-u-s-says-new-report-payment-reform-telehealth-expansion-state-and-federal-policy-changes-recommended.

2. National Association of Community Health Centers, "Closing the Primary Care Gap: How Community Health Centers Address the Nation's Primary Care Crisis," February 2023, https://www.nachc.org/wp-content/uploads/2023/06/Closing-the-Primary-Care-Gap_Full-Report_2023_digital-final.pdf.

3. On lower salaries, see Walter R. Hsiang, Cary P. Gross, Sean Maroongroge, and Howard P. Forman, "Trends in Compensation for Primary Care and Specialist Physicians after Implementation of the Affordable Care Act," *JAMA Network Open* 3, no. 7 (July 28, 2020), https://doi.org/10.1001/jamanetworkopen.2020.11981. On burnout, see J. S. Gerteis, C. Brooker, C. Brach, and J. De La Mare, "Burnout in Primary Care: Assessing and Addressing It in Your Practice," Agency for Healthcare Research and Quality, February 2023, https://

www.ahrq.gov/sites/default/files/wysiwyg/evidencenow/tools-and-materials/burnout-in-primary-care.pdf.

4. On choosing to work in primary care, see Neha Paralkar, Nancy LaVine, Saoirse Ryan, Rosemarie Conigliaro, Jason Ehrlich, Aisha Khan, and Lauren Block, "Career Plans of Internal Medicine Residents from 2019 to 2021," *JAMA Internal Medicine* 183, no. 10 (September 28, 2023): 1166–67, https://doi.org/10.1001/jamainternmed.2023.2873. On quitting, see Ethan Popowitz, "Addressing the Healthcare Staffing Shortage," *Definitive Healthcare*, September 2023, https://www.definitivehc.com/resources/research/healthcare-staffing-shortage.

5. American Hospital Association, "Fast Facts on U.S. Hospitals, 2024," accessed January 30, 2025, https://www.aha.org/statistics/fast-facts-us-hospitals.

6. American Hospital Association, "Hospital-At-Home," accessed January 2, 2025, https://www.aha.org/hospitalathome.

7. Nathaniel Meyersohn, "Why Urgent Care Centers Are Popping up Everywhere," *CNN*, January 28, 2023, https://edition.cnn.com/2023/01/28/business/urgent-care-centers-growth-health-care/index.html.

8. David Hyun and Rachel Zetts, "Antibiotics Are Overprescribed in Urgent Care," Pew Charitable Trusts, July 16, 2018, https://www.pewtrusts.org/en/research-and-analysis/articles/2018/07/16/antibiotics-are-overprescribed-in-urgent-care.

9. Nicolas Shanosky, Daniel McDermott, and Nisha Kurani, "How Do US Healthcare Resources Compare to Other Countries?," Peterson-KFF Health System Tracker, August 12, 2020, https://www.healthsystemtracker.org/chart-collection/u-s-health-care-resources-compare-countries.

10. Melissa E. Cyr, Anna G. Etchin, Barbara J. Guthrie, and James C. Benneyan, "Access to Specialty Healthcare in Urban Versus Rural US Populations: A Systematic Literature Review," *BMC Health Services Research* 19, no. 1 (December 18, 2019), https://doi.org/10.1186/s12913-019-4815-5.

11. For 2016, see Pranav Puri, James A. Yiannias, Aaron R. Mangold, David L. Swanson, and Mark R. Pittelkow, "The Policy Dimensions, Regulatory Landscape, and Market Characteristics of Teledermatology in the United States," *JAAD International* 1, no. 2 (December 2020): 202–7, https://doi.org/10.1016/j.jdin.2020.09.004. For pandemic restrictions, see Peter Elsner, "Teledermatology in the Times of COVID-19—A Systematic Review," *JDDG: Journal Der Deutschen Dermatologischen Gesellschaft* 18, no. 8 (July 27, 2020): 841–45, https://doi.org/10.1111/ddg.14180.

12. Megan Duffy, "Driving Outcomes with Doula Support: Maven's Research on Virtual Doula Care," Maven Clinic, December 6, 2023, https://www.mavenclinic.com/post/virtual-doula-care-research.

13. Kaiser Family Foundation, "Total Number of Medical School Graduates," April 2024, https://www.kff.org/other/state-indicator/total-medical-school-graduates.

14. Robert Rosseter, "Nursing Workforce Fact Sheet," American Association of Colleges of Nursing, April 2024, https://www.aacnnursing.org/news-data/fact-sheets/nursing-workforce-fact-sheet.

15. Chaunie Brusie, "Nurse Practitioner Is the Fastest Growing Profession, 10-Year Predictions Show," *Nurse.org News*, November 14, 2013, https://nurse.org/articles/nurse-practitioner-fastest-growing-profession.

16. Alan M. Adelman and Marie Graybill, "Integrating a Health Coach into Primary Care: Reflections from the Penn State Ambulatory Research Network," *Annals of Family Medicine* 3, no. 2 (July 3, 2005): S33–35, https://doi.org/10.1370/afm.317.

17. Joel Kreisberg and Reggie Marra, "Board-Certified Health Coaches? What Integrative Physicians Need to Know," *Integrative Medicine: A Clinician's Journal* 16, no. 6 (December 2017): 22–24, https://pmc.ncbi.nlm.nih.gov/articles/PMC6438087.

18. Paul Starr, *The Social Transformation of American Medicine. Internet Archive* (Basic Books, 1982).

19. Robert Pear "Doctors Assert There Are Too Many of Them," *New York Times*, March 1, 1997, https://www.nytimes.com/1997/03/01/us/doctors-assert-there-are-too-many-of-them.html.

20. American Medical Association, "AMA Successfully Fights Scope of Practice Expansions That Threaten Patient Safety," May 15, 2023, https://www.ama-assn.org/practice-management/scope-practice/ama-successfully-fights-scope-practice-expansions-threaten.

21. Jonathan Sidhu, "Exploring the AMA's History of Discrimination," *ProPublica*, July 16, 2008, https://www.propublica.org/article/exploring-the-amas-history-of-discrimination-716.

22. Association of American Medical Colleges, "Physician Supply and Demand—a 15-Year Outlook: Key Findings," May 2021, https://www.aamc.org/media/54686/download.

23. Rebecca C. Hendrickson, Roisín A. Slevin, Katherine D. Hoerster, Bernard P. Chang, Ellen Sano, Catherine A. McCall, Gillian R. Monty, Ronald G. Thomas, and Murray A. Raskind, "The Impact of the COVID-19 Pandemic on Mental Health, Occupational Functioning, and Professional Retention Among Health Care Workers and First Responders," *Journal of General Internal Medicine* 37, no. 12 (December 16, 2021): 397–408, https://doi.org/10.1007/s11606-021-07252-z.

24. Melanie Hanson, "Average Cost of Medical School," Education Data Initiative, November 9, 2024, https://educationdata.org/average-cost-of-medical-school.

25. Justin Nabity, "How Much Does Malpractice Insurance Cost?," Physicians Thrive, December 9, 2020, https://physiciansthrive.com/malpractice-insurance/costs.

26. Karolina Kruczaj, Ewa Krawczyk, and Magdalena Piegza, "Medical Malpractice Stress Syndrome in Theory and Practice—a Narrative Review," *Medycyna Pracy* 74, no. 6 (December 29, 2023): 513–26, https://doi.org/10.13075/mp.5893.01425.

27. David Blumenthal, "Private Equity's Role in Health Care," Commonwealth Fund, November 17, 2023, https://doi.org/10.26099/3kcn-8j78.

28. Jake Miller, "What Happens When Private Equity Takes over a Hospital," *Harvard Medical School News and Research*, December 26, 2023, https://hms.harvard.edu/news/what-happens-when-private-equity-takes-over-hospital.

29. Kevin Holloran, "Operating Margins Reset a Potential 'Pain Point' for U.S. NFP Hospitals," *Fitch Ratings*, January 29, 2024, https://www.fitchratings.com/research/us-public-finance/operating-margins-reset-potential-pain-point-for-us-nfp-hospitals-29-01-2024.

30. Bharath Krishnamurthy, "Margin Misconceptions: What Do Break-Even Hospital Margins Mean for Patient Care?," American Hospital Association, August 1, 2023, https://www.aha.org/news/blog/2023-08-01-margin-misconceptions-what-do-break-even-hospital-margins-mean-patient-care.

31. Starr, *Social Transformation*.

32. James Harvey Young, *The Toadstool Millionaires: A Social History of Patent Medicines in America Before Federal Regulation* (Princeton University Press, 1961).

33. On the Hill-Burton Act of 1946, see Health Resources and Services Administration, "Hill-Burton Free and Reduced-Cost Health Care," September 2023, https://www.hrsa.gov/get-health-care/affordable/hill-burton. On new hospital beds see, Andrea Park Chung, Martin Gaynor, and Seth Richards-Shubik, "Subsidies and Structure: The Lasting Impact of the Hill-Burton Program on the Hospital Industry," *Review of Economics and Statistics* 99, no. 5 (February 2016): 1–96, https://doi.org/10.3386/w22037.

34. Alan Condon, "Nearly 80 Percent of Physicians Now Employed by Hospitals, Corporations: 5 Things to Know," *Becker's Hospital Review*, April 11, 2024, https://www.beckershospitalreview.com/hospital-physician-relationships/nearly-80-physicians-now-employed-by-hospitals-corporations-report-finds.html.

35. Elisabeth Rosenthal, "Why Many Nonprofit (Wink, Wink) Hospitals Are Rolling in Money," *KFF Health News*, July 29, 2024, https://kffhealthnews.org/news/article/commentary-nonprofit-hospitals-rolling-in-money.

36. Derek Jenkins and Vivian Ho, "Nonprofit Hospitals: Profits and Cash Reserves Grow, Charity Care Does Not," *Health Affairs* 42, no. 6 (June 5, 2023): 866–69, https://doi.org/10.1377/hlthaff.2022.01542.

37. Jenkins and Ho. "Nonprofit Hospitals."

38. Cory E. Cronin, Berkeley Franz, Kelly Choyke, Vanessa Rodriguez, and Brian K. Gran, "For-Profit Hospitals Have a Unique Opportunity to Serve as

Anchor Institutions in the U.S," *Preventive Medicine Reports* 22 (April 3, 2021): 101372, https://doi.org/10.1016/j.pmedr.2021.101372.

39. Cornell Law School, "Public Benefit Corporation," Legal Information Institute, November 2020, https://www.law.cornell.edu/wex/public_benefit _corporation.

40. Katherine Keisler-Starkey and Lisa N. Bunch, "Health Insurance Coverage in the United States: 2023 Current Population Reports Acknowledgments," US Consensus Bureau. US Government Publishing Office, September 2024, https://www2.census.gov/library/publications/2024/demo/p60-284.pdf.

41. US Bureau of Labor Statistics, "Employee Tenure Summary," September 26, 2024, https://www.bls.gov/news.release/tenure.nro.htm.

42. US Congress, "United States Code: Stabilization Act of 1942, 50a U.S.C. § 968 (Suppl. 1 1946)," Library of Congress, 1946, https://www.loc.gov/item /uscode1946-006050a020.

43. Kaiser Family Foundation, "2023 Employer Health Benefits Survey," October 18, 2023, https://www.kff.org/report-section/ehbs-2023-section-8-high -deductible-health-plans-with-savings-option.

44. Gary Claxton, Matthew Rae, and Aubrey Winger, "Employer-Sponsored Health Insurance 101," Kaiser Family Foundation, May 28, 2024, https://www .kff.org/health-policy-101-employer-sponsored-health-insurance

45. Keisler-Starkey and Bunch, "Health Insurance Coverage in the United States."

46. Elizabeth Hinton and Jada Raphael, "10 Things to Know About Medicaid Managed Care," Kaiser Family Foundation, May 1, 2024, https://www.kff.org /medicaid/issue-brief/10-things-to-know-about-medicaid-managed-care.

47. Interestingly, more and more eligible people have been opting for private Medicare Advantage plans, which are administered by commercial insurers who receive payments from the government for covering Medicare services. In 2023, for the first time ever, more than half of all people eligible for Medicare were enrolled in private Medicare Advantage plans. The reasons behind this trend span from extensive Medicare Advantage marketing to rising Medicare Part D prescription premiums.

48. Jennifer Tolbert, Sammy Cervantes, Clea Bell, and Anthony Damico, "Key Facts about the Uninsured Population," Kaiser Family Foundation, December 18, 2024, https://www.kff.org/uninsured/issue-brief/key-facts-about -the-uninsured-population.

49. Tolbert et al. "Key Facts about the Uninsured Population."

50. Melanie Evans, Anna Wilde Matthews, and Tom MGinty, "Hospitals Often Charge Uninsured People the Highest Prices, New Data Show," *Wall Street Journal*, July 6, 2021, https://www.wsj.com/articles/hospitals-often -charge-uninsured-people-the-highest-prices-new-data-show-11625584448.

51. Keisler-Starkey and Bunch. "Health Insurance Coverage in the United States."

52. Caitlin Owens, "Major Health Insurance Companies Are Nearing Too Big to Fail Status," *Axios*, April 19, 2024, https://www.axios.com/2024/04/19/health-insurance-companies-uhg-aetna-cigna.

53. Centers For Medicare and Medicaid Services, "Medical Loss Ratio," September 10, 2024, https://www.cms.gov/marketplace/private-health-insurance/medical-loss-ratio.

54. Administration for Community Living, "Medical Loss Ratio Tip Sheet," February 2014, https://acl.gov/sites/default/files/programs/2017-03/Medical_Loss_Ratio_Tip_Sheet_Final.pdf.

55. Martha A. Roherty, "The Medical Loss Ratio Has Become a Barrier to Preventive Care," *STAT News*, April 30, 2024, https://www.statnews.com/2024/04/30/medical-loss-ratio-barrier-preventive-care.

56. Anne Somers Hogg, "Is the Medical Loss Ratio an Innovation Friend or Foe?," Christensen Institute, August 20, 2024, https://www.christenseninstitute.org/blog/is-the-medical-loss-ratio-an-innovation-friend-or-foe.

57. Karen Pollitz and Kaye Pestaina, "Could Consumer Assistance Be Helpful to People Facing Medical Debt?," Kaiser Family Foundation, July 14, 2022, https://www.kff.org/policy-watch/could-consumer-assistance-be-helpful-to-people-facing-medical-debt.

58. US Department of Health and Human Services, "Medicare and Medicaid Programs; Patient Protection and Affordable Care Act; Interoperability and Patient Access for Medicare Advantage Organization and Medicaid Managed Care Plans, State Medicaid Agencies, CHIP Agencies and CHIP Managed Care Entities, Issuers of Qualified Health Plans on the Federally—Facilitated Exchanges, and Health Care Providers," Federal Register—Rules and Regulations 85, no. 85 (May 1, 2020), https://www.govinfo.gov/content/pkg/FR-2020-05-01/pdf/2020-05050.pdf.

59. Jeff Lagasse, Jeff. ", "More than Half of Healthcare Consumers Not Fully Satisfied with Their Insurance."," *Healthcare Finance News*, August 18, 2023. https, https://www.healthcarefinancenews.com/news/more-half-healthcare-consumers-not-fully-satisfied-their-insurance.

60. Casey Ross and Bob Herman, "Denied by AI: How Medicare Advantage Plans Use Algorithms to Cut off Care for Seniors in Need," *STAT News*, March 13, 2023, https://www.statnews.com/2023/03/13/medicare-advantage-plans-denial-artificial-intelligence.

61. Katherine Smith, "A (Brief) History of Health Policy in the United States," *Delaware Journal of Public Health* 9, no. 5 (December 31, 2023): 6–10, https://doi.org/10.32481/djph.2023.12.003.

62. Jeffery St. Onge, "Operation Coffeecup: Ronald Reagan, Rugged Individualism, and the Debate Over 'Socialized Medicine,'" *Rhetoric and Public Affairs* 20, no. 2 (June 1, 2017): 223–52, https://doi.org/10.14321/rhetpublaffa.20.2.0223.

63. National Archives, "Medicare and Medicaid Act (1965)," February 8, 2022, https://www.archives.gov/milestone-documents/medicare-and-medicaid-act.

64. Susan Morse, "25 Biggest Provider-Sponsored Health Plans Include Some of the Nation's Biggest Systems," *Healthcare Finance News*, September 13, 2016, https://www.healthcarefinancenews.com/news/25-biggest-provider -sponsored-health-plans-include-some-nations-biggest-systems.

65. John McCormick, "Best health insurance companies of 2024," Insure.com, October 21, 2024, https://www.insure.com/best-health-insurance-companies.

66. Ashley Kirzinger, Alex Montero, Grace Sparks, Isabelle Valdes, and Liz Hamel, "Public Opinion on Prescription Drugs and Their Prices," Kaiser Family Foundation, October 4, 2024, https://www.kff.org/health-costs/poll-finding /public-opinion-on-prescription-drugs-and-their-prices.

67. Eric M. Tichy, James M. Hoffman, Mina Tadrous, Matthew H. Rim, Sandra Cuellar, John S. Clark, Mary Kate Newell, and Glen T. Schumock, "National Trends in Prescription Drug Expenditures and Projections for 2024," *American Journal of Health-System Pharmacy* 81, no. 14 (July 15, 2024): 583–98, https://doi .org/10.1093/ajhp/zxae105.

68. Lucas A. Berenbrok, Shangbin Tang, Nico Gabriel, Jingchuan Guo, Nasser Sharareh, Nimish Patel, Sean Dickson, and Inmaculada Hernandez, "Access to Community Pharmacies: A Nationwide Geographic Information Systems Cross-Sectional Analysis," *Journal of the American Pharmacists Association* 62, no. 6 (July 7, 2022): 1816–22, https://doi.org/10.1016/j.japh.2022.07.003.

69. Paula Forbes, "The Closest Starbucks Is Never More Than 170 Miles Away," *Eater*, October 4, 2012, https://www.eater.com/2012/10/4/6538669/the -closest-starbucks-is-never-more-than-170-miles-away.

70. On birth control, see Guttmacher Institute, "Pharmacist-Prescribed Contraceptives," November 8, 2024, https://www.guttmacher.org/state-policy /explore/pharmacist-prescribed-contraceptives. On COVID-19 treatments, see Rubin, Rita, "Pharmacists Allowed to Prescribe COVID-19 Antiviral," *JAMA* 328, no. 7 (August 16, 2022): 612, https://doi.org/10.1001/jama.2022.13679.

71. On burnout, see Dee, Jodie, Nabaa Dhuhaibawi, and John C. Hayden, "A Systematic Review and Pooled Prevalence of Burnout in Pharmacists," *International Journal of Clinical Pharmacy* 45, no. 1 (November 29, 2022): 1027–36, https:// doi.org/10.1007/s11096-022-01520-6. Many pharmacists are leaving retail settings for clinical roles in hospitals and healthcare systems, where they can focus more on direct patient care and less on meeting corporate performance metrics.

72. Sriparna Roy, "US Pharmacy Chain Rite Aid to Operate as a Private Company as It Emerges from Bankruptcy," *Reuters*, September 4, 2024, https:// www.reuters.com/business/healthcare-pharmaceuticals/rite-aid-operate -private-company-it-emerges-chapter-11-bankruptcy-2024-09-03.

73. On Walgreens, see Alina Selyukh, "CVS and Walgreens Are Ailing: Here's Why," *NPR*, October 16, 2024, https://www.npr.org/2024/10/16/nx-s1-5154129/

cvs-and-walgreens-closing-stores-why. On CVS, see Marcos, Coral Murphy, "CVS Will Close 900 Stores as It Looks Beyond Traditional Pharmacies," *New York Times*, November 18, 2021, sec. Business, https://www.nytimes .com/2021/11/18/business/cvs-store-closures.html.

74. Rachel Wittenauer, Parth D Shah, Jennifer L Bacci, and Andy Stergachis, "Locations and Characteristics of Pharmacy Deserts in the United States: A Geospatial Study," *Health Affairs Scholar* 2, no. 4 (March 16, 2024), https://doi .org/10.1093/haschl/qxae035.

75. T. Joseph Mattingly, II, David A. Hyman, and Ge Bai, "Pharmacy Benefit Managers: History, Business Practices, Economics, and Policy," *JAMA Health Forum* 4, no. 11 (November 3, 2023), https://doi.org/10.1001/jamahealthforum.2023.3804.

76. Matthew Fiedler, Loren Adler, and Richard G. Frank, "A Brief Look at Current Debates about Pharmacy Benefit Managers," Brookings Institution, September 7, 2023, https://www.brookings.edu/articles/a-brief-look-at -current-debates-about-pharmacy-benefit-managers.

77. US Federal Trade Commission, "Pharmacy Benefit Managers: The Powerful Middlemen Inflating Drug Costs and Squeezing Main Street Pharmacies Interim Staff Report," *Office of Policy Planning*, July 2024, https://www.ftc.gov /system/files/ftc_gov/pdf/pharmacy-benefit-managers-staff-report.pdf.

78. US Federal Trade Commission, "Pharmacy Benefit Managers."

79. Matthew Cunningham-Cook, "The PBM-Insurer Mafia Comes for Community Pharmacies," *Health Care Un-covered*, March 20, 2024, https:// healthcareuncovered.substack.com/p/the-pbm-insurer-mafia-comes-for -community.

80. The Biden White House, "Roundtable on Lowering Healthcare Costs and Bringing Transparency to Prescription Drug Middlemen," YouTube, March 4, 2024, https://www.youtube.com/watch?v=DiA6hAslOFg.

81. "Behind the Counter Video Series," *STAT News*, accessed November 4, 2024, https://www.statnews.com/behind-the-counter-video-series-high-drug -prices.

82. Elizabeth Seeley, "The Impact of Pharmaceutical Wholesalers on U.S. Drug Spending," Commonwealth Fund, July 20, 2022, https://www .commonwealthfund.org/publications/issue-briefs/2022/jul/impact-pharmaceutical -wholesalers-drug-spending.

83. Seeley, "The Impact of Pharmaceutical Wholesalers on U.S. Drug Spending."

84. Fangjun Zhou, Tara C. Jatlaoui, Andrew J. Leidner, Rosalind J. Carter, Xiaoyu Dong, Jeanne M. Santoli, Shannon Stokley, Demetre C. Daskalakis, and Georgina Peacock, "Health and Economic Benefits of Routine Childhood Immunizations in the Era of the Vaccines for Children Program—United States, 1994–2023," *MMWR Morbidity and Mortality Weekly Report* 73, no. 31 (August 8, 2024): 682–85, https://doi.org/10.15585/mmwr.mm7331a2.

85. Frank R. Lichtenberg, "The Effect of Pharmaceutical Innovation on Longevity: Evidence from the U.S. and 26 High-Income Countries," *Economics and Human Biology* 46 (August 2022): 101124, https://doi.org/10.1016/j.ehb.2022.101124.

86. Duxin Sun, Wei Gao, Hongxiang Hu, and Simon Zhou, "Why 90 Percent of Clinical Drug Development Fails and How to Improve It?," *Acta Pharmaceutica Sinica B* 12, no. 7 (February 11, 2022): 3049–62, https://doi.org/10.1016/j.apsb.2022.02.002.

87. Fred Ledley, Ekaterina Cleary, and Matthew Jackson, "US Tax Dollars Funded Every New Pharmaceutical in the Last Decade," Institute for New Economic Thinking, September 2, 2020, https://www.ineteconomics.org/perspectives/blog/us-tax-dollars-funded-every-new-pharmaceutical-in-the-last-decade.

88. Mulcahy, Andrew W, "Prescription Drug Prices in the United States Are 2.56 Times Those in Other Countries," RAND, January 28, 2021, https://www.rand.org/news/press/2021/01/28.html. These higher prices are driven by brand-name drugs; for generic drugs, we pay less than other countries.

89. European Medicines Agency, "The European Regulatory System for Medicines," Luxembourg: The Publications Office of the European Union, 2023, https://www.ema.europa.eu/en/documents/leaflet/european-regulatory-system-medicines_en.pdf.

90. Patented Medicine Prices Review Board, "About the PMPRB," accessed January 30, 2025, https://pmprb-cepmb.gc.ca.

91. Peter Kolchinsky, *The Great American Drug Deal: A New Prescription for Innovative and Affordable Medicines* (Encounter Books, 2020).

92. Neeraj Sood, "Flow of Money through the Pharmaceutical Distribution System," USC Leonard D. Schaeffer Center for Health Policy & Economics, June 6, 2017, https://healthpolicy.usc.edu/research/flow-of-money-through-the-pharmaceutical-distribution-system.

93. Alexander Schuhmacher, Markus Hinder, Nikolaj Boger, Dominik Hartl, and Oliver Gassmann, "The Significance of Blockbusters in the Pharmaceutical Industry," *Nature Reviews Drug Discovery*, December 12, 2022, https://doi.org/10.1038/d41573-022-00213-z.

94. "AI's Potential to Accelerate Drug Discovery Needs a Reality Check," *Nature*, October 10, 2023, https://www.nature.com/articles/d41586-023-03172-6.

95. Jeffrey M. Jones, "Grocery, Restaurant Industry Images Slide in U.S.," Gallup, September 12, 2024, https://news.gallup.com/poll/650318/grocery-restaurant-industry-images-slide.aspx.

96. Sriparna Roy and Jahnavi Nidumolu, "Nasal Spray Alternative to EpiPen Faces Setback as FDA Seeks Fresh Study," *Reuters*, September 20, 2023, https://www.reuters.com/business/healthcare-pharmaceuticals/us-fda-declines-approve-ars-emergency-nasal-spray-allergic-reactions-2023-09-20.

97. US Food and Drug Administration, "Counterfeit Medicine," May 15, 2024, https://www.fda.gov/drugs/buying-using-medicine-safely/counterfeit-medicine.

98. World Health Organization, "Substandard and Falsified Medical Products," January 31, 2018, https://www.who.int/news-room/fact-sheets/detail/substandard-and-falsified-medical-products.

99. US Capitol Visitor Center, "The Pure Food and Drug Act," accessed January 30, 2025, https://www.visitthecapitol.gov/exhibitions/congress-and-progressive-era/pure-food-and-drug-act.

100. Robert Gaynes, "The Discovery of Penicillin—New Insights after More than 75 Years of Clinical Use," *Emerging Infectious Diseases* 23, no. 5 (May 23, 2017): 849–53, https://doi.org/10.3201/eid2305.161556.

101. Michelle Meadows, "Promoting Safe and Effective Drugs for 100 Years," U.S Food and Drug Administration, 2006, https://www.fda.gov/files/Promoting-Safe-and-Effective-Drugs-for-100-Years-%28download%29.pdf.

102. On the cost of bringing a new drug to market, see Aylin Sertkaya, Trinidad Beleche, Amber Jessup, and Benjamin D. Sommers, "Costs of Drug Development and Research and Development Intensity in the US, 2000–2018," *JAMA Network Open* 7, no. 6 (June 28, 2024), https://doi.org/10.1001/jamanetworkopen.2024.15445. On the time it takes, see Bernard Lo and Marilyn J. Field, *The Pathway from Idea to Regulatory Approval: Examples for Drug Development* (National Library of Medicine, National Academies Press, 2009), https://www.ncbi.nlm.nih.gov/books/NBK22930.

103. Goshen David Miteu, "Patenting: The Bayh–Dole Act and Its Transformative Impact on Science Innovation and Commercialization," *Annals of Medicine and Surgery* 86, no. 6 (April 15, 2024): 3192–95, https://doi.org/10.1097/ms9.0000000000002047.

104. Bayh-Dole Coalition, "New Coalition Launches to Celebrate and Protect the Bayh-Dole Act—the Bayh-Dole Coalition," February 19, 2020, https://bayhdolecoalition.org/new-coalition-launches-to-celebrate-and-protect-the-bayh-dole-act.

105. US Food and Drug Administration, "Hatch-Waxman Letters," Abbreviated New Drug Application, February 3, 2022, https://www.fda.gov/drugs/abbreviated-new-drug-application-anda/hatch-waxman-letters.

106. Alfred Engelberg, "Unaffordable Prescription Drugs: The Real Legacy of the Hatch-Waxman Act," *STAT News*, December 16, 2020, https://www.statnews.com/2020/12/16/unaffordable-prescription-drugs-real-legacy-hatch-waxman-act.

107. Mattingly et al., "Pharmacy Benefit Managers."

108. Andy Coghlan, "Blockbuster Challenge," *New Scientist*, June 12, 2004, https://www.newscientist.com/article/mg18224515-800-blockbuster-challenge.

109. Julie Donohue, "A History of Drug Advertising: The Evolving Roles of Consumers and Consumer Protection," *Milbank Quarterly* 84, no. 4 (December 2006): 659–99, https://doi.org/10.1111/j.1468-0009.2006.00464.x.

110. Ben Adams, "The Top 10 Pharma Drug Ad Spenders for 2022," *Fierce Pharma*, May 1, 2023, https://www.fiercepharma.com/special-reports/top-10 -pharma-drug-brand-ad-spenders-2022.

3. HEALTHCARE'S SLEEPING GIANT

1. "Failure to thrive" is a controversial diagnosis to describe a decline in physical, cognitive, and functional abilities in adults. Critics argue this term may be used as a shortcut to suggest social rather than medical reasons for hospital admission. Regardless of intent, such labels can be harmful and are associated with delays in care.

2. Malay Gandhi and Teresa Wang, "Digital Health Consumer Adoption: 2015," Rock Health, October 19, 2015, https://rockhealth.com/insights/digital -health-consumer-adoption-2015.

3. Shaun Callaghan, Martin Losch, Anna Pione, and Warren Teichner, "Feeling Good: The Future of the $1.5 Trillion Wellness Market," McKinsey and Company, April 8, 2021, https://www.mckinsey.com/industries/consumer -packaged-goods/our-insights/feeling-good-the-future-of-the-1-5-trillion -wellness-market.

4. National Academies of Sciences, "Factors That Affect Health-Care Utilization," *Health-Care Utilization as a Proxy in Disability Determination* (National Academies Press, 2018), https://www.ncbi.nlm.nih.gov/books/NBK500097.

5. Lunna Lopes, Alex Montero, Marley Presiado, and Liz Hamel, "Americans' Challenges with Health Care Costs," Kaiser Family Foundation, March 1, 2024, https://www.kff.org/health-costs/issue-brief/americans-challenges-with -health-care-costs.

6. National Association of Community Health Centers. "Closing the Primary Care Gap: How Community Health Centers Address the Nation's Primary Care Crisis," February 2023, https://www.nachc.org/wp-content/uploads/2023/06 /Closing-the-Primary-Care-Gap_Full-Report_2023_digital-final.pdf.

7. Rabia Shahid, Muhammad Shoker, Luan Manh Chu, Ryan Frehlick, Heather Ward, and Punam Pahwa, "Impact of Low Health Literacy on Patients' Health Outcomes: A Multicenter Cohort Study," *BMC Health Services Research* 22, no. 1 (September 12, 2022), https://doi.org/10.1186/s12913-022-08527-9.

8. Michael Darden and Mario Macis, "Trust and Health Care-Seeking Behavior," National Bureau of Economic Research, January 2024, https://doi .org/10.3386/w32028.

9. Michael A. Jaeb and Kristen E. Pecanac, "Shame in Patient-Health Professional Encounters: A Scoping Review," *International Journal of Mental Health Nursing* 33, no. 5 (March 18, 2024): 1158–69, https://doi.org/10.1111/inm.13323.

10. Rebecca J. Schwei, Timothy P. Johnson, Alicia K. Matthews, and Elizabeth A. Jacobs, "Perceptions of Negative Health-Care Experiences and Self-Reported Health Behavior Change in Three Racial and Ethnic Groups," *Ethnicity and Health* 22, no. 2 (October 17, 2016): 156–68, https://doi.org/10.1080/13557858.2016.1244621.

11. On better outcomes, see Centers for Disease Control and Prevention, "Patient Engagement," June 21, 2024, https://www.cdc.gov/health-literacy/php/research-summaries/patient-engagement.html. On higher satisfaction, see Sima Marzban, Marziye Najafi, Arjola Agolli, and Ensieh Ashrafi, "Impact of Patient Engagement on Healthcare Quality: A Scoping Review," *Journal of Patient Experience* 9, no. 23743735221125439 (September 16, 2022), https://doi.org/10.1177/23743735221125439.

12. Centers for Disease Control and Prevention, "Up to 40 Percent of Annual Deaths from Each of Five Leading US Causes Are Preventable," *CDC Newsroom*, May 1, 2014, https://archive.cdc.gov/www_cdc_gov/media/releases/2014/p0501-preventable-deaths.html.

13. Michele Peters, Caroline M. Potter, Laura Kelly, and Ray Fitzpatrick, "Self-Efficacy and Health-Related Quality of Life: A Cross-Sectional Study of Primary Care Patients with Multi-Morbidity," *Health and Quality of Life Outcomes* 17, no. 37 (February 14, 2019), https://doi.org/10.1186/s12955-019-1103-3.

14. Garrett R. Beeler Asay, Kakoli Roy, Jason E. Lang, Rebecca L. Payne, and David H. Howard, "Absenteeism and Employer Costs Associated with Chronic Diseases and Health Risk Factors in the US Workforce," *Preventing Chronic Disease* 13, no. 150503 (October 6, 2016), https://doi.org/10.5888/pcd13.150503.

15. Fred Kleinsinger, "The Unmet Challenge of Medication Nonadherence," *Permanente Journal* 22, no. 18-033 (July 5, 2018), https://doi.org/10.7812/tpp/18-033.

16. Dr. Darrin Menard, interview by Halle Tecco, October 2024.

17. Open Secrets, "Ranked Sectors," October 24, 2024, https://www.opensecrets.org/federal-lobbying/ranked-sectors?cycle=2023.

18. Matthew Hill, Gary Wayne Kelly, Brandon Lockhart, and Robert A. Van Ness, "Determinants and Effects of Corporate Lobbying," *Financial Management* (June 16, 2009), http://dx.doi.org/10.2139/ssrn.1420224.

19. Open Secrets, "Data on Campaign Finance, Super Pacs, Industries, and Lobbying," 2024, https://www.opensecrets.org.

20. On state tax dollars, see National Association of State Budget Officers, "2024 State Expenditure Report," 2024, https://www.nasbo.org/reports-data/state-expenditure-report. On federal tax dollars, see Center on

Budget and Policy Priorities, "Policy Basics: Where Do Our Federal Tax Dollars Go?," July 18, 2024, https://www.cbpp.org/research/federal-budget/where-do-our-federal-tax-dollars-go.

21. Jacqueline A. Fiore, Andrew J. Madison, John A. Poisal, Gigi A. Cuckler, Sheila D. Smith, Andrea M. Sisko, Sean P. Keehan, Kathryn E. Rennie, and Alyssa C. Gross, "National Health Expenditure Projections, 2023–32: Payer Trends Diverge as Pandemic-Related Policies Fade," *Health Affairs* 43, no. 7 (June 12, 2024), https://doi.org/10.1377/hlthaff.2024.00469.

22. Rachel Effros, "Analysis of High Deductible Health Plans," RAND, October 12, 2009, https://www.rand.org/pubs/technical_reports/TR562z4/analysis-of-high-deductible-health-plans.html.

23. Kaiser Family Foundation, "2024 Employer Health Benefits Survey," July 13, 2025, https://www.kff.org/report-section/ehbs-2024-section-8-high-deductible-health-plans-with-savings-option/.

24. Amy Lotven, "Individual Coverage HRAs Gaining Momentum, Reports Say," HRA Council, August 10, 2023, https://hracouncil.org/news/13241739.

25. Noah Tong, "Oscar Health Growth Ambitions: Doubled Footprint, Planned ICHRA Products Launch and More," *Fierce Healthcare*, June 7, 2024, https://www.fiercehealthcare.com/payers/oscar-health-growth-ambitions-doubling-its-footprint-planned-ichra-products-launch-and-more.

26. Steve Maas, "The Impact of High Deductibles on Health Care Spending," *The Digest*, National Bureau of Economic Research, December 1, 2015, https://www.nber.org/digest/dec15/impact-high-deductibles-health-care-spending.

27. Press Ganey, "Consumer Experience in Healthcare," 2025, https://info.pressganey.com/e-books-research/cx-report#main-content.

28. Karen Pollitz, Kaye Pestaina, Lunna Lopes, Rayna Wallace, and Justin Lo Published, "Consumer Survey Highlights Problems with Denied Health Insurance Claims," Kaiser Family Foundation, September 29, 2023, https://www.kff.org/affordable-care-act/issue-brief/consumer-survey-highlights-problems-with-denied-health-insurance-claims.

29. American Society of Anesthesiologists, "Anthem Blue Cross Blue Shield Won't Pay for the Complete Duration of Anesthesia for Patients' Surgical Procedures," *ASA News*, November 14, 2024, https://www.asahq.org/about-asa/newsroom/news-releases/2024/11/anthem-blue-cross-blue-shield-will-not-pay-complete-duration-of-anesthesia-for-surgical-procedures.

30. On Johnson & Johnson, see Daniel Wiessner, "J&J Faces Class Action over Employees' Prescription Drug Costs," *Reuters*, February 6, 2024, https://www.reuters.com/legal/litigation/jj-faces-class-action-over-employees-prescription-drug-costs-2024-02-05. On Wells Fargo, Daniel Wiessner, "Wells Fargo Sued Over Employee Prescription Drug Costs," *Reuters*, July 30, 2024, https://www.reuters.com/legal/wells-fargo-sued-over-employee-prescription-drug-costs-2024-07-30.

31. Kaiser Family Foundation, "2024 Employer Health Benefits Survey."

32. Matthew McGough, Emma Wagner, Aubrey Winger, Nirmita Panchal, and Lynne Cotter, "How Has U.S. Spending on Healthcare Changed Over Time?," Peterson-KFF Health System Tracker, December 20, 2024, https://www .healthsystemtracker.org/chart-collection/u-s-spending-healthcare-changed-time.

33. On federal tax dollars, Emily Wielk and Rachel Snyderman, "It's Officially Tax Season: Do You Know Where Your Federal Tax Dollars Go?," *Bipartisan Policy Center* (blog), January 31, 2024, https://bipartisanpolicy.org/blog /do-you-know-where-your-tax-dollars-go-tr. On state tax dollars, see National Association of State Budget Officers, "2024 State Expenditure Report," 2024, https://www.nasbo.org/reports-data/state-expenditure-report.

34. RAND Corporation, "Burden of Health Care Payments Is Greatest Among Americans with the Lowest Incomes," RAND, January 27, 2020, https:// www.rand.org/news/press/2020/01/27.html.

35. Seema Verma, "Empowered Patients Are the Future of Health Care," The White House, May 3, 2018, https://trumpwhitehouse.archives.gov/articles /empowered-patients-future-health-care.

36. Jessica Buchter, Jenny Cordina, and Jillian Eckroate, "Consumers Rule: Driving Healthcare Growth with a Consumer-Led Strategy," McKinsey and Company, April 15, 2024, https://www.mckinsey.com/industries/healthcare/our -insights/consumers-rule-driving-healthcare-growth-with-a-consumer-led-strategy.

37. Collective Health, "Collective Health Cuts Healthcare Cost Trend by 50 Percent for Studied Customers," *Collective Health* (blog), June 2, 2023, https://collectivehealth.com/blog/under-the-hood/collective-health-cuts -healthcare-cost-trend.

38. On mail-in DNA tests, see Taylor Orth, "DNA Tests: Many Americans Report Surprises and New Connections," YouGov, February 24, 2022, https:// today.yougov.com/society/articles/41232-dna-tests-many-americans-report- surprises-and-new-. On health-tracking devices, see Madelyn Knowles, Sari Kaganoff, and Adriana Krasniansky, "Screenagers to Silver Surfers: How each generation clicks with care," Rock Health, March 17, 2025, https://rockhealth.com /insights/screenagers-to-silver-surfers-how-each-generation-clicks-with-care/.

39. Louise Wylie, "Health App Revenue and Usage Statistics (2023)," Business of Apps, accessed September 30, 2024, https://www.businessofapps.com /data/health-app-market.

4. WHAT DOES INNOVATION LOOK LIKE?

1. GoodRx, "What's the Deal with GoodRx? FAQs from Pharmacy Staff," May 27, 2021, https://www.goodrx.com/corporate/business/faqs-from-pharmacy -professionals.

2. Warby Parker, "The Whole Story Begins with You," accessed December 18, 2024, https://www.warbyparker.com/buy-a-pair-give-a-pair.

3. Centers for Medicare and Medicaid Services, "NHE Fact Sheet," December 18, 2024, https://www.cms.gov/data-research/statistics-trends-and-reports/national-health-expenditure-data/nhe-fact-sheet.

4. Steve Kraus, host, *The Heart of Healthcare*, podcast, "Lessons from an $11B Healthcare Exit," Massively Better Healthcare, February 24, 2025, https://art19.com/shows/the-heart-of-healthcare/episodes/5fe90515-8583-493b-82fd-552fde276195.

5. Anna M. Roth and Thomas H. Lee, "Health Care Needs Less Innovation and More Imitation," *Harvard Business Review*, November 19, 2014, https://hbr.org/2014/11/health-care-needs-less-innovation-and-more-imitation.

5. WHERE DOES INNOVATION COME FROM?

1. Wikipedia, s.v., "COVID Tracking Project," accessed November 7, 2024, https://en.wikipedia.org/wiki/COVID_Tracking_Project.

2. Anita Williams Woolley, Ishani Aggarwal, and Thomas W. Malone, "Collective Intelligence and Group Performance," *Current Directions in Psychological Science* 24, no. 6 (2015): 420–24, https://www.jstor.org/stable/44318880.

3. Francesco D'Acunto, Geoffrey A. Tate, and Liu Yang, "Entrepreneurial Teams: Diversity of Skills and Early-Stage Growth," Center for Economic Studies, U.S. Census Bureau, November 20, 2020, http://dx.doi.org/10.2139/ssrn.3750982.

4. Pierre Azoulay, Benjamin F. Jones, Daniel Kim, and Jaier Miranda, "Research: The Average Age of a Successful Startup Founder Is 45," *Harvard Business Review*, July 11, 2018, https://hbr.org/2018/07/research-the-average-age-of-a-successful-startup-founder-is-45.

5. Melissa Lee, "3 Ways Tidepool Has Made Change Happen," *Tidepool* (blog), October 13, 2020, https://www.tidepool.org/blog/3-ways-tidepool-has-made-change-happen-in-diabetes.

6. Kim Parker, "About a Third of U.S. Workers Who Can Work from Home Now Do So All the Time," Pew Research Center, March 30, 2023, https://www.pewresearch.org/short-reads/2023/03/30/about-a-third-of-us-workers-who-can-work-from-home-do-so-all-the-time.

7. Kevin Dowd, "Mapping VC Activity: Texas Gains Ground in Q1, but California Still Reigns," Carta, May 23, 2023, https://carta.com/data/venture-shifts-california-texas.

8. Susan Hsu, Collin Anderson, and Kyle Stanford, "Capital Concentration and Its Effect on the VC Ecosystem," PitchBook, February 16, 2023, https://files.pitchbook.com/website/files/pdf/Q1_2023_PitchBook_Analyst_Note_Capital_Concentration_and_Its_Effect_on_the_VC_Ecosystem.pdf.

9. Jacqueline A. Fiore, Andrew J. Madison, John A. Poisal, Gigi A. Cuckler, Sheila D. Smith, Andrea M. Sisko, Sean P. Keehan, Kathryn E. Rennie, and Alyssa C. Gross, "National Health Expenditure Projections, 2023–32: Payer Trends Diverge as Pandemic-Related Policies Fade," *Health Affairs* 43, no. 7 (June 12, 2024), https://doi.org/10.1377/hlthaff.2024.00469.

10. Laura Medford-Davis, Rupal Malani, Chelsea Snipes, and Pieter Du Plessis, "The Physician Shortage Isn't Going Anywhere," McKinsey and Company, September 10, 2024, https://www.mckinsey.com/industries/healthcare /our-insights/the-physician-shortage-isnt-going-anywhere.

11. Lisa M. Haddad, Tammy J. Toney-Butler, and Pavan Annamaraju, "Nursing Shortage," National Library of Medicine, February 13, 2023, https:// www.ncbi.nlm.nih.gov/books/NBK493175.

12. Tom Murphy, "Pharmacist Shortages and Heavy Workloads Challenge Drugstores Heading into Their Busy Season," *AP News*, October 7, 2023, https://apnews.com/article/cvs-walgreens-pharmacists-drug-shortages -c7a94430a2c9d11779a684c2bcfc4c2c.

13. Health Care Payment Learning and Action Network, "Our Work," accessed December 1, 2024, https://hcp-lan.org.

14. Meghan Gabriel, Tricia Lee Rolle, and Chelsea Richwine, "A Decade of Data Examined: The Evolution of Electronic Prescribing," *Health IT Buzz*, July 15, 2024, https://www.healthit.gov/buzz-blog/health-data/a-decade-of-data-examined -the-evolution-of-electronic-prescribing.

15. Kate E. Trout, Li-Wu Chen, Fernando A. Wilson, Hyo Jung Tak, and David Palm, "The Impact of Meaningful Use and Electronic Health Records on Hospital Patient Safety," *International Journal of Environmental Research and Public Health* 19, no. 19 (September 30, 2022), https://doi.org/10.3390/ijerph191912525.

16. Assistant Secretary for Technology Policy, "Information Blocking," HealthIT.gov, 2024, https://www.healthit.gov/topic/information-blocking.

17. Pew Research Center, "Internet/Broadband Fact Sheet," November 13, 2024, https://www.pewresearch.org/internet/fact-sheet/internet-broadband.

18. Federal Communications Commission, "Studies and Data Analytics on Broadband and Health," January 16, 2024, https://www.fcc.gov/health/sdoh /studies-and-data-analytics.

19. Risa Gelles-Watnick, "Americans' Use of Mobile Technology and Home Broadband," Pew Research Center, January 31, 2024, https://www .pewresearch.org/internet/2024/01/31/americans-use-of-mobile-technology -and-home-broadband.

20. Emily Mullin, "The Era of Fast, Cheap Genome Sequencing Is Here," *Wired*, September 29, 2022, https://www.wired.com/story/the-era-of-fast-cheap -genome-sequencing-is-here.

21. Ashwini Nagappan, Madelyn Knowles, and Adriana Krasniansky, "Put a Ring on It: Understanding Consumers' Year-Over-Year Wearable Adoption

Patterns," *Rock Health*, August 5, 2024, https://rockhealth.com/insights/put-a-ring
-on-it-understanding-consumers-year-over-year-wearable-adoption-patterns/.

22. Art Markman, "Test Yourself to Learn Better," *Psychology Today*,
August 23, 2011, https://www.psychologytoday.com/us/blog/ulterior-motives
/201108/test-yourself-learn-better.

23. CVS Health, "CVS Health to Acquire Signify Health," September 5,
2022, https://www.cvshealth.com/news/company-news/cvs-health-to-acquire
-signify-health.html.

6. HEALTHCARE IS HARD, SO MAKE HARD YOUR MOAT

1. Zoë Slote Morris, Steven Wooding, and Jonathan Grant, "The Answer
Is 17 Years, What Is the Question: Understanding Time Lags in Translational
Research," *Journal of the Royal Society of Medicine* 104, no. 12 (December 2011):
510–20, https://doi.org/10.1258/jrsm.2011.110180.

2. James B. Rebitzer and Robert S, Rebitzer, *Why Not Better and Cheaper?*
(Oxford University Press, 2023).

3. Bureau of Labor Statistics, "Employee Tenure in 2024," Washington,
DC: US Department of Labor, September 26, 2022, https://www.bls.gov/news
.release/pdf/tenure.pdf.

4. All-In Podcast, "All-in Summit: Bill Gurley Presents 2,851 Miles," YouTube,
September 15, 2023, https://www.youtube.com/watch?v=F9cO3-MLHOM.

5. Matthew D. Mitchell, "Certificate of Need Laws in Health Care: Past,
Present, and Future," *Inquiry* 61 (May 10, 2024), https://doi.org/10.1177
/00469580241251937.

6. Sergei Polevikov, "Please Help Me Fix American Healthcare," *AI Healthcare Uncut* (blog), June 25, 2024, https://sergeiai.substack.com/p/please-help
-me-fix-american-healthcare.

7. Catherine Ho, "Kaiser Nurses Protest Use of AI That Could Put Patient
Safety at Risk," *San Francisco Chronicle*, April 22, 2024, https://www.sfchronicle
.com/health/article/kaiser-nurses-protest-use-ai-put-patient-safety-19412379.php.

8. Basavana Gouda Goudra et al, "SEDASYS[®], Airway, Oxygenation, and
Ventilation: Anticipating and Managing the Challenges," *Digestive Diseases and
Sciences* 59, no. 5 (2014): 920–27, doi:10.1007/s10620-013-2996-z.

9. Todd C. Frankel, "New Machine Could One Day Replace Anesthesiologists," *Washington Post*, May 11, 2015, https://www.washingtonpost.com
/business/economy/new-machine-could-one-day-replace-anesthesiologists
/2015/05/11/92e8a42c-f424-11e4-b2f3-af5479e6bbdd_story.html.

10. Tom Simonite, "Automated Anesthesiologist Suffers a Painful Defeat,"
MIT Technology Review, March 29, 2016, https://www.technologyreview.com/2016
/03/29/161269/automated-anesthesiologist-suffers-a-painful-defeat.

11. LTV/CAC compares how much a customer spends over time (lifetime value) to the cost of acquiring them as a customer (customer acquisition cost). A higher ratio means you're making more money from customers than it costs to acquire them. Also see Sofia Guerra and Steve Kraus, "State of Health Tech 2023," Bessemer Venture Partners, October 9, 2023, https://www.bvp.com /atlas/state-of-health-tech-2023.

7. WHEN INNOVATION FAILS

1. Sarah Buhr, "UBiome Is Jumping into Therapeutics with a Healthy $83 Million in Series C Financing" *TechCrunch*, September 21, 2018, https:// techcrunch.com/2018/09/21/ubiome-is-jumping-into-therapeutics-with-a -healthy-83-million-in-series-c-financing.

2. Fast Company, "The World's Most Innovative Companies 2018: Data Science Honorees," accessed January 5, 2025, https://www.fastcompany.com /most-innovative-companies/2018/sectors/data-science.

3. United States Attorney's Office, "UBiome Co-Founders Charged with Federal Securities, Health Care Fraud Conspiracies," U.S Department of Justice, Northern District of California, March 18, 2021, https://www.justice.gov /usao-ndca/pr/ubiome-co-founders-charged-federal-securities-health-care -fraud-conspiracies.

4. Synapse, "From UCSF Start-up to Fugitives from Justice," *UCSF Synapse*, February 28, 2022, https://synapse.ucsf.edu/articles/2022/02/28/ucsf-start-fugitives -justice.

5. David Vatchev, "How to Be in the 10 percent, When 90 Percent of Start-ups Fail," *Startups Magazine*, accessed January 5, 2025, https://startupsmagazine .co.uk/article-how-be-10-when-90-startups-fail.

6. U.S. Department of Justice, "Office of Public Affairs: Three Former Executives Sentenced for $1B Corporate Fraud Scheme, United States Department of Justice," Office of Public Affairs, July 1, 2024, https://www.justice.gov/opa /pr/three-former-executives-sentenced-1b-corporate-fraud-scheme.

7. Heather Landi, "Ex-Cerebral Executive Files Lawsuit Claiming the Startup Overprescribed ADHD Meds," *Fierce Healthcare*, April 29, 2022, https://www .fiercehealthcare.com/health-tech/former-cerebral-executive-files-lawsuit -alleging-unsafe-prescribing-practices.

8. Anna Werner and Jessica Kegu, "Young Man's Death Leads to Questions About an Adderall Prescription Obtained Online," *CBS News*, December 6, 2022, https://www.cbsnews.com/news/adderall-online-prescription-cerebral -mental-health-elijah-hanson.

9. U.S. Federal Trade Commission, "Proposed FTC Order Will Prohibit Tele-health Firm Cerebral from Using or Disclosing Sensitive Data for Advertising

Purposes, and Require It to Pay $7 Million," April 15, 2024, https://www.ftc.gov/news-events/news/press-releases/2024/04/proposed-ftc-order-will-prohibit-telehealth-firm-cerebral-using-or-disclosing-sensitive-data.

10. Rolfe Winkler, "Cerebral Says It Will Stop Prescribing Most Controlled Substances," *Wall Street Journal*, May 17, 2022, https://www.wsj.com/articles/cerebral-says-it-will-stop-prescribing-most-controlled-substances-11652773258.

11. Jessica Kegu, "Former Cerebral CEO Kyle Robertson Says Investors Pushed Prescribing of Stimulants and Used Him as a 'Scapegoat'," *CBS News*, November 15, 2022, https://www.cbsnews.com/news/former-cerebral-ceo-kyle-robertson-says-health-startup-investors-pushed-prescribing-stimulants.

12. U.S. Office of Public Affairs, "Founder/CEO and Clinical President of Digital Health Company Arrested for $100M Adderall Distribution and Health Care Fraud Scheme," U.S. Department of Justice, June 13, 2024, https://www.justice.gov/opa/pr/founderceo-and-clinical-president-digital-health-company-arrested-100m-adderall-distribution.

13. Saul McLeod, "Stanley Milgram Shock Experiment," *Simply Psychology*, October 3, 2024, https://www.simplypsychology.org/milgram.html.

14. Giles Bruce, "Epic's Revenue over the Past 5 Years," *Becker's Hospital Review*, July 19, 2024, https://www.beckershospitalreview.com/ehrs/epics-revenue-over-the-past-5-years.html.

15. Maria Armental, "Pear Therapeutics to Go Public in Roughly $1.6 Billion SPAC Deal," *Wall Street Journal*, June 22, 2021, https://www.wsj.com/articles/pear-therapeutics-to-go-public-in-roughly-1-6-billion-spac-deal-11624359600.

16. Corey McCann, "Today Is a Difficult Day for Pear Therapeutics," Linkedin, April 7, 2023, https://www.linkedin.com/feed/update/urn:li:activity:7050137359002038272.

17. Katie Jennings, "Pear Therapeutics Looks for a Buyer as It Struggles," *Forbes*, March 17, 2023, https://www.forbes.com/sites/katiejennings/2023/03/17/pear-therapeutics-looks-for-a-buyer-as-it-struggles-to-get-paid-for-prescription-apps.

18. John Toussaint, "Why Haven Healthcare Failed," *Harvard Business Review*, January 6, 2021, https://hbr.org/2021/01/why-haven-healthcare-failed.

19. CB Insights, "Venture Capital Funnel Shows Odds of Becoming a Unicorn Are About 1 Percent," CB Insights Research Briefs, September 6, 2018, https://www.cbinsights.com/research/venture-capital-funnel-2.

8. RULE 1: WORK FROM THE INSIDE OUT, NOT THE OUTSIDE IN

1. Harry Stebbings, host, *The Twenty Minute VC*, podcast, "Vinod Khosla on the Art of Disagreeing Agreeably, Why the Best VCs are Company Builders

Not Financiers, Why the Best CEOs are Paranoid Optimists and the Two Ways to Build Truly Generational Companies," April 24, 2020, https://www.khoslaventures.com/the-twenty-minute-vc-with-vinod-khosla/.

2. Quoteresearch, "Quote Origin: My Customers Would Have Asked for a Faster Horse," Quote Investigator, July 28, 2011, https://quoteinvestigator.com/2011/07/28/ford-faster-horse.

3. Goodreads, "Henry Ford „ Quotes „ Quotable Quote," https://www.goodreads.com/quotes/108918-if-there-is-any-one-secret-of-success-it-lies.

4. Apple Inc., "Inclusion & Diversity," accessed December 1, 2024, https://www.apple.com/diversity.

5. Emily A. Vogels, "About One-In-Five Americans Use a Smart Watch or Fitness Tracker," Pew Research Center, January 9, 2020, https://www.pewresearch.org/short-reads/2020/01/09/about-one-in-five-americans-use-a-smart-watch-or-fitness-tracker.

6. Michael W. Sjoding, Robert P. Dickson, Theodore J. Iwashyna, Steven E. Gay, and Thomas S. Valley, "Racial Bias in Pulse Oximetry Measurement," *New England Journal of Medicine* 383, no. 25 (December 16, 2020): 2477–78, https://doi.org/10.1056/nejmc2029240.

7. Ashraf Fawzy, Tianshi David Wu, Kunbo Wang, Matthew L. Robinson, Jad Farha, Amanda Bradke, Sherita H. Golden, Yanxun Xu, and Brian T. Garibaldi, "Racial and Ethnic Discrepancy in Pulse Oximetry and Delayed Identification of Treatment Eligibility Among Patients with COVID-19," *JAMA Internal Medicine* 182, no. 7 (July 1, 2022): 730–38, https://doi.org/10.1001/jamainternmed.2022.1906.

8. Healthcare IT Today, "Fax Today: Fictions and Facts," *Healthcare IT Today*, August 28, 2024, https://www.healthcareittoday.com/2024/08/28/fax-today-fictions-and-facts.

9. Sheng Wang and Raymond A. Noe, "Knowledge Sharing: A Review and Directions for Future Research," *Human Resource Management Review* 20, no. 2 (November 25, 2009): 115–31, https://doi.org/10.1016/j.hrmr.2009.10.001; Élizabeth Côté-Boileau, "How Openness Serves Innovation in Healthcare?," *International Journal of Health Policy and Management* 11, no. 12 (November 14, 2022): 3129–32, https://doi.org/10.34172/ijhpm.2022.7517.

9. RULE 2: ALIGN THE MARGIN AND THE MISSION

1. Daniel L. Riddle, William A. Jiranek, and Curtis W. Hayes, "Using a Validated Algorithm to Judge the Appropriateness of Total Knee Arthroplasty in the United States: A Multi-Center Longitudinal Cohort Study," *Arthritis and Rheumatology* 66, no. 8 (August 1, 2015): 2134–43, https://doi.org/10.1002/art.38685.

2. James Clear, *Atomic Habits: An Easy and Proven Way to Build Good Habits and Break Bad Ones* (Avery, 2018).

3. Steve Kraus, host, *The Heart of Healthcare*, podcast, episode 152, "The Southwest Airlines Theory of Healthcare Transformation | Iora Health Co-Founder Rushika Fernandopulle," December 9, 2024, https://podcasts.apple.com/us /podcast/the-southwest-airlines-theory-of/id1575404727?i=1000679716274.

4. Hims and Hers Q3, "Q3 2024 Shareholder Letter," 2024, https://s27.q4cdn .com/787306631/files/doc_financials/2024/q3/FINAL-Q3-2024-Shareholder -Letter.pdf.

5. 2023 Employer Health Benefits Survey," KFF, October 18, 2023, https:// www.kff.org/report-section/ehbs-2023-section-8-high-deductible-health -plans-with-savings-option/.

6. Kyle Bryant, Madelyn Knowles, and Adriana Krasniansky, "2022 Year-End Digital Health Funding: Lessons at the End of a Funding Cycle," Rock Health, January 9, 2023, https://rockhealth.com/insights/2022-year-end-digital-health -funding-lessons-at-the-end-of-a-funding-cycle.

7. The most common medical code system in the United States is the Current Procedural Terminology (CPT®) code system, which is managed by the American Medical Association (AMA).

8. Vijay Nair and Jordan Harmon of Hospital for Special Surgery, interview by Halle Tecco, March 6, 2024.

9. Centers for Medicare and Medicaid Services, "Value-Based Care," March 26, 2024, https://www.cms.gov/priorities/innovation/key-concepts/value -based-care.

10. Michael Bailit and Christine Hughes, "Key Design Elements of Shared Savings Payment Arrangements," *Commonwealth Fund* 20, no. 1539 (August 2011), https://www.commonwealthfund.org/sites/default/files/documents/___ media_files_publications_issue_brief_2011_aug_1539_bailit_key_design _elements_sharedsavings_ib_v2.pdf.

11. Halle Tecco, *Heart of Healthcare*, podcast, episode 153, "The Big Healthcare Reset | SCAN Group and Health Plan President and CEO Dr. Sachin Jain," December 16, 2024, https://podcasts.apple.com/us/podcast/the-big-healthcare -reset-scan-group-health-plan/id1575404727?i=1000680522421.

12. Laura Dyrda, "Why Intermountain Ditched the Term 'Value-Based Care.'" *Becker's Hospital Review*, August 29, 2024, https://www.beckershospitalreview .com/finance/why-intermountain-ditched-the-term-value-based-care.html.

13. Jonathan Slotkin, "Refunds to Dissatisfied Patients Drives Process Improvement," *The Value Initiative*. American Hospital Association, October 2018, https://www.aha.org/system/files/2018-10/18-value-initiative-case-study -geisinger-refunds.pdf.

14. On PANZYGA®, see Pfizer, "The Pfizer Pledge Warranty Program for Adult Patients with CIDP Starting PANZYGA," accessed January 30, 2025,

https://panzyga.pfizerpro.com/support/cidp-warranty-program. On XALKORI®, see Pfizer, "Xalkori Crizotinib: Explore What's Possible," February 2022, https://www.xalkori.com/files/PP-XLK-USA-1122_XALKORI_Patient-Brochure-Digital_Pledge_Update.pdf.

15. Outpatient Surgery, "Stryker Guarantees Its Sponge-Scanning System Will Prevent Retained Items," March 23, 2016, https://www.aorn.org/outpatient-surgery/article/2016-March-stryker-guarantees-its-sponge-scanning-system-will-prevent-retained-items.

16. Natalie Sherman, "Juul's Rise to a $38bn Vaping Phenomenon," *BBC News*, January 5, 2019, https://www.bbc.com/news/business-46654063.

17. Robert K. Jackler, Cindy Chau, Brook D. Getachew, Mackenzie M. Whitcomb, Jeffrey Lee-Heidenreich, Alexander M. Bhatt, Sophia H.S Kim-O'Sullivan, Zachary A. Hoffman, Laurie M. Jackler, and Divya Ramamurthi, "JUUL Advertising over Its First Three Years on the Market," Stanford Research into the Impact of Tobacco Advertising, January 31, 2019, https://tobacco-img.stanford.edu/wp-content/uploads/2021/07/21231836/JUUL_Marketing_Stanford.pdf.

18. Chris Kirkhan, "Juul Disregarded Early Evidence It Was Hooking Teens," *Reuters*, November 5, 2019, https://www.reuters.com/investigates/special-report/juul-ecigarette.

19. On students' use of e-cigarettes, see Teresa W. Wang, Linda J. Neff, Eunice Park-Lee, Chunfeng Ren, Karen A. Cullen, and Brian A. King, "E-Cigarette Use Among Middle and High School Students—United States, 2020," *Morbidity and Mortality Weekly Report* 69, no. 37 (September 18, 2020): 1310–12, https://doi.org/10.15585/mmwr.mm6937e1. On the popularity of Juul, see Shivani Mathur Gaiha, Lauren Kass Lempert, Karma McKelvey, and Bonnie Halpern-Felsher, "E-Cigarette Devices, Brands, and Flavors Attract Youth: Informing FDA's Policies and Priorities to Close Critical Gaps," *Addictive Behaviors* 126, no. 107179 (November 14, 2021), https://doi.org/10.1016/j.addbeh.2021.107179.

20. Gaiha, et al. "E-Cigarette Devices, Brands, and Flavors Attract Youth."

21. Aimee Picchi, "Juul Labs CEO Kevin Burns Has a Message to Parents of Kids Who Vape: 'I'm Sorry,'" *CBS News*, July 15, 2019, https://www.cbsnews.com/news/juul-ceo-kevin-burns-tells-parents-of-kids-who-vape-im-sorry.

22. On the class action settlement in 2024, see Robbins Geller Rudman & Dowd LLP, "$255 Million Settlement with JUUL Approved by Court," September 26, 2023, https://www.rgrdlaw.com/news-item-255-Million-Settlement-with-JUUL-Approved-by-Court.html. On Juul's market share, see Eloise Trenda, "E-Cigarette Market Share by Brand U.S. 2020," Statista, June 12, 2024, https://www.statista.com/statistics/1097004/e-cigarette-market-share-us-by-brand.

23. Heather Lyu, Tim Xu, Daniel Brotman, Brandan Mayer-Blackwell, Michol Cooper, Michael Daniel, Elizabeth C. Wick, Vikas Saini, Shannon Brownlee, and Martin A. Makary, "Overtreatment in the United States," *PLoS One* 12, no. 9 (September 6, 2017): e0181970, https://doi.org/10.1371/journal.pone.0181970.

10. RULE 3: BE A GOOD STEWARD OF HEALTH DATA

1. Katie Palmer, "Health Data Breaches Hit an All-Time High in 2023," *STAT News,* December 21, 2023, https://www.statnews.com/2023/12/21/health -data-breaches-all-time-high-in-2023.

2. Sara Rosenbaum, "Data Governance and Stewardship: Designing Data Stewardship Entities and Advancing Data Access," *Health Services Research* 45, no.5,part2(October2010):1442–55,https://doi.org/10.1111/j.1475-6773.2010.01140.x.

3. Susan Baird Kanaan and Justine M. Carr, "Health Data Stewardship: What, Why, Who, How an NCVHS Primer," National Committee on Vital and Health Statistics, September 2009, https://www.ncvhs.hhs.gov/wp-content /uploads/2014/05/090930lt.pdf.

4. Christophe Weber, "Data and Trust: The Two Pillars of Value-Based Healthcare," World Economic Forum, January 17, 2024, https://www.weforum .org/stories/2024/01/value-based-healthcare-data-trust.

5. Clemens Suter-Crazzolara, "Better Patient Outcomes Through Mining of Biomedical Big Data," *Frontiers in ICT* 5 (December 2, 2018), https://doi .org/10.3389/fict.2018.00030.

6. World Economic Forum, "4 Ways Data Is Improving Healthcare," December 5, 2019, https://www.weforum.org/stories/2019/12/four-ways-data -is-improving-healthcare. Marissa Plescia, "Health Exec: 97 percent of Health-care Data Isn't Used," *MedCity News,* October 30, 2023, https://medcitynews. com/2023/10/health-exec-97-of-healthcare-data-isnt-used. H. J. Kong, "Man-aging Unstructured Big Data in Healthcare System," *Healthcare Informat-ics Research* (January 2019), PMID: 30788175, https://pmc.ncbi.nlm.nih.gov /articles/PMC6372467.

7. Laura L. Adams, "Health Care's Failure to Share Data: An Issue of Culture or a Crisis of Integrity?," Academy Health, September 12, 2019, https:// academyhealth.org/blog/2019-09/health-cares-failure-share-data-issue -culture-or-crisis-integrity.

8. Lucia Savage, Martin Gaynor, and Julia Adler-Milstein, "Digital Health Data and Information Sharing: A New Frontier for Health Care Competi-tion?," *Antitrust Law Journal* 82, no. 2 (April 2019): 592–621, https://www .researchgate.net/publication/332530889_Digital_Health_Data_and_Information _Sharing_A_New_Frontier_for_Health_Care_Competition.

9. Will Maddox, "Why Medical Data Is 50 Times More Valuable Than a Credit Card," *D Magazine,* October 15, 2019, https://www.dmagazine.com /healthcare-business/2019/10/why-medical-data-is-50-times-more-valuable -than-a-credit-card.

10. Emery Csulak and Theresa Meadows, "Report on Improving Cybersecu-rity in the Health Care Industry," *Health Care Industry Cybersecurity Task Force,*

June 2017, https://www.phe.gov/Preparedness/planning/CyberTF/Documents/report2017.pdf.

11. Emily Olsen, "Healthcare Is an 'Easy Victim' for Ransomware Attacks: How Hospitals Can Mitigate the Damage," *Healthcare Dive*, July 18, 2024, https://www.healthcaredive.com/news/how-hospitals-can-mitigate-ransomware-attacks-healthcare/719751.

12. Khristopher J. Brooks, "UnitedHealth Paid Ransom after Massive Change Healthcare Cyberattack," *CBS News*, April 23, 2024, https://www.cbsnews.com/news/unitedhealth-ransom-paid-change-healthcare-attack.

13. Bruce Japsen, "UnitedHealth Group Cyberattack Costs to Hit $2.3 Billion This Year," *Forbes*, July 16, 2024, https://www.forbes.com/sites/bruce-japsen/2024/07/16/unitedhealth-group-cyberattack-costs-to-eclipse-23-billion-this-year.

14. Claire C. McGlave, Hannah Neprash, and Sayeh Nikpay, "Hacked to Pieces? The Effects of Ransomware Attacks on Hospitals and Patients," *Social Science Research Network* (October 4, 2023), https://doi.org/10.2139/ssrn.4579292.

15. Christian Dameff, Jeffrey Tully, Theodore C. Chan, Edward M. Castillo, Stefan Savage, Patricia Maysent, Thomas M. Hemmen, Brian J. Clay, and Christopher A. Longhurst, "Ransomware Attack Associated with Disruptions at Adjacent Emergency Departments in the US," *JAMA* 6, no. 5 (May 8, 2023): e2312270, https://doi.org/10.1001/jamanetworkopen.2023.12270.

16. *Individually identifiable health information* (IIHI) is any health-related data that can be linked to a specific person, including their physical or mental health status, healthcare services received, or payment for those services, along with personal identifiers. It's called *protected health information* (PHI) when in the custody of an entity legally responsible for protecting it.

17. Stephanie Mulrine, Mwenza Blell, and Madeleine Murtagh, "Beyond Trust: Amplifying Unheard Voices on Concerns About Harm Resulting from Health Data-Sharing," *Medicine Access Point Care* 5 (October 1, 2021), https://doi.org/10.1177/23992026211048421.

18. Maya Sabatello, Daphne O. Martschenko, Mildred K. Cho, and Kyle B. Brothers, "Data Sharing and Community-Engaged Research," *Science* 378, no. 6616 (October 14, 2022): 141–43, https://doi.org/10.1126/science.abq6851.

19. Joe Corkery, "Google and Harris Poll Healthcare Interoperability Survey," *Google Cloud* (blog), July 20, 2021, https://cloud.google.com/blog/topics/healthcare-life-sciences/google-and-harris-poll-healthcare-interoperability-survey.

20. Jordan Everson, Nathaniel Hendrix, Robert L. Phillips, Julia Adler-Milstein, Andrew Bazemore, and Vaishali Patel, "Primary Care Physicians' Satisfaction with Interoperable Health Information Technology," *JAMA Network Open* 7, no. 3 (March 26, 2024), https://doi.org/10.1001/jamanetworkopen.2024.3793.

21. Office for Civil Rights, "Understanding Some of HIPAA's Permitted Uses and Disclosures," U.S. Department of Health and Human Services, February 12, 2016, https://www.hhs.gov/hipaa/for-professionals/privacy/guidance/permitted-uses/index.html.

22. Assistant Secretary for Technology Policy, "Information Blocking," accessed November 4, 2024, https://www.healthit.gov/topic/information-blocking.

23. Cheryl Mason, "Understand the Four Levels of Interoperability in Healthcare," Wolters Kluwer, September 22, 2023, https://www.wolterskluwer.com/en/expert-insights/understand-the-four-levels-of-interoperability-in-healthcare.

24. The HIPAA Security Rule requires covered entities and their business associates to conduct risk assessments. The Office of the National Coordinator for Health Information Technology and U.S. Department of Health and Human Services have developed a downloadable Security Risk Assessment tool to help guide you through the process, which you can access at healthit.gov.

25. Office for Civil Rights, "Covered Entities and Business Associates," U.S. Department of Health and Human Services, August 21, 2024, https://www.hhs.gov/hipaa/for-professionals/covered-entities/index.html.

26. U.S. Department of Health and Human Services, "Cases Currently Under Investigation," accessed November 4, 2024, https://ocrportal.hhs.gov/ocr/breach/breach_report.jsf.

27. U.S, Federal Trade Commission, "FTC Gives Final Approval to Order Banning BetterHelp from Sharing Sensitive Health Data for Advertising, Requiring It to Pay $7.8 Million," July 14, 2023, https://www.ftc.gov/news-events/news/press-releases/2023/07/ftc-gives-final-approval-order-banning-betterhelp-sharing-sensitive-health-data-advertising.

28. U.S. Department of Health and Human Services, "HHS Office for Civil Rights and the Federal Trade Commission Warn Hospital Systems and Telehealth Providers About Privacy and Security Risks from Online Tracking Technologies," July 20, 2023, https://public3.pagefreezer.com/browse/HHS.gov/02-01-2024T03:56/https://www.hhs.gov/about/news/2023/07/20/hhs-office-civil-rights-federal-trade-commission-warn-hospital-systems-telehealth-providers-privacy-security-risks-online-tracking-technologies.html.

29. Meghan Hufstader Gabriel, Chelsea Richwine, Catherine Strawley, Wesley Barker, and Jordan Everson, "Interoperable Exchange of Patient Health Information Among U.S. Hospitals: 2023," Office of the National Coordinator for Health Information Technology, May 2024, https://www.healthit.gov/data/data-briefs/interoperable-exchange-patient-health-information-among-us-hospitals-2023.

30. John Lewin, "A New HHS Rule Takes a Far Too Narrow Approach to Health Care Data Interoperability," STAT News, January 18, 2024, https://www.statnews.com/2024/01/18/health-care-data-interoperability-hhs-rule-cures-act.

11. RULE 4: INVEST IN EVIDENCE

1. Shaminie J. Athinarayanan, Rebecca N. Adams, Sarah J. Hallberg, Amy L. McKenzie, Nasir H. Bhanpuri, Wayne W. Campbell, Jeff S. Volek, Stephen D. Phinney, and James P. McCarter, "Long-Term Effects of a Novel Continuous Remote Care Intervention Including Nutritional Ketosis for the Management of Type 2 Diabetes: A 2-Year Non-Randomized Clinical Trial," *Frontiers in Endocrinology* 10 (June 4, 2019), https://doi.org/10.3389/fendo.2019.00348.

2. Sean Day, Veeraj Shah, Sari Kaganoff, Shannon Powelson, and Simon C. Mathews, "Assessing the Clinical Robustness of Digital Health Startups: Cross-Sectional Observational Analysis," *Journal of Medical Internet Research* 24, no. 6 (June 20, 2022), https://doi.org/10.2196/37677.

3. Jonathan Sander, Catijn Schierbeek, and Antoine Nguyen, "How to Generate Value with Evidence-Led Digital Health Technologies," PwC, 2023, https://www.pwc.ch/en/insights/health-industries/evidence-led-digital-health-technologies.html.

4. On time, see Grayson Mullen and Nicolas Davidenko, "Time Compression in Virtual Reality," *Timing and Time Perception* 9, no. 4 (May 3, 2021): 377–92, https://doi.org/10.1163/22134468-bja10034. On pain, see Aliaa Rehan Yossef, Mohammed Gumaa, and Marcin Czub, "Virtual Reality for Pain Management," *Frontiers in Pain Research* 4 (August 31, 2023), https://doi.org/10.3389/fpain.2023.1274613.

5. Tabitha V. Craig, Ryan E. Rhodes, and Wuyou Sui, "Examining and Comparing the Energy Expenditure of Two Modes of a Virtual Reality Fitness Game (Supernatural): Indirect Calorimetry Study," *JMIR Serious Games* 12, no. 1 (April 6, 2024), https://doi.org/10.2196/53999.

6. Stephen D. Herrmann, Erik A. Willis, Barbara E. Ainsworth, Tiago V. Barreira, Mary Hastert, Chelsea L. Kracht, John M. Schuna, et al., "2024 Adult Compendium of Physical Activities: A Third Update of the Energy Costs of Human Activities," *Journal of Sport and Health Science* 13, no. 1 (January 1, 2024): 6–12, https://doi.org/10.1016/j.jshs.2023.10.010.

7. When I was in school, I learned this as the Triple Aim. More recently, people have added a fourth measure of improved provider experience (the work life of healthcare workers). I like to broaden that fourth aim to also encompass patients and caregivers.

8. Key terms for understanding medical test results: (1) true positive: correctly identifies an existing condition; (2) false positive: incorrectly indicates a condition that's not present; (3) true negative: correctly shows no condition when none exists; and (4) false negative: fails to detect an existing condition.

9. Elkin V. Lemos, Dongmu Zhang, Bradley J. Van Voorhis, and X. Henry Hu, "Healthcare Expenses Associated with Multiple vs Singleton Pregnancies

in the United States," *American Journal of Obstetrics and Gynecology* 209, no. 6 (December 2013): p586.e1–586.e11, http://dx.doi.org/10.1016/j.ajog.2013.10.005.

10. Progyny, "Proven Impact, Superior Outcomes," accessed November 4, 2024, https://progyny.com/for-employers/benefits-at-work.

12. GO FORTH AND FIX HEALTHCARE

1. Hallie Levine, "Stick with It: 18 Fun Facts About the History of BAND-AID® Brand Adhesive Bandages," Johnson and Johnson, April 9, 2017, https://www.jnj.com/our-heritage/18-facts-about-the-history-of-band-aid-brand-adhesive-bandages.

2. National Museum of American History Behring Center, "Predictor Pregnancy Test—Design Prototype," Smithsonian, 2015, https://americanhistory.si.edu/collections/object/nmah_1803285.

3. Wikipedia, s.v., "Orphan Drug Act of 1983," accessed November 30, 2024, https://en.wikipedia.org/wiki/Orphan_Drug_Act_of_1983.

4. Rahul Kumar, "UM Professor and Creator of EpiPen Discusses Entrepreneurship, Career Advice," *Miami Hurricane*, September 25, 2020, https://themiamihurricane.com/2020/09/25/um-professor-and-creator-of-epipen-discusses-entrepreneurship-career-advice.

5. U. S. Capitol Visitor Center, "The Pure Food and Drug Act," 2024, https://www.visitthecapitol.gov/exhibitions/congress-and-progressive-era/pure-food-and-drug-act.

6. Ellison C. Piece, "Looking Back: Doctor Pierce Reflects," Anesthesia Patient Safety Foundation, 2007, https://www.apsf.org/article/looking-back-doctor-pierce-reflects.

7. Robert K. Stoelting, "APSF History," Anesthesia Patient Safety Foundation, 2025, https://www.apsf.org/about-apsf/apsf-history.

8. Michael Dowling, "Coopetition," *Business and Management*, Oxford University Press, April 30, 2020, https://oxfordre.com/business/display/10.1093/acrefore/9780190224851.001.0001/acrefore-9780190224851-e-9.

9. Office of Disease Prevention and Health Promotion, "The Diabetes Advocacy Alliance and Healthy People: Putting Diabetes on the National Agenda," U.S. Department of Health and Human Services, November 10, 2020, https://odphp.health.gov/news/202011/diabetes-advocacy-alliance-and-healthy-people-putting-diabetes-national-agenda.

10. Xiangmin Liu, Li Bai, Xiaoning Leng, Yexiang Yao, Yue Yang, Debao Li, and Haobo Yin, "Coopetition, Exploration and Exploitation Capabilities, and Growth Performance in Digital Healthcare Ventures," *Frontiers in Public Health* 12, no. 1369885 (June 19, 2024), https://doi.org/10.3389/fpubh.2024.1369885.

11. Rosabeth Moss Kanter, "Change Is Hardest in the Middle," *Harvard Business Review*, August 12, 2009, https://hbr.org/2009/08/change-is-hardest-in-the-middl.

12. Natee Amornsiripanitch, Paul A. Gompers, George Hu, William Levinson, and Vladimir Mukharlyamov, "Failing Just Fine: Assessing Careers of Venture Capital-Backed Entrepreneurs via a Non-Wage Measure," *NBER Working Paper Series*, no. 30179 (June 2022), https://doi.org/10.2139/ssrn.4145818.

13. National Association of Community Health Centers, "Closing the Primary Care Gap: How Community Health Centers Address the Nation's Primary Care Crisis," February 2023, https://www.nachc.org/wp-content/uploads/2023/06/Closing-the-Primary-Care-Gap_Full-Report_2023_digital-final.pdf.

INDEX

Prozac antidepressant, 52
public benefit corporation (PBC), 29
public health system, social
    determinants of health and
    underfunding of, 12
public reporting, negative
    externalities and, 217
PubMed.gov, 206
Pure Food and Drug Act (1906), 51

QOL. *See* quality-of-life
QSEHRA. *See* Qualified Small
    Employer Health Reimbursement
    Arrangement
quadruple aim, of healthcare
    innovation, 210, 219
Qualified Small Employer Health
    Reimbursement Arrangement
    (QSEHRA), 32
quality-of-life (QOL): patient
    engagement and higher, 62; WHO
    screening questions for, 205
quality ratings, as payer challenge, 37

racial discrimination, AMA history
    of, 24
RAND Corporation, 147
randomized controlled trials (RCTs),
    206-7
R&D. *See* research and development
reactive approach, to healthcare, 14;
    as healthcare expenditures factor,
    6; proactive approach versus,
    11-12; vicious cycle of, 15
real-world data (RWD), 208; data
    sources, 207; from EHR, 207;
    RCTs and, 206-7
reforms: for Medicare and Medicaid,
    37; proposals of 1970s on health, 39
registered nurses: Circulation and
    flu shots on-demand by, 113;
    credentialing of, 22

regulations, 204; for innovation
    negative externalities, 216-17
regulatory approval, 106
regulatory capture, healthcare
    innovation difficulty, 120, 129;
    CON laws and, 123-24; Polevikov
    on, 124
regulatory drivers, 109-10
regulatory issue, of healthcare data
    interoperability, 193
regulatory pressure, as payer
    challenge, 37
reimbursement, in B2C2B business
    model, 172; medical and
    diagnostic codes, 171
relentlessly pursuing meaningful
    problems, as healthcare
    innovation ingredient, 98, 101-3,
    116; Tidepool.org, of Look, 102-3
reputation: as payer challenge, 37-38;
    as pharma challenge, 50
research: clinical of Vita Health, 206;
    healthcare data protection and
    accelerated, 191; study of problem
    with resources, 148; on VBC by
    Intermountain Health, 179
research and development (R&D):
    blockbuster drugs offset of costs
    of, 52; for breakthrough solutions,
    83; of pharma, 41, 51
reserve requirements, for self-
    insured plans, 32
right place, as healthcare innovation
    ingredient, 98, 103-6, 116
right time, as healthcare innovation
    ingredient, 98; for breakthrough
    solutions, 107; of Circulation, of
    Brownstein, 113; for competitive
    solutions, 106; for creative
    solutions, 106; inflection
    points, 107-8, 108; market
    drivers, 109; market readiness,

GPSR Authorized Representative: Easy Access System Europe, Mustamäe tee
50, 10621 Tallinn, Estonia, gpsr.requests@easproject.com

www.ingramcontent.com/pod-product-compliance
Lightning Source LLC
Chambersburg PA
CBHW051727260326
41914CB00040B/2005/J